"Just a Housewife"

DATE DUE

"JUST A HOUSEWIFE"

The Rise and Fall of Domesticity in America

GLENNA MATTHEWS

OXFORD UNIVERSITY PRESS
New York · Oxford

Oxford University Press

Oxford   New York   Toronto
Delhi   Bombay   Calcutta   Madras   Karachi
Petaling Jaya   Singapore   Hong Kong   Tokyo
Nairobi   Dar es Salaam   Cape Town
Melbourne   Auckland

and associated companies in
Berlin   Ibadan

Library of Congress Cataloging-in-Publication Data

Matthews, Glenna.
"Just a housewife."

Includes bibliographical references and index.
1. Women—United States—Social conditions.
2. Housewives—United States—History—19th century.
3. Housewives—United States—History—20th century.
I. Title.
HQ1410.M38   1987   305.4′2′0973   86-33318
ISBN 0-19-503859-2
ISBN 0-19-505925-5 (pbk)

4 6 8 10 9 7 5

Printed in the United States of America

To my parents, Glen Ingles and Alberta Nicolais Ingles,
and to the memory of my grandmother,
Annie Delullo Nicolais

Preface

THE READERS of the following pages will soon deduce that I have more than a passing interest in the plight of the housewife: I was a suburban housewife for a number of years. Coming of age in the late 1950s, I followed the path of much of my age cohort, a path that included early marriage and early motherhood. Through a combination of incredible naïveté and considerable ignorance, I somehow maintained the belief that I would go on to do graduate work despite this. I was rarely frustrated, because it never occurred to me that I had forfeited the chance to have an academic career. At the same time, I noticed that my sister housewives and I were accorded little respect in the culture, and that frequently made me angry. So it is not surprising that, after a struggle to obtain a doctorate, the likes of which I never would have dreamed of in advance, I have written a book about housewives and the lack of respect from which we all suffered.

I was fortunate indeed to be able to attend Stanford University for my graduate work and to study with Carl Degler. He was one of the few established historians in the country, I am sure, who was prepared to take a "re-entry" woman seriously in 1969. Beyond this obvious fact, he and the other historians with whom I studied at

Stanford set a standard of intellectual vitality and passion for our discipline for which I will always be grateful. I think of my graduate school career as having provided intellectual capital upon which I will be able to draw for the rest of my life.

Upon graduating, I moved to Stillwater, Oklahoma, where I taught at Oklahoma State University. I will always be grateful, too, to supportive colleagues and administrators there. In a time of financial stringency, I received generous research support. My colleague H. James Henderson shared with me his breadth of knowledge about colonial America and critiqued an early version of Chapter 1. Conversations with Adelia Hanson sharpened my ideas about the role of the housewife. Another great boon resulting from my Oklahoma years was the chance to become acquainted with Angie Debo, a much-loved friend and much-esteemed role model as a pioneering woman historian.

These are the general circumstances from which this book arose. The specific circumstances are as follows. In 1978 I gave a birthday party for a historian friend, and after dinner a group of us—by coincidence, all historians—sat around discussing *The Feminization of American Culture* by Ann Douglas. As the talk swirled around me, I wondered to myself who could speak for the housewife in this discourse, and I then resolved to do the job myself when I felt ready. Conversations early on with Kathryn Kish Sklar and George Fredrickson were useful in focusing my ideas.

In 1982–83 I received an ACLS Fellowship to support my research and embarked on a year of travel. During this year I was the beneficiary of help from librarians and archivists who gave of their time to point me in the right direction and also from friends who gave me hospitality while I was on the road. In particular, I join the ever-growing list of scholars who regard the Schlesinger Library of Women's History at Radcliffe as a second home, because its superb staff is so welcoming. Barbara Haber, Patricia King, Elizabeth Shenton, and Eva Moseley are justly celebrated as representing the highest professional and the warmest human standards. Friends who entertained me during this year—sometimes for unconscionably lengthy stays—include Sandra Mahoney, Larry Mahoney, Debbie Harvey, Michel Dahlin, David Ruchman, Roderick McDonald, Lynn McDonald, Deborah Gardner, Pat Hills, and Kevin Whitfield.

In addition to help from Oklahoma State University and the ACLS Fellowship, the writing of this book was possible because of a legacy from my late aunt, Thelma Ingles. I can only hope that she would have approved of it. She herself was a remarkable woman whose nursing career was devoted to upgrading the standing of nurses in the medical profession and to upgrading the standard of nursing in Third World countries.

I have benefited greatly from the help of friends and colleagues who read all or part of the manuscript. Susan Harris read the first seventy pages in rough draft and gave me criticism that was as useful as it was tough-minded. She then read the entire first draft, as did Meredith Marsh. Londa Schiebinger read Chapter 5 (on Darwinism), which I subsequently presented to an audience of Darwinists at the Seventeenth International History of Science Congress in Berkeley in August 1985. Mark Kornbluh, Mary Kelley, and Estelle Freedman read the manuscript at a later stage. Needless to say, I am solely responsible for the various interpretations—error-ridden as some of my critics may deem them to be! My editor at Oxford University Press, Sheldon Meyer, showed faith in the project from our earliest conversation on the subject and sustained me throughout the writing of the book, and Stephanie Sakson-Ford did an excellent job of copyediting. Jackie Stevens gathered the data in the Appendix, and Dan Silin arranged them in tabular form. Karen Matthews and Dan Silin helped with the proofreading.

A book on the subject of domesticity clearly owes much to domesticity shared and to friendship. In addition to the friends named above I want to thank Barbara Baer, Monica Loewi, John Snetsinger, Jan Duffy, Dorothy Schrader, Etta Perkins, and Nathanael Silin because all of them have made a difference in my life.

Lastly, I want to thank my family for their encouragement and support. The dedication only begins to suggest what I owe to my parents and to my late grandmother. Other family members whose loving support has been important are my aunt, Norma Cook, and my cousins, Robert Nicolais and the late John Nicolais. My two children, Karen and David, made—and continue to make, as they come home for visits with their friends—my own experience of domesticity a wonderful part of my life.

Berkeley, California   G. M.
January 1987

Contents

Introduction

STARTED THIS BOOK with the dawning realization that while American women were relegated to a separate domestic sphere in 1850, it was a sphere that was central to the culture. One hundred years later, most American women were still functioning as housewives in some fashion, but the home was no longer central, and this made the role of housewife much more problematic for those who filled it. In fact, by the mid-twentieth century many women had begun to think of themselves as "just a housewife."*

In 1850 a housewife knew she was essential not only to her family but also to her society. History would be affected by the cumulative impact of women creating good homes. Advice books, popular novels, and even the writings of male intellectuals set forth this theme and elaborated the ideal of the "notable housewife." In 1950, the suburban, middle-class housewife was doubly isolated: physically, by the nature of housing patterns, and spiritually, because she had become merely the general factotum for her family. She was a cog in the economic machine, necessary for the maintenance of national pros-

* See the Appendix for statistics about percentages of women in the work force. Only 5.6 percent of married women were gainfully employed outside the home as late as 1900.

perity but overlooked in discussions of the gross national product. The desperate letters sent to Betty Friedan after she identified "the problem that has no name"—that is, the emptiness of many housewives' lives—testify to the damage inflicted by the twentieth-century version of domesticity.[1]

I think it is obvious from the above that feminists need to take a serious, sustained, and sympathetic interest in the home because it is too valuable an institution to leave to Phyllis Schlafly and others who take a negative view of feminism. In the first place, women are less likely to convince those with whom they share households to become equal partners in the performance of domestic duties—as opposed to "helping" with the housework—if they denigrate and devalue these duties. In the second place, I think that a humane society has a stake in the optimal performance of domestic duties; in short, that the home truly does have important social functions that have been undervalued for several generations. Children need not only to be nurtured but also to be trained to be caring and socially responsible adults. Adults of both sexes need to receive emotional refreshment—as well as give it—in order to be effective as citizens and workers. Moreover, men and women who live alone can create hospitable homes that they share with friends, thereby also creating socially valuable institutions.

Women themselves have unquestionably been the big losers in the devaluation of domesticity. Homes may be more or less elaborate, housework may be more or less professionalized, but there will always remain an irreducible residue of effort required to maintain the place where people live. If such work is despised, it will be performed by someone whose sex, class, or race—perhaps all three— consign her to an inferior status. If such work is despised, we will be much more likely to allow corporate America to manipulate the nature of homes and of housework. There was, for instance, no technological imperative in the Industrial Revolution that insured that in 1960 a middle-class housewife would serve TV dinners while spending an inordinate amount of time acting as chauffeur for the rest of her family. This came about because women's traditional skills and women's time were both undervalued.

It should be pointed out, too, that valuing the home and the skill involved in performing domestic duties that have traditionally been female does not mean endorsing the position that those duties should always be performed by a woman. In a society with a completely egalitarian gender system, both sexes could perform work around the house and take pride in doing a good job. After all, domestic tasks, other than the most menial, can have more of an immediate emotional "payoff" than most jobs in complex organizations. What has made domestic tasks especially obnoxious has been the fact that they have been ascribed only to women and that women have thereby been put in the position of rendering non-reciprocal personal service to those they love.

I hope that the ensuing pages will contribute to the discussion of what "home" can and should represent to feminists now. This is because we have a rich heritage from the past. For example, in the nineteenth century—before domesticity suffered its decline—Antoinette Brown Blackwell spoke of how women could move from "bound to rebound" between home and the world with energies for both. She understood that this would be possible only if men were to enter into a fair share of responsibility for the life of the home. Moreover, in a letter to Lucy Stone, she spoke of wanting "to give and take some home comfort" herself. It seems to me that Blackwell's vision of giving and taking home comfort while participating actively in the world is peculiarly appropriate for women of today. Blackwell's ideas demonstrate, too, that one can enthusiastically support the value of "home" without endorsing a program of sexual asymmetry.

And now a word about my sources and general approach. In order to cover a substantial sweep of time and examine the status of domesticity as it was affected by such critical developments as industrialization, secularization, the culture of professionalism, and the appearance of consumerism, I have opted for cultural, as opposed to social, history. By this I mean that I have not used "history-from-the-bottom-up" sources because to do so for the period of time covered by this study would be the labor of a lifetime. Where I used manuscript or archival material, it reflected the experiences of well-known women like Elizabeth Cady Stanton, Susan B. Anthony, or Harriet

Beecher Stowe rather than those of a typical housewife. I am necessarily painting with a broad brush, and subsequent scholars will no
doubt refine—if they do not discard!—my generalizations. This is an
exploratory essay on a huge subject, rather than a definitive statement.

At the same time I must point out that my sources go beyond the
ideas of a highly educated elite. In addition to Emerson, Hawthorne,
and Darwin, I have read potboilers, best-selling cookbooks, popular
magazines, and advice books. In general, I asked myself where the
images of home and of housewife would be most reliably reflected.
Moreover, I made pilgrimages to a number of old kitchens and was
allowed to go "backstage" at the Smithsonian and handle some of
the utensils so as to have a better understanding of them than merely
looking at them would permit. In other words, I tried to be as imaginative as possible in thinking about the interaction between material
culture and ideas.

Nonetheless, I must freely acknowledge that my sources are principally confined to the middle class. The ideology of domesticity
arose in the middle class and may well have been one of the principal
means by which the middle class assumed a self-conscious identity
in the antebellum period. Much more research must be done before
we know the extent to which working-class families subscribed to
the ideology. I am especially curious about the existence of the ideal
among slave families. Since black women did so much of the skilled
cookery in the southern states, one would like to know if they were
able to develop a craft tradition or if the conditions under which
they worked were simply too oppressive for this development to take
place.

Finally, let me explain my use of the word "housewife" rather
than the more modern term "homemaker." "Housewife" had a long
and honorable history, even if the women who filled the position
were denied full participation in their society. It is the argument of
this study that, in the nineteenth century, American housewives
even contrived to occupy a relatively respected position in the culture. I suspect that the term "homemaker" made its appearance more
or less simultaneously with the devaluation of domesticity, a public

relations gesture to cover up the loss of prestige for the job. In the utopian future of which I dream, neither term would be appropriate since all adults would perform a fair share of the work involved in maintaining the domestic environment.

"Just a Housewife"

ONE

The Emergence of a New Ideology

$\mathcal{I}$N 1750 THE COLONIAL AMERICAN HOME was an essential locus
of production for the entire society. The overwhelming majority of
colonists lived outside the cities and made many of the items that
later Americans would routinely buy in stores. Soap required home
manufacture, bread must be baked at home, bacon cured, and clothing pieced together for growing families, because consumer goods
were not commercially available. This in turn created a demanding
job for the housewife. A small percentage of wealthy women may
have escaped performing domestic duties, but for most women chores
were arduous and unending. The housewife was, however, in charge
of a team that kept the household supplied and functioning. Many
housewives had help from a "hired" girl even if they had no full-
time servants, and they could count on regular assistance from members of their own families.[1] Even children had routine chores to
perform that added to the productive capacity of the household. This
"team" helped make the economy function smoothly, too.

The importance of home production for the survival of the society
does not mean, however, that either the home or the person in charge
of domestic tasks was highly valued at the time. A leading scholar of
the eighteenth-century woman, Mary Beth Norton, argues that be-

3

fore the American Revolution women were frequently apologetic about their roles. To be a good housewife "was conceived to be an end in itself, rather than as a means to a greater or more meaningful goal."[2] Hence women described their work as "my Narrow sphere," "my humble duties," or "my little Domestick affairs."[3] In other words, a home was seen as serving the purely private ends of providing for the needs of those who lived in it, and the housewife had no reason to think of herself as vitally linked with the world outside the home. With that world her connection was limited principally to church attendance and local market activities. In fact, Norton speaks of a "dichotomy between male public activity and female private passivity."

If the home was taken for granted, so too was the fact that the distribution of power within the home was hierarchical. Although the wife might supervise the day-by-day performance of domestic chores, the weight of authority in the household clearly rested with the husband, who was seen as a moral arbiter as well as the ultimate decision-maker in the marriage. As husband was to wife, so father was to child with respect to being the source of moral authority. The emotional ties between mother and child were much less salient than they were to become in the nineteenth century because discipline rather than nurturing warmth was the prime consideration in parental treatment of children. Finally, the father's authority within the family reflected patriarchal patterns of authority in other aspects of colonial American culture.[4]

Another generalization that can be offered about the colonial home in 1750 has to do with the distribution of chores. Much has been made of the separation of male and female spheres of activity under the impact of industrialization. It seems increasingly clear, however, that while the two sexes may have been working in physical proximity in pre-industrial America, their jobs were highly differentiated. Men tended the orchards, for example, while women preserved the fruit. Men or boys chopped the firewood, while women tended the fires. Each sex stuck to its own tasks except under conditions of duress, such as the absence or illness of a spouse.[5]

The physical appearance of the home might vary from colony to colony because of the differences in culture and in available building materials. For the tiny minority of colonists who lived in cities, homes had a more elaborate style of architecture as well as more gracious appointments. What the homes had in common, however, except for the small number of those belonging to the wealthy, was their modest size, especially considering the dimensions of the typical household of parents, several children, hired help, and possibly apprentices. The notion of a "room of one's own" was unknown to colonial society, and privacy was an unheard-of luxury.

Moreover, there is reason to believe that in 1750 the ordinary home was only beginning to have enough consumer goods to make possible a comfortable style of domesticity. Scholars who have studied probate inventories suggest that most homes in colonial America beyond those of the luxury-owning elite were equipped with only sparse necessities until some time in the mid-eighteenth century.[6] Around 1750, tea services, for example, began to show up in non-elite households.[7] These in turn would have enhanced the style of female sociability possible in ordinary homes.

In 1750 cooking was done over an open hearth with relatively few and unspecialized utensils.[8] For all but the households of the wealthy, the diet was plain and possessed little variety. In New England, salt meat provided most of the animal protein, and peas porridge was the other staple. Bread was usually "rye 'n injun"—cornmeal was then known as Indian meal—because wheat flour was scarce. Dairy products were needed to make up part of the protein requirements of the very utilitarian diet, hence butter was rarely available for fancy baking. Vegetables showed up as afterthought in the meals, rather than as part of a carefully thought-out menu. Such cookbooks as existed had been published in Britain and were unlikely to be consulted beyond the urban elite. In consequence of all of this, cooking was a purely utilitarian function and not a highly prized skill: there is no evidence to suggest that women thought in terms of "culinary art." Rather, they would put a meal to simmer over the fire in the open hearth and go about their other business.[9] Hence, for a variety of reasons, in 1750 domestic chores were likelier to be approached as matter-of-fact routines than as occasions for displays of female prowess or as possessing ceremonial meaning.

The colonial home, then, was both essential and mundane, mundane because it had no transcendent functions. What is more, nothing in the culture reflected glory on the woman in charge of the home. Literary heroines of eighteenth-century British novels, for example, were noteworthy for their purity and gentleness and not for their domestic skills.

By 1850 all of this had changed. The home was so much at the center of the culture that historians speak of a "cult" of domesticity in the early to mid-nineteenth century. Women in their homes were the locus of moral authority in the society. Further, in the 1850s women could read an outpouring of novels in which housewives figured in highly positive terms. Best-selling cookbooks of the day reveal a much more varied cuisine, even for middle-class households, than had prevailed in the colonial period. In short, domesticity was both more elaborate and more valued, and this, in turn, meant that the housewife had access to new sources of self-esteem. How did the changes come about?

Perhaps the most important factor in elevating the status of the home was the role home played in the polity after the American Revolution. In fact, the intermingling of the domestic and the political began even earlier than the war itself, with the boycott of British-made goods. What had been viewed by men and women alike as a set of petty concerns—the kind of cloth to be employed in making a suit, for example—acquired a whole new political relevance. The boycotts would not have worked without the cooperation of women acting within their own households, and this gave women a new self-respect and a rationale for entering into political discussions. In consequence, "the public recognition accorded the female role irreversibly altered its inferior status."[10]

But it was the widespread concern over how best to socialize citizens after the war that had the largest impact. There were no precedents for a republic on the scale of the United States. Many people believed that the new nation would require the support of a uniquely public-spirited citizenry. If citizens must learn to place a high value on the public interest, this was a lesson they would need to begin in childhood. Thus the home became crucial to the success of the nation and women—whose education began to be taken much more seriously than ever before—gained the role of "Republican Mother," to use the term coined by Linda Kerber. Kerber asserts:

> The notion that a mother can perform a political function represents the recognition that a citizen's political socialization takes place at an early age, that the family is a basic part of the system of political communication and that patterns of family authority influence the general political culture. Yet most premodern political societies—and even some fairly modern democracies—maintained unarticulated, but nevertheless very firm, social restrictions that isolated the female domestic world from politics. The willingness of the American woman to overcome this ancient separation brought her into the all-male political community. In this sense Republican Motherhood was a very important, even revolutionary, invention. It altered the female domain in which most women had always lived out their lives; it justified women's absorption and participation in the civic culture.[11]

The home in effect gained a function so political that the domestic sphere could influence the outcome of history. Indeed, the home already *had* influenced the outcome of history during the 1770s when patriots had put pressure on the British by altering the pattern of colonial consumption. What this meant was that the female sphere was no longer entirely private. Catharine Beecher's *A Treatise on Domestic Economy* of 1841, a prime document of the cult of domesticity because it combined citations from the work of Tocqueville with explicit instructions on laundry, may be seen as the logical outgrowth of the politicization of the home after the Revolution.

That the political culture engendered by the Revolution found its way into American homes is particularly well demonstrated by the first American cookbook, which appeared in Hartford in 1796. Amelia Simmons's *American Cookery* exemplifies both the changing culinary standards of the eighteenth century and a strongly patriotic sensibility. By the 1790s American cuisine had diverged from that of the mother country because it utilized many native ingredients. It had also begun to be more elaborate because the society was becoming more prosperous. Thus in keeping with the new interest in vegetables documented by culinary historians, for example, Simmons gives recipes for more than a dozen different varieties, including artichokes as well as beans and peas. Several recipes called for that quintessentially American ingredient, Indian meal. Writing in an American vernacular, she included recipes for Indian pudding, johnnycake, slapjacks, pumpkin pie, and cranberry sauce. She employed the terms "cooky" and "slaw," borrowed from the Dutch. In the second edition of her work, published in 1800, she not only gave recipes for Election Cake, Independence Cake, and Federal Pan Cake, but also for "rye 'n injun," the first appearance of this bread in a published cookbook. In short, during the first decade of the new nation's existence, the first published cookbook based on a distinctive American cuisine appeared, and it reflected not only a more varied diet than had obtained earlier but also a patriotic impulse in ingredients, language, types of recipes, and names of dishes.[12]

It is worth pointing out that contrary to a hardy myth about the inexactness of measurement before the twentieth century, perhaps originally concocted by the home economists, the recipes in *American Cookery* are by and large neither slapdash nor haphazard. Exact quantities of most ingredients other than spices are specified; for example, the recipe for flour pudding calls for seven eggs, one-fourth pound of sugar, and a teaspoon of salt. Ironically, this book, which both borrowed from English sources and codified the preparation of characteristic American dishes, foreshadowed the de-skilling trends of the future in its utilization of chemical leavening as an ingredient in cookies. According to Mary Tolford Wilson in her introduction to the 1958 facsimile edition, this was the first time in the Anglo-American world that a published recipe called for chemical leavening, in this case pearlash, a derivative of potash. Throughout most of the nineteenth century, cookbooks would reflect a tension between the old style of using eggs for leavening and the new, which permitted the use of cheaper ingredients and required less skill on the part of the baker.

If the colonial home had been viewed as mundane and lacking vital connections to the realm of historical development, it had also received relatively little notice for its role in people's emotional lives. This was because patriarchal patterns of authority discouraged interest in maternal nurture and the emotional warmth to be found at home. Yet by the 1830s, the home had begun to be sentimentalized to an unprecedented degree. It is difficult to pinpoint the timing of this change with precision because there was no clearly identifiable event such as the American Revolution that precipitated the change. Nonetheless we can point to the culmination of a number of long-term trends operating in the Anglo-American world to explain this phenomenon. In the first place childhood began to garner more attention. In a provocative interpretation of the culture of late eighteenth-century America, Jay Fliegelman argues that John Locke's *Education* was "perhaps the most significant text of the Anglo-American Enlightenment" because it taught people to place a new value on nurture and to esteem a consensual rather than authoritarian style of parenting.[13] Locke's empiricism, with its view of the human mind as a tabula rasa at birth, implicitly made the affectionate home the molder of intelligence as well as character. Only a fully affectionate home would be able to produce the desired results. Such late eighteenth-century works as *Clarissa* by Samuel Richardson and *La Nouvelle Heloise* by Jean-Jacques Rousseau taught educated Americans to condemn parental tyranny.

If the highest duty of loving parents was to create an affectionate home so as to provide optimal nurture for their children, so, too, scholars have discerned a new pattern for marriage coming into being at about the same time. Carl Degler dates the emergence of the modern American family, characterized by "companionate" norms for marriage, as occurring between the American Revolution and about 1830.[14] Echoing the findings of Lawrence Stone writing about eighteenth-century England,[15] Degler argues that the importance of emotion was fundamental in creating new expectations for marriage. The relationship became more egalitarian and was based on mutual esteem and respect rather than on family property considerations. Young people gained greater autonomy in choosing a marriage partner. Above all, "The woman in the marriage enjoyed an increasing degree of influence or autonomy within the family."[16]

The combination of the new value placed on nurture, the new style of marriage, and changes in the material world—to be discussed shortly—all coalesced to create a new style of motherhood. This style was much more intense and demanded more of the mother emotionally than was required in previous generations. On this topic alone books can be—and have been—written.[17] With this added emotional charge, rather than being defined matter-of-factly as the place to eat and sleep, home began to acquire such sentimental overtones that it could inspire outbursts of rhapsody, especially after the changes in American society ushered in during the 1830s.

Turmoil and instability in the Jacksonian Age of the 1830s penetrated into a wide range of institutions and created great concern about social cohesion. Universal white manhood suffrage meant that class deference was no longer a political norm, although racial and gender inequities remained. The cultural hegemony that had been enjoyed by the clergy of a few denominations was being undermined by the proliferation of new denominations and the destruction of the last vestiges of an established church. Mass immigration was beginning to create a more heterogeneous population. Given this, the growing cities were becoming increasingly disorderly. People were moving farther west and thus placing more distance between themselves and the historic guardians of cultural stability in the older centers of population. Factories were appearing on the landscape. Above all, the cash nexus was at the base of an increasing number of human relationships outside the family. Not surprisingly, the home came to be seen as an especially potent symbol of integration at this time, valuable because it seemed to represent a haven of stability.

The home's capacity to play this heightened emotional role was enhanced by changes in the material underpinnings of domesticity that had come to full fruition by the Age of Jackson. In essence, the changes added up to the following: middle-class women had both more time and a greater profusion of utensils and other artifacts with which to create the good home. In turn, novels, advice books, and periodicals all began to reflect a highly positive image of the "notable housewife" in action. By the 1850s there was an entire genre of "domestic novel," written by, about, and for women, that depicted heroines demonstrating remarkable initiative in creating homes. In sum, the home gained a role both in women's lives and in their reading matter as an arena for the display of prowess.

That nineteenth-century American women had more time for tasks that were ornamental or ceremonial than had their colonial counterparts was because an increasing percentage of families lived in cities or towns by 1830, and the trend continued throughout the century. This transition in itself eliminated many onerous tasks, for urban women could now purchase a number of basic commodities that had previously been produced at home, commodities that were commercially available because of the beginnings of industrialization, the other major source of change for women. A number of historians have demonstrated what it meant for women's lives when women were no longer required to spend a vast amount of time producing cloth, for example. Although this was the most important development, there were other items, too, like soap, that could be purchased by the mid-nineteenth century—at a considerable savings of time to the housewife.

Her time was also more abundant because of the increasing availability of domestic servants by the 1830s and because of changing attitudes about the allocation of tasks between mistress and maid. In essence, there began to be more social distance between the two and a greater differentiation in the tasks they performed. Says Faye Dudden in her recent book, *Serving Women*:

> Beginning in the 1820s and more noticeably in the 1830s, Americans began to hire more servants to work in an explicitly domestic sphere. Abandoning the language of help, they began to call them "domestic servants" or just "domestics." The difference was more than semantic; it reflected altered relationships. . . .[18]

Dudden argues that this change enabled middle-class women to devote time to "the elaboration of domestic space and rituals." Moreover, supervising a servant—as opposed to working with help—gave housewives a more elevated status. "In hiring domestics middle-class women found the means to make domesticity more flexible, accommodating roles of authority and activity, rather than passivity and isolation."[19]

Furthermore, all the evidence indicates a striking growth in the variety and complexity of household objects and utensils for the middle-class housewife by the 1830s. The second quarter of the nineteenth century was a time of explosive economic growth, and the material culture of ordinary households began to reflect the new abundance. Even in fairly remote areas, a woman might have been able proudly to display a China tea set.[20] In the cities the possibilities for acquiring such objects were much greater. In Philadelphia in 1850, for example, a hardware store offered its customers two hundred and fifty kitchen tools.[21] Presumably, these tools could give the woman in charge of the household an enhanced sense of craft and mastery. What we know with certainty is that women clung to their familiar household objects with determination as they packed for the Overland Trail, and they parted with them only with the greatest reluctance.[22]

Another technological change that had profound consequences for the style of domesticity was the development of the stove. The transition from open-hearth cookery to cook stove was effected in the middle decades of the nineteenth century. In her *Treatise on Domestic Economy* of 1841, for example, Catharine Beecher gave instructions for the hearth, while in *The American Woman's Home*, published in 1869, she and her sister Harriet Beecher Stowe discussed the stove.[23] Affordable for almost all American households, the cast-iron stove made it easy to carry on several different cooking operations simultaneously—a feat much more difficult to accomplish over an open hearth—and thus contributed to a more varied menu in nonelite households. In short, the stove led to the demise of the one-pot meal.[24]

Dudden's argument and our growing understanding of material culture accord well with what we know about changes in cookery and needlework in the second quarter of the nineteenth century. In both these areas, available evidence indicates that a greater number of women outside the elite class participated in producing more elaborate concoctions—whether in the kitchen or with a needle—than ever before. Not surprisingly, given the technological changes, the economic growth and the increasing urbanization, there was a proliferation of cookbooks in this period. As we have seen, Amelia Simmons's *American Cookery* had codified the preparation of a number of characteristic American dishes and had embodied a careful approach to ingredients and measurement. What it did not have, however, was a venturesome attitude toward anything exotic. "Garlicks, tho' used by the French, are better adapted to the uses of medicine than cookery," Simmons observed, for example.[25] Conversely, many of the cookbooks of the second quarter of the nineteenth century contained recipes calling for such items as garlic, artichoke bottoms, and curry powder.[26] They also called for lavish ingredients in baking. Later in the century, the cuisine was to deteriorate as chemical leavenings came into greater use, cheap sugar made its appearance and was widely utilized, and factory-made flour replaced stone-ground flour on the housewife's shelf.[27]

For most of the nineteenth century, Eliza Leslie's *The Lady's Receipt Book* was the best-selling cookbook in the United States.[28] Leslie included a recipe for temperance plum pudding, but in many other instances she gave recipes calling for wine and brandy. In other words, she took a far-from-abstemious approach to gastronomy. An even livelier palate was encouraged in *The Virginia Housewife* by Mary Randolph.[29] Randolph gave a recipe for fish chowder with two cups of white wine, for example, and also one for gazpacho, the cold vegetable soup that is a classic of Spanish cuisine. *The Housekeeper's Book* of 1838 discussed a "mode of dressing cauliflowers with Parmesan cheese."[30] Other antebellum cookbooks included recipes for sauce Italian (with mushrooms, bay leaf, onion, and white wine) and sauce piquante. Finally, the sumptuousness of some cakes in the days before baking powder is indicated by a recipe for white cake that calls for the whites of twenty eggs, one pound of butter, one pound of flour, one pound of loaf sugar, and one pound of blanched almonds crushed fine.[31]

There is reason to believe that baking was the nineteenth-century housewife's particular pride. Said one antebellum writer, "There is nothing in any department of cooking that gives more satisfaction to a young housekeeper than to have accomplished what is called a good baking."[32] There were probably several reasons for this phenomenon. In the first place, a housewife with adequate help might turn over the day-in and day-out preparation of meals to a cook and reserve the baking for special occasions to herself. In the second place, baking called for more skill than any other department of cookery. Heating an oven so that it would be uniformly hot was a very delicate undertaking. Manufacturing one's own yeast for bread required great skill. Beating eggs so that they would have enough volume to support the other ingredients in a cake, especially with the mammoth proportions of those days, was no easy task. In short, every step of the baking process required an apprenticeship and a great deal of practice before the housewife could expect to be an accomplished baker.

Thus the inchoate developments of the early nineteenth century became well-established realities by mid-century. More time, better equipment, more abundant ingredients, and more widely available cookbooks gave middle-class women the opportunity to approach cookery in a wholly new spirit. As Mary Ryan writes in *Cradle of the Middle Class*, by the 1850s "[t]he universal function of cooking . . . had become something more than simply preparing food for human consumption. Even publications addressed to farm women contained increasingly elaborate recipes for cakes and cookies and desserts, all recommended as symbols of domesticity as well as for their nutritional value."[33] Women treasured this expertise, and domestic writers took very seriously the matter of how it might be transferred from mother to daughter.

It was just this sense of an inherited craft tradition that many novelists celebrated. Harriet Beecher Stowe gave a vivid account of the preparations for a New England Thanksgiving in *Oldtown Folks*, for example:

> We also felt its approach in all departments of the household,— the conversation at this time beginning to turn on high and solemn culinary mysteries and receipts of wondrous power and virtue. New modes of elaborating squash pies and quince tarts were now ofttimes carefully discussed at the evening fireside by Aunt Lois and Aunt Keziah, and notes seriously compared with the experiences of certain other Aunties of high repute in such matters. I noticed that on these occasions their voices often fell into mysterious whispers, and that receipts of especial power and sanctity were often communicated in tones so low as entirely to escape the vulgar ear.[34]

There is a gentle humor in this passage but also genuine respect for the collective wisdom of the "aunties."

Susan Warner's *The Wide, Wide World* provides a valuable source for studying attitudes toward a female craft tradition in housewifery both because it was so popular—published in late 1850, it may have been the first novel to sell one million copies—and because it contains a complex sub-theme with respect to domesticity. The young heroine, Ellen Montgomery, loses her mother, a mother who never kept house herself, and goes to live with her aunt, Miss Fortune. Aunt Fortune, the character with the greatest proficiency at housewifery, is not especially sympathetic. Indeed, she treats her motherless niece with great severity. Nonetheless, Aunt Fortune knows her way around a kitchen. The first breakfast Ellen eats after arriving at her aunt's farm sets the tone. Ellen is awakened by the smells and sounds of someone frying at the hearth. Going downstairs she sees her aunt, "crouching by the pan turning her slices of pork."

> In a few minutes the pan was removed from the fire, and Miss Fortune went on to take out the brown slices of nicely fried pork and arrange them in a deep dish, leaving a small quantity of clear fat in the pan. Ellen, who was greatly interested, and observing every step most attentively, settled in her own mind that this would be thrown away. . . .[35]

But instead she sees her aunt make gravy, pouring cream into the pan and then "a fine white shower of flour." Soon the mixture has been transformed "as if by magic to a thick white froth."

Despite her aunt's harshness, Ellen cannot resist being fascinated by so much dazzling prowess. Happily for Ellen, there are other women characters she can observe in the performance of domestic duties without the risk attendant on observation of her aunt, a risk occasioned by her aunt's sharp tongue and imperious demands. She watches her surrogate mother, Alice Humphreys, make tea cakes, for example, and also watches a kindly neighbor, Mrs. Van Brunt, in action. Mrs. Van Brunt serves her "splitters," "a kind of rich short-cake baked in irons, very thin and crisp, and then split in two and buttered, whence their name."[36]

Thus, in addition to the narrative tension created by the unfolding of melodramatic events in this novel—which some scholars claim to have inaugurated the very concept of "best-seller"—there is an under-lying tension created as the reader wonders how many trials Ellen will undergo before she learns the housewifely arts. Even mundane physical details are important. Ellen expresses repugnance about cleaning up after other people:

> "Look here," said Miss Fortune,—"don't you let me hear no more of that, or I vow I'll give you something to do you won't like. Now put the spoons here, and the knives and forks to-gether here; and carry the salt-cellar and the pepper-box and the butter and the sugar into the buttery."
>
> "I don't know where to put them," said Ellen.
>
> "Come along then, and I'll show you; it's time you did."
>
> . . . This was Ellen's first introduction to the buttery; she had never dared to go in there before. It was a long light closet or pantry, lined on the left side, and at the further end, with wide shelves up to the ceiling. On these shelves stood many capa-cious pans and basins, of tin and earthen ware, filled with milk and most of them coated with superb yellow cream.[37]

In the end there is no satisfactory resolution to the issue of how Ellen will be inducted into the female craft tradition because the young heroine is whisked off to an aristocratic never-never land in Scotland where she has a whole new set of problems. Nonetheless, it is not hard to imagine that one of the reasons for the book's unprecedented success was the fact that hundreds of thousands of American women were fascinated by Ellen's pre-Scotland plight: her aunt extracts a high price for the domestic apprenticeship; Alice dies, as had Ellen's beloved if unskilled mother, and Mrs. Van Brunt comes from too different a social class to replace Alice.[38]

It is important to juxtapose the cookbooks with the novels because taken together they give us a sense of a craft tradition not only as it was practiced but as it was savored by its practitioners. Moreover, if we juxtapose surviving nineteenth-century needlework with nineteenth-century women's magazines we can glimpse a similar phenomenon. In her beautifully illustrated history of American needlework, Susan Swan argues that by mid-century, middle-class women had more time than ever before for fancy work, with the result that they became "zealous needleworkers." They were aided by the fact that widely circulating magazines like *Godey's Lady's Book* published needlework patterns and instructions, thus disseminating skilled techniques beyond an elite. Women could do the needlework and also see their effort validated in a respected national publication.[39] They could aspire to perfect their skills.

That changes in the material foundations of domesticity turned the middle-class house into a home contributed to strengthening the emotional role that could be played by the domestic sphere. The newly potent emotional content of "home" in turn created a religious function for the domestic sphere, one celebrated by the leading Protestant spokespeople of the mid-nineteenth century. In order to understand how home came to be viewed in so transcendent a fashion, however, we need to undertake a brief survey of the changes that had taken place in American Protestantism by 1850.

In its seventeenth-century manifestation, Calvinism—the dominant strand in the colonial religious fabric—was rigorous, demanding, and patriarchal both in theology and in governance. In Calvinist thought, God the Father predestined some to be saved and more to be damned. The fearful sinner could hope for enough signs of divine grace to enable him or her to live a godly life, as, in fact, a "visible saint." But underneath there was bound to be a powerful anxiety because the sermons one heard every Sunday emphasized human shortcomings and depravity. If God the Father was merciful but just in His infinite wisdom, so too should His earthly representative in the community, the clergyman, be merciful but just. For women the prescribed role was to accept clerical authority with meek submission, as they accepted the authority of their husbands within the family.[40]

By the nineteenth century, there had been dramatic changes. The Great Awakening of the eighteenth century had destroyed the unity of Calvinism. This, in turn, undermined the authority of the clergy in the established churches. Human agency began to assume a greater role in theology, too. In fact, by the nineteenth century, mainstream Protestants accepted a view of the individual's capacity to take an active role in his or her own salvation that would have been heresy in the seventeenth century. At the same time, the eighteenth century had also seen an increasingly rational approach to religion gaining acceptance. Deism, a view of God as the clockmaker who started the universe in motion but who is remote from daily lives, was espoused by many Americans, the most prominent being Thomas Jefferson.

A leading scholar of American evangelical religion, William McLoughlin, divides the nineteenth century into the following periods. Between 1800 and 1835 there was a counter-revolution against deism but with much of the bite of seventeenth-century Calvinism gone. Charles Grandison Finney, exponent of the possibilities for human perfectibility, was one of the leading preachers of the day. Another important figure was Lyman Beecher, "a major transitional figure in the adjustment of the churches from the established religion of the colonial period to the new era of voluntarism and denominational competition." The second period, between 1835 and 1875, McLoughlin calls Romantic Evangelicalism. The two leading figures were Horace Bushnell and Henry Ward Beecher. After 1875, liberal Evangelicals began to espouse the Social Gospel.[41]

Thus Romantic Evangelicalism was at its height during the exact period when domesticity enjoyed its greatest esteem. Clearly, this was no coincidence, because what Bushnell and Beecher, among others, did was to create a religious role for the home that made it an even more important institution. The leading theologian of his day, Horace Bushnell presented a view of the importance of nurture in which such vast claims were made for the role of Christian parents in inculcating piety that the home virtually replaced the cross as the central Christian symbol. Reacting to the revivals that flourished in the Age of Jackson, with their heavy emphasis on a single act of conversion, Bushnell set out to describe an alternative route to salvation. Building on the foundation of Scottish common sense philosophy—the Scottish thinkers had placed great stress on cultivating the moral capacity—he offered a "genial reconstruction of theology" in which the child became a "center of hope."[42] According to Bushnell, children should begin to learn about Christ in their early years, but their instruction should be very different from that of an adult. He thought that Christ should be "infused into the childish mind; in other words, that the house, having a domestic spirit of grace dwelling in it, should become the church of childhood, the table and hearth a holy rite and life an element of saving power."[43] Indeed, home and religion are inextricably intertwined in Bushnell's view: "Home and religion are kindred words: names both of love and reverence; home because it is the seat of religion; religion because it is the sacred element of home."[44]

If Horace Bushnell was the most famous American theologian, Henry Ward Beecher was the most famous clergyman during the middle decades of the nineteenth century. Like Bushnell, Beecher espoused a romantic, Christ-centered theology. Like Bushnell, he, too, placed great emphasis on the role of the Christian home. One difference between them lay in the fact that Beecher tended to stress the conjugal relationship rather than the nurture of children. Many nineteenth-century Protestants saw love as the essence of spiritual life, and this led directly to seeing marriage as a "holy sacrament" for the enjoyment of divine grace.[45] There are numerous passages in Beecher's writings that exemplify this phenomenon, but his novel, Norwood (1867), exemplifies it best. When one of the characters becomes engaged, for example, Beecher's narrator remarks: "From the hour of his engagement, Cathcart was a different man. Every faculty was quickened, but most, his moral nature." After marriage, "[h]e worshipped Rachel with love; he came to her as one comes to an altar or shrine."[46] Describing the home of another set of characters, the narrator says:

> But stop. Turn back. We have neglected the heart of home, the mother's room! The old temple had no such holy of holies. The mother's room! Here came she a bride. Here only God's angels and her own husband have heard what words the inmost heart of love can coin.[47]

It is useful to compare the approach of Bushnell and Beecher with that of the seventeenth-century Puritan Cotton Mather. Like nineteenth-century writers, Mather believed that children should receive instruction in a Christian home. In his diary, he left a detailed description of his own practice of family education. More than one hundred years before the heyday of domesticity, the approach was unabashedly patriarchal: "I first beget in them a high opinion of their father's love to them, and of his being best able to judge what shall be good for them."[48] This is in decided contrast to Beecher's view of the mother's room as the "holy of holies." In the mid-nineteenth century mothers, not fathers, were the moral arbiters.

Very different from evangelical Protestantism was Unitarianism, a liberal creed that emerged in New England in the early nineteenth century and emphasized "the goodness of God and the dignity of man," while de-emphasizing the divinity of Christ. Indeed, there were a series of bitter battles between clergy of the two persuasions in the early 1800s.[49] What the two had in common, however—and this indicates how pervasive the cult of domesticity was in American culture—was agreement on the value of home and the importance of mother. Theodore Parker, a leading Unitarian clergyman in the antebellum period (and a militant abolitionist) dilated on these subjects in more than one sermon. "Home is the dearest spot in the world," Parker maintained, and mother, "the dearest name that mortal lips can ever speak." Indeed, we know God through our mothers. "Her conscience went before us as a great wakening light. . . ." A

motherly woman can even educate her husband, he asserted.[50] Thus
we see that by the antebellum years, for both evangelical and liberal
Protestants, home had acquired a transcendence that it had lacked in
the eighteenth century.

Not surprisingly, the new valorization of "home," "mother," and
"wife" had profound consequences for American women. With home
seen as the front line of action to produce virtuous citizens, women
would need adequate training for their new tasks. More than one
scholar has demonstrated how significant the ideology of Republican
Motherhood was in promoting better education for women.[51] In the
words of Benjamin Rush:

> I beg pardon for having delayed so long to say any thing of the
> separate and peculiar mode of education proper for women in
> a republic. I am sensible that they must concur in all our plans
> of education for young men . . . they should not only be in-
> structed in the usual branches of female education, but they
> should also be taught the principles of liberty and government;
> and the obligations of patriotism should be inculcated upon
> them. The opinions and conduct of men are often regulated by
> the women in the most arduous enterprizes of life; and their
> approbation is frequently the principal reward of the hero's
> dangers, and the patriot's toils. Besides, the first impressions
> upon the mind of children are generally derived from the
> women. Of how much consequence, therefore, is it in a repub-
> lic that they should think justly upon the great subject of lib-
> erty and government.[52]

So many Americans agreed with Rush that by 1860 there was little
discernible difference in the literacy rates of the two sexes. What is
more, girls were just about as likely to be found in school as boys.[53]
All of this represented a sharp break with the colonial past.

The growing number of educated, urban women created a market
for advice books and novels—as well as for cookbooks—and both of
these genres then reflected the new possibilities for female self-
esteem available by the antebellum period. We have already examined *The Wide, Wide World* in some detail. Susan Warner's "best-
seller" was part of a veritable flood of domestic novels in the 1850s,

many of them setting forth extremely positive views of the housewife. For decades these novels have been ignored, patronized, or dismissed with contempt.[54] Now both the novels and their authors are being placed under the historical scrutiny they deserve, considering their enormous popularity.[55]

What is most striking about the novels when one reads a number of them at a time is the fact that, by and large, marriage is rarely depicted as the solution to a woman's problems. Rather, the heroine has to learn to develop her own resources and to display pluck in order to keep body and soul together. In many instances, she becomes a professional writer. In one clearly autobiographical novel, Fanny Fern's *Ruth Hall*, the widowed heroine is reduced to doing laundry before she discovers her writing talent and goes on to fame and fortune. The heroine of E. D. E. N. Southworth's *The Deserted Wife* becomes a professional singer, and with her income restores her ancestral home and gets her husband back on her own terms. Still unable to read about other women's activities in newspapers or history books, women could now read novels that depicted such activities—activities beyond what appertained merely to the realm of romance, and that often gave minute character analyses of their female protagonists. This phenomenon, in turn, validated female experience in a wholly unprecedented way.

Like the novels, the advice books presented a highly positive view of the housewife's role. One can, in fact, discern a strengthening of this tendency within a very short period of time. We begin with *Domestic Duties* by Frances Parkes. Originally published in England, the third edition was revised for the American market and published in the United States in 1829. Parkes claimed unequivocally: "The world corrupts; home should refine. . . ."[56] The self-interestedness fostered by the former injures the mind, tarnishing it with "a rust which nothing can better remove than home, when it is properly organized. . . ." She thought that because contemporary women were better educated than hitherto, they enjoyed an esteem that produced greater delicacy of conduct by men and would lead to the decay of such customs as the post-dinner segregation of the sexes. In these regards, she was a woman of her time and even prescient about the future. In other ways, however, the book looked backward to the eighteenth century. Parkes denounced the new practice of "shopping" as a "fashionable method of killing time," which was unfair to the shopkeepers.[57] Further, she thought that woman's employments in the home, however useful, did not challenge the mind as did male employments. At its height many exponents of the cult of domesticity would present an altogether different argument, claiming that a housewife might well benefit from an understanding of the principles of chemistry, for example, to say nothing of the depth of moral and religious training she needed. Parkes's book is valuable in that she presents an inchoate vision of what others would later develop more fully and state more forcefully.

Another early writer on domesticity was the feminist-abolitionist, Lydia Maria Child. Because she engaged in a voluminous correspondence, which has been preserved and even indexed, we are fortunate enough to be able to juxtapose her prescriptions for "the American Frugal Housewife" with her descriptions of her own housewifely experiences. Students of Child's life have pointed out that Child's marriage to a man who tended to be improvident meant that she had less domestic help than was usual for a middle-class woman.[58] What is more, she and David Child spent several years living apart, evidently for financial reasons. Therefore her close study of the best way to achieve frugality, reflected in her popular advice book of 1829, was no affectation.

Child wrote *The American Frugal Housewife* during the first year of her marriage, and from then until the end of her long life she wrote and published almost constantly. Her letters reflect the strain of carrying the "double burden" of heavy domestic responsibilities and writing—writing not as an avocation but in order to support herself and her husband. One of the chief publicists for the cult of domesticity, she often expressed the longing for a chance to enjoy a home herself in a more unqualified way. For example, after twenty years of marriage, she wrote to her husband, "Oh, if we only *could* have ever so small a home, where you could be contented and have no dreams about Congress!"[59] In a letter to her mother-in-law written eighteen years earlier, she had mentioned their "pecuniary troubles" and had exclaimed, "Sometimes I get a little fidgety because I want to go to housekeeping so much—and it is such a long, long way out of the woods yet."[60] Letters to friends, written in the intervals when she actually had the responsibility for a home, frequently enumerated a set of extremely arduous chores, including, in addition to cooking, sewing, and washing, such items as mending rat-gnawed meal bags, whitewashing the house, and mending old carpets. At one point she wrote, "I often think if we could graze in the fields, like the cows, and have a pretty feathered suit for our life-time, like the dear little birds, it would be vastly convenient."[61]

The American Frugal Housewife reflects a practical, no-nonsense tone. Every object and process in the home should be studied for ways to save either time or money, Child suggests. Girls as young as six can begin to contribute to the household economy by braiding straw for their own bonnets. "Economical people will seldom use preserves, except for sickness. They are unhealthy, expensive, and useless to those who are well."[62] She gives no recipe for pound cake, stating that "cup cake is about as good as pound cake, and is cheaper." On the other hand, "There is a kind of tea cake still cheaper."[63] In addition to the recipes there is advice on everything, from how to get rid of warts to how to get rid of red ants.

Like *Domestic Duties*, Child's book contains elements of both old and new. In its practical tone and unsentimental approach to advice giving, *The American Frugal Housewife* resembles a latter-day *Poor Richard's Almanac*. At one point Child even quoted one of Dr. Franklin's maxims: "Nothing is cheap that we do not want."[64] Yet in her view of the importance of a good education for women she was articulating one of the tenets of the new style of domesticity and anticipating arguments that Catharine Beecher would present more systematically a dozen or so years later: "There is no subject so much connected with individual happiness and national prosperity as the education of daughters." Girls require a sound *domestic* education, however, so that they can cultivate their own happiness and that of others: "The difficulty is, education does not usually point the female heart to its only true resting-place. That dear English word home is not half so powerful a talisman as the world. Instead of the salutary truth, that happiness is *in* duty, they are taught to consider the two things totally distinct; and that whoever seeks one, must sacrifice the other."[65]

Catharine Sedgwick's novel, *Home*, published in 1835, provides a particularly valuable source for examining the characteristics of the early cult of domesticity because its tone is so didactic as to reveal clearly the author's own views. In a work possessing little literary merit but evidently resonating in the minds of Jacksonian Americans, Sedgwick chronicled the fortunes of the Barclay family, with an eye to providing precise details about an exemplary home. She describes the food, conversation, and interaction at the Barclay dinner table and then sets a parallel scene in a chaotic household so that her readers can learn what to do and what not to do. Mr. and Mrs. Barclay regard meals as three opportunities a day for teaching "punctuality, order, neatness, temperance, self-denial, kindness, generosity, and hospitality." The food may be frugal, but the table is set with "scrupulous neatness."[66] Meals proceed at a deliberate pace so that Mr. Barclay may instruct along the way. Boldly asserting the value of good works as well as church attendance—the Barclays go to public worship on Sunday mornings and engage in charitable activities in the afternoon—Sedgwick also describes the way both husband and wife spend time on the Sabbath inculcating Irish immigrants with American values. Mrs. Barclay says that while her husband gives instruction in the responsibilities of citizenship, "I take upon myself the more humble, womanly task of directing their domestic affections and instructing them, as well as I am able, in their everyday home duties."[67] Again we see an intermingling of old and new, with Mr. Barclay viewed in rather patriarchal a light, relative to the literature of mid-century.

Although she, too, published domestic advice in the 1830s, the Hartford poet Lydia Sigourney represents a somewhat later stage in the evolution of the cult of domesticity. Rather than conceding that household duties call forth only a limited range of abilities, she asserts, "The science of housekeeping affords exercise for the judgment and energy, ready recollection and patient self-possession that are the characteristics of a superior mind."[68] In particular, "Cookery it is surely the business of the mistress of a family either to do, or to see well done. . . . Neither is it a despicable discipline of the mind. Its details are almost endless. . . ."[69] While deprecating the idea that women might share in the actual administration of government, she clearly believes in the value of Republican Mothers: "The aid of the weaker vessel is now invoked by legislators and sages. It has been discovered that there are signs of disease in the body politick, which can best be allayed, by the subordination taught in families and through *her* agency to whom is committed the moulding of the whole mass of mind in its first formation."[70] Indeed, she advances a specifically historical generalization to validate the role of the Republican Mother: "It has been remarked that almost all illustrious men have been distinguished by love for their mother."[71]

In yet another way did Sigourney foreshadow themes that would be set forth in the 1840s and 1850s: "Homes should be the centre but not the boundary of our duties; the focus of sympathy, but not the point where it terminates. The action of the social feelings is essential to a well-balanced character. Morbid diseases are generated by an isolated life. . . ."[72] In other words, there is no antithesis between concern for one's home and concern for one's society. The world outside the home is more than a source of danger to be avoided or a corrupting influence; it should properly be the recipient of charitable energies that spill over from one's home life.

As for the attitudes of male writers toward domesticity, the examination of how leading male intellectuals felt toward the home belongs to the next chapter, on the epic stage of domesticity. In looking at the emergence of the new ideology, it is important to note, however, that early on there were men who gave advice about the home to other men. The type of advice they gave explains, in part, how the cult could empower women. That is, the fact that middle-class men were being told to respect the domestic sphere and to subordinate some portion of self in order to achieve the optimum home makes comprehensible the leverage that gave women more influence—at least potentially—in their own households than had been the case in the colonial period.

One of the most prolific dispensers of advice was William Andrus

Alcott. A physician and the author of some thirty books and pamphlets, Alcott wrote for the young husband as well as for the young wife. Achieving a happy Christian home was the supreme felicity for both sexes, he thought. "I have seen bliss begun below. . . . I have known a husband who regarded home, not as a prison—a place of irksome restraint—and its inmates fellow-prisoners, but as a scene of the highest delight."[73] While he ascribed the preponderance of authority in making decisions to husbands, he thought that marriage should be a "school" for both parties. Husbands owed consideration to their wives; for example, they should be careful about bringing dirt into the house. Alcott thought that, in general, husbands did not render enough help to their wives.

Another prolific writer of the Victorian period, Timothy Shay Arthur, author of *Ten Nights in a Barroom,* among other novels, gave the ideology of Republican Motherhood an unusual twist in his advice to young men. If writers of the early Republic had urged that women be well educated so that they could train good citizens, thereby giving the home an expressly political function, Arthur went so far as to argue that no man could be a good citizen unless he were to have a good home:

> Indeed, the more perfectly a man fulfills all his domestic duties, the more perfectly in that very act, has he discharged his duty to the whole . . . those who have least regard for home—who have indeed, no home, no domestic circle—are the worst citizens.[74]

Indeed, the domestic sphere was special for men as well as women. "Home is man's true place."[75]

Home might be "man's true place," but most Americans probably would have agreed with Henry Clarke Wright that, above all, it was the "empire of the mother," to use the title of one of Wright's books. Like Alcott and Arthur, Wright was an enormously popular writer who extolled the value of the home. Like many of his contemporaries, such as Alcott, he believed that the best home was the purest home, and that meant that sex should be for procreation only. Thus we see another means by which the cult of domesticity gave women leverage within families: Wright and others were counseling men that it was so important that a mother's rule be respected that a husband should learn to curb his sexual appetite in deference to her presumed passionlessness. The man who thinks of marriage primarily as a means to sensual gratification will never have a pure and happy home, Wright asserted. Further:

> The details of domestic economy can never be repulsive to the true husband. On the contrary, to relieve the wants and cares of the wife, in any way, and help her to bear the burdens of household labor, is not to serve as a menial, but to cherish her and to sustain her as a husband.[76]

The point in examining these three male authors is not to suggest that their advice was invariably or literally followed. It is well known that prescriptive literature cannot be taken as a description of social reality. Moreover, the internal dynamics of any marriage, including the distribution of power between husband and wife, will depend on a number of factors such as the strength of personality of the two people involved and the legal rights of both. But when a culture enshrines the home and the moral authority of the mother to the extent that American culture did in the mid-nineteenth century, a wife has a rationale for advancing her claims.

We do have one body of evidence that suggests that the new prescriptions affected behavior: the decreasing family size in the nineteenth century. Daniel Scott Smith coined the term "domestic feminism"—which means, in essence, women using domestic credentials to enhance their position in the family or in the society—in order to account for the declining birth rate during that period from an average of seven children per married white woman in 1800 to an average of three and a half in 1900. He speculates that husbands, newly respectful of their wives' autonomy, cooperated in the attempt to have fewer children, an interpretation endorsed by Carl Degler.[77] Nancy Cott has delineated the ideological means by which this reduction in family size may well have come about. According to the tenets of the emerging cult of domesticity and in the view of writers like Alcott and Wright, as we have discovered, women were seen as lacking sexual passion—in contrast to earlier Protestant views of Eve as a temptress—and therefore husbands were expected to keep their sexual appetites under tight control.[78] Whether sexual withholding from their husbands may have exacted too high a price from the women themselves is, of course, an important issue and one that will no doubt be subject to scholarly debate.

That declining family size not only reflected the strength of the cult of domesticity but also enhanced that strength as the century wore on and the average family grew ever smaller in number must be understood, too. In the colonial period, a woman spent the preponderance of her adult life pregnant, lactating, or with responsibility for somewhat older children. This placed a heavy burden on her health and energy. Moreover, a housewife's capacity to approach domestic tasks as aesthetic activities was undercut by the burden of her reproductive responsibilities to her family. An exhausted woman needing to sew for a family of eight children, for example, could not devote her time to fancy needlework or fancy baking. She also had less time to read, whether advice books, cookbooks, or novels.

In discussing the formulation of the cult of domesticity, one wishes to know how much impact the newly valorized role of the home had on women's concepts of self. In truth, knowing the extent to which the cult enhanced women's self-esteem would require the examination of a large number of surviving letters and diaries in order to approach an adequate answer. There are indications, though, that the new value conferred on the home gave women a greater chance to feel satisfied about doing important work than had been the case in the eighteenth century.

One nineteenth-century woman whose diary reflected high self-esteem about her performance as a housewife was Harriet Robinson. The wife of an editor whose worldly success was never great, she took considerable pride in being "a good poor man's wife." She knew that her skills were essential to the family economy and thought that it took "a woman of Genius" to be a good housewife and that cooking was "one of the fine arts." Robinson sewed for her family and was especially pleased with herself when she was able to recycle garments. One daughter's hooded red cape was cut down from an old dress and dyed, for example. Her biographer, Claudia Bushman, has this to say about Harriet Robinson: "Harriet was competent, maybe even inspired in her job as housewife. She had mastered her calling and could not help thinking well of herself."[79] It should be noted that she did have "daily" help with the heavier chores and that "her major duties were managerial rather than manual."[80]

But even if the valorization of the home made it likely that domesticity was an "adequate prop" for female self-esteem, we must not quit our discussion of the emergence of the new values without acknowledging how hard many women's lives still were in the nineteenth century. If we examine just one family—and that a family of outspoken advocates of the cult of domesticity—we can gain insight into the sheer onerousness of the housewife's job. Harriet Beecher Stowe wrote the best-selling novel of the nineteenth century, *Uncle Tom's Cabin,* but in addition she also wrote books and articles on the good home and how to achieve it. No one wrote more feelingly than she about the joy of nurturing young creatures (even plants). Yet before she wrote *Uncle Tom's Cabin* and became world-famous and while she was in fact immersed in domesticity with a number of young children to care for, she was much less positive about her own tasks. In fact, Stowe may have suffered acutely from the disjunction between the ideal of marriage and family life that she celebrated in her novels and her own experience as a wife and mother. At one point while her children were small, she took the water cure for nearly a year, thus escaping from all domestic responsibilities and also insuring that she would not become pregnant during this interval. Shortly before she took the cure, she had written that she was "sick of the smell of sour milk, and sour meat, and sour everything, and then the clothes *will* not dry, and no wet thing does, and everything smells mouldy; and altogether I feel as if I never wanted to eat again."[81]

A member of one of the best-known families in the country, Stowe nonetheless endured many of the problems that confronted other women who were less well known. Her husband Calvin Stowe, a clergyman and professor, had difficulty earning enough money to support his family above the level of genteel poverty in the early days of the marriage. Thus the family was unable to afford a level of domestic help adequate to relieve Stowe's heavy burdens. She bore several children within the space of a few years, including twin girls. Her time was fragmented between the necessities of child care and housework and the need to write in order to bring in extra money. In her memoir of Stowe, Annie Fields describes an episode in which another woman friend was urging the young writer to complete a story. Stowe is said to have replied to the friend:

> "But, my dear, here is a baby in my arms and two little pussies by my side, and there is a great baking down in the kitchen, and there is a 'new girl' for 'help,' besides preparations to be made for housecleaning next week. It is really out of the question, you see."[82]

While frequently complaining about being overburdened, Stowe at least preserved her health. In this respect, she was more fortunate than her sister-in-law, Eunice, wife of Henry Ward Beecher. Too much work and too many pregnancies robbed Eunice Beecher of both health and spirits, and she spent the last several decades of her life as a sickly and querulous semi-invalid. Nonetheless she joined her husband and sisters-in-law in writing domestic advice, *All Around the House; or How To Make Homes Happy*.[83]

With such examples before her, Catharine Beecher, Stowe's sister and author of the best-known treatises on domestic economy of the nineteenth century, advanced sweeping generalizations about the extent of female invalidism in the United States. She first sounded the warning in *A Treatise on Domestic Economy*. Young American girls had delicate constitutions to begin with, she thought, and when they had to deal with the "trials of domestic life," they were often incapacitated.[84] A dozen years later Beecher published *Letters to the People on Health and Happiness*, in which she maintained that, according to her personal study of dozens of communities, sick women outnumbered the well by a three-to-one margin.[85] In other words, despite her warm advocacy of domesticity, she worried that these responsibilities took a heavy toll on American women.

Those housewives who escaped overwork all too often did so at the expense of other women, that is, by the exploitation of servants. As the century wore on and there were increasing class differences between mistress and maid—and eventually ethnic and racial differences as well—women who worked as domestics were increasingly likely to be excluded from the benefits of domesticity they provided for others. In an earlier day, when housewives used "help" rather than employing "servants," mistress and maid had worked side by side, with the latter knowing that she could realistically aspire to having a comfortable establishment of her own some day. Not so by mid-century. Domestics were most often immigrants and part of the working class for their entire lives. The extent to which working-class families participated in the ideology of domesticity—or created their own variant of the middle-class norm—is worth a book in itself. What can be known with certainty is that a working-class woman was at least as likely as Harriet Beecher Stowe or Eunice Beecher to be overworked and overburdened, whether she was a domestic in some one else's home or a married woman with a family of her own.[86]

Moreover, the ideal may well have outstripped the real with respect to companionate marriage. Carl Degler and others have argued that new, egalitarian norms for marriage became widely diffused in the United States by about 1830, norms that both precipitated the creation of the cult of domesticity and promoted its continuance. A recent study by Suzanne Lebsock reminds us that, companionate marriage notwithstanding, the law gave husbands by far the greater share of power within a marriage in the antebellum years. In studying the free women of Petersburg, Virginia, between 1784 and 1860, she was struck by the number of common-law disabilities that encumbered married women. In addition, men did not often make their wives the executors of their wills.[87] It is useful to be reminded that, while the culture reflected an image of the woman as moral arbiter, until well into the nineteenth century the law gave men the power of a patriarch. This was accomplished by the restrictions on a married woman's property rights and also on her right to custody of her own children in the event of a divorce.

It must also be acknowledged that the ideology of domesticity was narrow in many ways, especially in its early phase. It had not only been primarily generated by New England writers to reflect the concerns of white, Anglo, middle-class women,[88] but its exponents usually made a series of invidious assumptions about women of other classes, regions, and ethnic origins, to say nothing of other colors. The figure of the New England housewife was singled out so often for special mention that it is clear that she was becoming a stock character in American literature as well as the standard of excellence in the manuals. We find Sigourney, for example, warning that it is difficult to combine being a truly excellent housekeeper with a literary career, *especially in New England*.[89] In other words, New England women were assumed to have higher standards than women in the rest of the country. In *Home* Sedgwick took it for granted that her readers would share her frame of reference when she wrote about the way Mrs. Barclay spent Sunday afternoons instructing Irish women in "domestic affections" and "everyday home duties." When Irish immigrant women began to flock into domestic service there were repeated references in the advice literature to the tedium of teaching "green Erin" the domestic graces. The assumption was that these young women, coming from homes too poor to enjoy many comforts, were ignorant of the very meaning of "home" as it was then being apotheosized.

No doubt women in the more settled parts of the country had an easier time creating homes—in the fullest sense of the word—than on the frontier, although the evidence is accumulating to suggest that "westering" women sought to recreate the same domestic sphere they had left behind when they reached the new country.[90] In her recent book on southern women, Catharine Clinton suggests that plantation mistresses had a much more tenuous hold on the cult of domesticity than had their northern counterparts. This was because female virtue in the South was still defined primarily in terms of chastity. A southern woman might perform very onerous work, but the regional norm defined her only as a lady (or not a lady) and not as a "frugal housewife."[91] Thus the stock New England housewife might have had a certain basis in reality, but there seems to be no empirical foundation strong enough to justify the negative stereotypes of housewives outside the favored area and class that were so freely put forth.

Finally, although the cult of domesticity did not create an asymmetrical gender system—as we have seen male and female tasks were highly differentiated in the pre-industrial period, for example—it did little or nothing to challenge the idea of sexual asymmetry. Valorizing home does not necessarily entail ascribing domestic tasks only to women. In fact, at mid-century a few people were moving toward the position that both sexes should share domestic tasks. But most Americans tied a heightened appreciation of home to an ideology of sex roles in which women were seen as by nature more gentle, more loving, and more willing to sacrifice than men. What was new about the cult was that, for the first time in American history, both home and woman's special nature were seen as uniquely valuable.

Therefore, despite all the limitations and the gaps between the ideal and the real, the cult of domesticity had a favorable impact on women. Wherever a middle-class housewife turned—whether to her minister's words from the pulpit or to her favorite reading matter—she could see and hear her value and the value of the home for which she was responsible being affirmed. Moreover, Harriet Beecher Stowe, overworked and worn out as she may have felt herself to be at some stages of her life, had an influence on American culture and on the course of American history that no woman before had ever enjoyed—and not many since. This influence came about because Stowe used the moral authority of the housewife to justify speaking out against slavery. The cult of domesticity was predicated in part on the idea that the home has an expressly political function. The political impact of *Uncle Tom's Cabin*, filled as it is with domestic imagery, demonstrated how the influence of home on the world could manifest itself.

TWO

The Golden Age of Domesticity

W HEN THE HOME acquired so diverse and expanded a set of roles in the early nineteenth century—political, religious, emotional, and social—it ceased to be automatically taken for granted by men. Indeed, by 1850 the home had become a mainstay of the national culture. Many scholars have discussed women's culture in the nineteenth century and have related it to the strength of the cult of domesticity.[1] What has been insufficiently recognized, however, is the extent to which men, too, entered into the ideology of domesticity, helping to create and perpetuate it. In so doing they took the home beyond the boundaries of "woman's sphere" and into the national arena. Moreover, in so doing, they and the female exponents of the cult created yet another role for the home, an epic one in which the home provided a touchstone of values for reforming the entire society. The epic style of domesticity then resonated in the minds of middle-class women and impelled them to participate in crusades outside the home. In fact, when the cult of domesticity reached its height, middle-class women began to organize for exerting influence in the world as never before and in such a way that public and private values were genuinely intermingled rather than being dichotomized. Hence the designation "Golden Age" for the mid-nineteenth century.

Furthermore, the intermingling of public and domestic spheres in turn created the possibility of establishing a symmetrical gender system—although such was not to be the case for generations and is still not fully realized. Eighteenth-century America had seen highly differentiated spheres, with all glory and honor being accorded to the public realm. The cult of domesticity created a new respect for the private sphere, and when certain of its exponents, male and female, began to carry domestic values outside the home, they also carried a rationale for private, "indoors" people—that is, women—to be publicly active. This, then, solved the problem of how to mediate between two spheres that were not only geographically distinct but also populated by entirely different groups of people once industrialization took male work away from the home.

This problem was well depicted in one of Lydia Maria Child's short stories. In "Home and Politics," Child, whose own domestic life was troubled and unhappy owing to the fecklessness of her husband, delineated an unbridgeable gap between the realms of the two sexes. The fictional husband, an enthusiast for Henry Clay, becomes so absorbed in politics that he neglects his domestic responsibilities. His wife eventually goes mad. Citing this story to demonstrate the difficulty of reconciling home values and worldly values, Kirk Jeffrey says, "Essentially, Mrs. Child is here wrestling with the same difficulty: experience in the world inevitably changes a person, but the cult of home demanded that one return absolutely intact."[2] Yet as the epic style of domesticity developed, this difficulty was addressed because women, too, began to speak out on public issues—in the name of the home—while many men proclaimed the salience of domestic values.

It was not just evangelical Christian men like Horace Bushnell and Henry Ward Beecher who waxed eloquent about the home. Indeed, we have already encountered some of Theodore Parker's thoughts on the subject. But the most important male writer to deal with the home was Ralph Waldo Emerson, who was unquestionably the most influential American thinker of his time. It is well known that Emerson hoped to precipitate the creation of a unique American culture with his book *Nature*. What has been ignored for decades is the fact that he also gave thought to the moral foundations of the just household in a democratic society. This is not to say that domesticity was a major component of his work. Nonetheless, what he wrote about the home in the essay "Domestic Life" was striking and original.

In the first place, he advocated a distribution of household tasks that would reflect democratic values:

> I think it plain that this voice of communities and ages, "Give us wealth, and the good household shall exist," is vicious, and leaves the whole difficulty untouched. It is better, certainly, in this form, "Give us your labor, and the household begins." I see not how serious labor, the labor of all and every day is to be avoided. . . .[3]

Taken in its most literal fashion, this passage would seem to indicate an absolutely egalitarian approach to housework. It is unlikely, however, that the sage of Concord was prepared to do laundry. In fact, there are other passages in the essay which reflect the view that domestic chores belong to women. What he was attempting, rather, was to combat the application of invidious caste distinctions to domestics. In his judgment, Americans needed to rethink their approach to manual labor:

> . . . many things betoken a revolution of opinion and practice in regard to manual labor that may go far to aid our practical inquiry. . . . But the reform that applies itself to the household must not be partial. It must correct the whole system of our social living. It must come with plain living and high thinking; it must break up caste and put domestic service on another foundation.[4]

We know that Emerson tried to put this approach into practice in his own household, developing an interest in the daily allocation of work, for example, and attempting to persuade the Irish cook to take her meals with the family.[5]

If the just household must free itself from caste, it must also embody other virtues such as charity and hospitality. Emerson urged his

countrymen and -women to go beyond material comfort and pru-
dence in envisioning the ideal home:

> With these [purely material] ends housekeeping is not beau-
> tiful; it cheers and raises neither the husband, the wife, nor
> the child; neither the host nor the guest; it oppresses women.
> A house kept to the end of display is impossible to all but a
> few women, and their success is dearly bought.[6]

In the second place Emerson's emphasis on the importance of hospitality is so marked that it seems clear that he was trying to mediate
between the public and private spheres in this fashion. On the one
hand, he pointed out that domestic life is more salient to most of us
than the public life of the world outside the home: "Domestic events
are certainly our affair. What are called public events may or may
not be ours." But on the other hand, he was astute enough to realize
that it would be bad for a society should families simply retreat into
their homes. Therefore, families should be hospitable: "Let a man
then say, My house is here in the county for the culture of the
county;—an eating-house and sleeping house for travellers it shall
be. . . ." Rather than being the castle of the man who dwells there,
the virtuous home will be a shrine radiating outward, "pulses of
thought that go to the borders of the universe." Thus the leading
American intellectual of the nineteenth century not only took the
home seriously but also tried explicitly to bridge the gap between
home and the world. That his writings had a contemporary impact
is suggested by the fact that in 1897, Lucy Salmon used Emerson's
thoughts about eliminating caste in the household as the frontispiece
for her book, *Domestic Service*.

Despite his wife's frequent ill health, Emerson offered hospitality
on the scale he himself advocated. Elizabeth Oakes Smith, a feminist
lecturer, stayed with the Emersons when she spoke to the Lyceum of
Concord. In her memoirs she recalled the experience as follows: "It
was indeed a model household." Everything was fresh, clean, and
well ordered, she remembered. The food was wholesome, and meals
were enhanced by "Mr. Emerson so quietly breathing out his precious aphorisms."[7]

Unfortunately, however, though Lidian Emerson took pride in her housekeeping and evidently did a good job as a hostess, she had to cope with bouts of invalidism throughout most of her adult life. Her frequent illnesses suggest that she found her role as the wife of a Great Man to provide insufficient nourishment for her own ego.[8] Thus we glimpse the darker side of domesticity. Despite the valorization of home, an entirely house-bound wife might be prey to debilitating depressions, and this even when her husband was, like Emerson, genuinely interested in the domestic sphere.

Emerson's Concord neighbor, Nathaniel Hawthorne, was another major male writer who drew upon the tenets of the ideology of domesticity. In *The House of the Seven Gables*, published in 1851 and hence contemporaneous with *The Wide, Wide World* and *Uncle Tom's Cabin*, he even drew on the conventions of the domestic novel. This is indeed ironic considering his well-known outburst against the "damned mob of scribbling women," whose novels were outselling his. Nonetheless, the ideology of domesticity was sufficiently pervasive that it found its way into his novel. In fact, a house and a housewife embody the moral polarities of *The House of the Seven Gables*.

This work is a chronicle of the Pyncheon family from its Puritan origins to its decline in the mid-nineteenth century. Hawthorne's imagination, haunted as it was by the impact of the past, created a house whose forbidding appearance bespeaks the rapacity and unhappiness that were the Pyncheon family heritage. How this should happen he explains on the first page:

> The aspect of the venerable mansion has always affected me like a human countenance, bearing the traces not merely of outward storm and sunshine, but expressive also of the long lapse of mortal life, and accompanying vicissitudes that have passed within.[9]

No physical detail of the house escapes his attention, from the architecture to the furnishings to the tea cups.

The Pyncheon family had acquired title to the land because of the death of its original owner, Matthew Maule. Colonel Pyncheon had collaborated in the witchcraft prosecution—and execution—of the rightful owner, and at the moment of death Maule had laid a curse on the Pyncheons. As the novel opens, the gloomy and decaying dwelling of an accursed family is being occupied by poor Hepzibah Pyncheon. Tall, angular, unmarried, and dried-up, Hepzibah is incapable of doing anything to combat the all-pervasive gloom and is, in fact, the antithesis of the good housewife. Hawthorne does show us, however, that she has a tender heart despite her scowling countenance.

Both the house and the family are thus in a state of decay when young Phoebe Pyncheon arrives for a visit. If Hepzibah is the antithesis, then cousin Phoebe is the prototype of the notable housewife:

> Little Phoebe was one of those persons who possess, as their exclusive patrimony, the gift of practical arrangement. It is a kind of natural magic that enables the favored ones to bring out the hidden capabilities of things around them; and particularly to give a look of comfort and habitableness to any place which, for however brief a period, may happen to be their home. A wild hut of underbrush, tossed together by wayfarers through the primitive forest, would acquire the home aspect by one night's lodging of such a woman. . . .[10]

Godey's itself could not have given a better description of the ideal housewife.

It soon appears that, if any human agency can redeem the Pyncheons, it will be that of loving yet capable Phoebe. At one point, Hepzibah even tells her that her housekeeping skills must have come from her mother's side, because "I never knew a Pyncheon that had any turn for them." Indeed, when Pyncheons are capable, their ability takes the form of evil-doing, as in the case of Judge Jaffrey Pyncheon, the villain, who has hounded Hepzibah and her brother, Clifford, for years. After a complicated series of plot turns, Hawthorne allows the novel to have a happy ending. Judge Pyncheon dies, Phoebe is united with her lover Holgrave, a descendant of the Maules, and the ineffectual Clifford Pyncheon is cleared of any suspicion of murder with respect to his cousin's death. The house itself is beyond redemption so Phoebe and Holgrave make plans to live in the judge's country home.

Just before the final resolution—after Judge Pyncheon's death but before its discovery—there is a scene in which Clifford and Hepzibah are fleeing from their home. Nearly unbalanced by the years of unhappiness betokened by the very appearance of the house of the seven gables, Clifford harangues a stranger on a train about the liberating possibilities of the railroad. Mankind will be able to return to a nomadic state, thanks to this invention, he proclaims. "It is as clear to me as sunshine—were there any in the sky—that the greatest possible stumbling blocks in the path of human happiness and improvement, are these heaps of bricks, and stones, consolidated with mortar, or hewn timber, fastened together with spike-nails, which men painfully contrive for their own torment, and call them house and home!"[11] No doubt Clifford denies the value of "home" because his own house embodies evil. But in giving this character a speech rejecting one of the most important values of the culture, Hawthorne clearly means to shock his readers into understanding the depths of Clifford's despair. So much is the cult of domesticity woven into the fabric of the novel, then, that it would be virtually impossible to understand Hawthorne's intention should the reader be ignorant of the centrality of the home to most Americans at the time it was written.

Taken together, Emerson's essay and Hawthorne's novel offer a program for the American home. It should be free of caste, hospitable, loving, and inhabited by a family whose way of life could be emulated by others. Hawthorne further demonstrated an acute sensitivity to the physical appearance of the home and its appurtenances. Not surprisingly, given the level of interest in the home at midcentury, thousands of Americans shared this interest in the physical characteristics of the house itself and were eager to buy books about architecture. As Henry Ward Beecher put it, "A house is the shape a man's thoughts take when he imagines how he should like to live. Its interior is the measure of his social and domestic nature. . . ."[12] Therefore, the question of design was suffused with moral significance.[13] Middle-class men and women wanted advice on this topic as they wanted advice on behavior from Catharine Beecher, Henry Clarke Wright, and others. Moreover, they sought help in this area for the same reason that they sought it with respect to styles of conduct: the United States was an experiment in a republican society. Not only would there be a new etiquette but pleasant housing would be diffused much more widely throughout the entire land than in the class-ridden Old World. What would houses look like?

Andrew Jackson Downing was perhaps the best known of several authors who wrote profusely illustrated books about the American home during this period. Indeed, his *Architecture of Country Houses* sold more than 16,000 copies by the end of the Civil War. A landscape architect in New York, Downing had firm ideas about how design could express the moral nature of the homeowner. A modest, unpretentious dwelling demonstrated that the owner was free of false ambition, for example. Moreover, he believed, "Something of a love for the beautiful, in the inmates, is always suggested by a vine-covered cottage, because mere utility would never lead any person to plant flowering vines."[14] Vines, thus, add to the "domestic expression" of the house and enhance the quality of "heart" it possesses. Downing also believed that every American dwelling could represent the "home of a virtuous citizen."[15] Here again we encounter the political overtones of the cult of domesticity. If well-educated mothers were to inculcate republican values in their offspring, they would be better able to do so in the appropriate domestic surroundings.

Literate people of both sexes, then, were reading books and periodicals in which the cult of domesticity found expression. Men had access to works reflecting domestic values by many of the leading writers of the age as well as to the numerous "pattern books" about domestic architecture. Nor should we assume that women alone read *Godey's* and the domestic novels. Catharine Sedgwick was flattered to learn that Chief Justice John Marshall was an admirer of her writing, for example.[16] But above all, the career of Sarah Josepha Hale, the editor of *Godey's*, reveals the extent to which men paid heed to a genre, the so-called woman's magazine, which would become "for women only" in the twentieth century.

One of the great editors in American history, Sarah Josepha Hale began her collaboration with Louis Godey in the 1830s. Together they launched *Godey's Lady's Book*, which she continued to edit until 1877, her ninetieth year. *Godey's* contained fiction, poetry, needlework patterns, designs for model homes, and illustrations of the latest fashions, as well as Hale's editorials. In its pages appeared the writing of Edgar Allan Poe, Nathaniel Hawthorne, Ralph Waldo Emerson, Oliver Wendell Holmes, Catharine Beecher, and Harriet Beecher Stowe, to cite only a few of its distinguished contributors. At its height *Godey's* had a circulation of 150,000, with a growth paralleling the growth of the domestic novel. Unquestionably, Hale was one of the two or three most influential American women of the nineteenth century.

No feminist by modern standards—she opposed woman suffrage and believed in clearly delineated separate spheres for the two sexes— Hale was nonetheless a forceful advocate of many improvements in woman's status. She campaigned for better education for women, including higher education. She campaigned for the admission of women to the medical profession. She campaigned for property rights for married women. The list of her favorite reforms would be a long one. Moreover, despite her aversion to women casting ballots, she did not draw the line at other forms of political activity such as writing letters to politicians. Indeed, in the pursuit of her most cherished goal of having the President set aside a national Thanksgiving Day, she fired off a constant barrage of letters to governors, senators, secretaries of state, and Presidents. Henry Clay wrote to thank her for her gifts to himself and his wife, concluding, "I also received the book and papers which you were good enough to send and I shall seize the earliest opportunity to peruse them."[17] Another instance of her impact on men is contained in a letter from Oliver Wendell Holmes, who went so far as to tell her, "Thank you for the 'Editor's Tables'— I read them all and agree with every word you say about women."[18] In 1863, President Lincoln rewarded her efforts on behalf of Thanksgiving Day by proclaiming it as a national holiday. This was an open acknowledgment not only of Hale's influence but also of the political ramifications of domesticity, because Hale had based her campaign for the holiday on the political benefits to be derived from a feast in which the whole nation could participate at once.

Although *Godey's* published both male and female authors and was evidently read by at least a few men, it was clearly designed for a female audience. Not so with *Hearth and Home,* a short-lived but remarkable periodical whose first issue appeared in December 1868, with Harriet Beecher Stowe listed as a co-editor. What makes *Hearth and Home* a revealing document of the Golden Age of Domesticity is the fact that, with so domestic a name, it was designed to appeal to both sexes. In addition to patterns and recipes, excerpts from *Old-town Folks,* and pieces by Rebecca Harding Davis and Thomas Wentworth Higginson, *Hearth and Home* published market information, agricultural advice, and national and international news. It also published a few overtly feminist articles. The issue of October 23, 1869, contained, for example, Grace Greenwood's reply to an anti-feminist statement by Horace Greeley. Greenwood asserted that not all women necessarily wanted to be household queens and that many preferred to be self-supporting. She thought young women should choose a career for themselves. Other issues contained discussions of the merits of cooperative housekeeping, and Harriet Beecher Stowe's forthright reply to an anti-suffrage diatribe by Horace Bushnell.[19] Thus we see that at the height of the Golden Age, a publication fundamentally celebrating domesticity did not confine itself to sentimentalizing narrowly prescribed roles for women but rather reached out to encompass both sexes and to incorporate divergent views on such matters as suffrage and woman's optimal role.

So uniformly accepted a symbol of middle-class values had the home become, then, by mid-century, that it was a logical rallying point for those who wanted to change the world and, in particular, improve the lot of women. Catharine Beecher used the home to justify opening up the profession of teaching to her sex and also to justify making women guardians of the public welfare. Harriet Beecher Stowe gave vivid depictions of notable housewives in her novels and then used the values these characters symbolized to launch a revolutionary attack on the values of the larger society. Antoinette

Brown Blackwell developed a view of the home as a source of renewal for reform energies and ultimately had the courage and imagination to envision a society in which both sexes might share domestic responsibilities as well as having access to the public sphere. Although these women were the leading exemplars of an epic style of domesticity, there were others, too, who shared their vision, in particular two members of the Unitarian clergy, Theodore Parker and Samuel May. The connection between home and world that found its first expression in the ideology of Republican Motherhood thus came to full fruition by the middle of the nineteenth century.

Catharine Esther Beecher was the oldest of the remarkable offspring of Lyman Beecher, a group that also included Harriet Beecher Stowe, the outspoken feminist Isabella Beecher Hooker, Henry Ward Beecher, and a number of other well-respected clergymen. Like many of her siblings, Catharine Beecher launched a rebellion against her father's Calvinist God (although the Calvinism in her father's thought was far less fierce than the seventeenth-century original). When she was twenty-one, her fiancé drowned at sea, a tragedy that required her to forge an independent life for herself and also made her unwilling to accept the traditional Calvinist world-view, a view that would have damned the unconverted Alexander Fisher to eternal punishment.[20] She went on not only to found her own schools for young women but also to launch a long campaign aimed at recruiting young women as teachers. She also dared to write theological treatises expressing her opinions on the importance of free will and human agency. She was perhaps best known in her own day, however, for *A Treatise on Domestic Economy*. In short, in creating her own identity she became an important female progenitor as teacher, as home economist, as architect, and as theologian.[21]

That so outstanding a pioneer and so forceful a personality held entirely traditional views on woman suffrage and woman's sphere should not surprise us. In fact, there was a continuum of opinion on such issues in the nineteenth century, and many of those—such as Sarah Josepha Hale—who crusaded for change in some areas were unwilling to endorse suffrage.[22] Her conservative views on women and ballots notwithstanding, Catharine Beecher, in her *Treatise* of

1841, made larger claims for American women than had ever been publicly made before with very few exceptions (such as the speeches and writings of Sarah and Angelina Grimké). Simply put, Beecher maintained that American democracy rose or fell on the efforts of its female members.

If the home, optimally a loving one, was the most universally shared institution in a hyper-competitive, atomized society, then it had the unique capacity to soften the asperities of life and to prevent society from fragmenting. As Kathryn Kish Sklar puts it in her biography of Beecher:

> Like other writers of the period including Sarah Josepha Hale and Horace Bushnell, Catharine Beecher believed that the values of the home stood in opposition to some other values, but unlike Bushnell and Hale, she wanted the same set of values to apply to both spheres, and she was far more aggressive in applying domestic values to the rest of society.[23]

As guardians of the home, women had a special role to play. All that they had to do was to surrender their claims to civil and political affairs and acknowledge a subordination in some regards. They could then claim their rightful place as moral leaders:

> In matters pertaining to the education of their children, in the selection and support of a clergyman, in all benevolent enterprises, and in all questions relating to morals or manners, they have a superior influence. In all such concerns, it would be impossible to carry a point contrary to their judgment and feelings; while an enterprise, sustained by them, will seldom fail of success.[24]

It is important to recognize just how political a formulation Beecher is offering here, despite having proclaimed that politics should be off-limits to women. It is political, in the broadest definition of the term, because there are other means of exerting influence in a society besides voting. In fact, she is reserving for women the preponderance of influence in education, in charitable activities, and in the selection of clergymen. This clearly represents a sharp break with Anglo-

American tradition as well as being virtually a program for women's voluntary activities in the nineteenth century.

Ten years after the publication of her treatise on domestic economy, having been embroiled in controversies over the funding of her schools, she was even more explicit about what women needed to do to advance their own cause: they must organize. Only "the organization of women as women" could "redress the deep wrongs that have so long and so heavily oppressed them."[25] The wrongs she had in mind were no doubt financial ones, a sore subject for one who was frequently hampered by the difficulty of raising money. Eventually she came around to the clearly proto-feminist idea that all women should possess the ability to support themselves:

> The ability to secure an independent livelihood and honorable employ suited to her education and capacities, are the only true foundation of the social elevation of women, even in the very highest classes of society. While she continues to be educated only to be somebody's wife, and is left without any aim in life till that somebody, either in love, or in pity, or in selfish regard, at last grants her the opportunity, she can never be truly independent.[26]

Yet despite this stance, she was very decided in the opinion that women need a good domestic education, too. Her numerous publications on the subject of domestic economy reflect the high value she placed on excellence, on expertise, in the performance of domestic duties. To compare the tone and content of Lydia Maria Child's *American Frugal Housewife* of 1829 with *A Treatise on Domestic Economy* (1841) offers a valuable perspective on the elevated status of home at mid-century. Child had given common-sense advice in a matter-of-fact tone with only a modicum of philosophizing about what the optimum home might be. Beecher, on the other hand, began with extensive quotations from Alexis de Tocqueville on the role of American women. Tocqueville had remarked that, although American women were confined to the domestic sphere, their influence was vast. Beecher then employed these remarks as the starting point for her own program for American women, a program that was both

domestic and political from the first page. Child had leaped from
topic to topic in a rather unsystematic fashion. Conversely, Beecher
attempted to give an organized and exhaustive compendium of everything that a housewife might need to know, replete with the latest
scientific information wherever applicable. In so doing, she enhanced
the home's ability to serve as an arena for the display of female
prowess.

If one examines her advice in just one area, laundry, one will be
struck by how much brain work is called for in addition to the physical effort. Making the soap, or purchasing it as the case might be,
was only the first step. Each type of fabric would benefit from treatment with a specific substance:

> Some persons wash calico in bran-water, without soap. For this
> purpose, boil four quarts of wheat bran in two pailfuls of
> water; strain it, and when lukewarm, divide it into two parts.
> Wash the calico first in one and then in the other water. Then
> rinse, wring hard, and hang out to dry. Potato-water is equally
> good.[27]

Standing on the firm foundation of the American home, Beecher
thus claimed for well-educated women the right to be guardians of
the public welfare in several ways. Women must have the superior
influence in charitable activities. Women must educate the young at
home and at school. And women, cultivating their domestic skills to
the highest possible degree of competence must preside over homes
so loving and well ordered that they could provide the cohesion for
the entire society. The only prerequisite for the woman in all of this
was the willingness to practice self-denial. It is only fair to point out,
however, that Beecher thought that men, too, should be self-sacrific-
ing. Indeed, the general rule should be that the stronger should
sacrifice for the weaker.[28] What is most important is the extent to
which the home and the world were intertwined in Beecher's formulation.

Where Beecher's work was implicitly political without referring to
specific legislative actions, the work of her sister Harriet was much

more explicitly political—the writing of *Uncle Tom's Cabin* was undertaken in direct response to the passage of the Fugitive Slave Act of 1850. Outrage over a law that gave incentives to judges to return men and women to bondage was coupled in Stowe's mind with compassion for slave mothers, who could so readily be separated from beloved children. Together, these sentiments transformed a woman who had written occasional pieces for *Godey's* into a major writer. Yet her powerful emotions in themselves would have been insufficient for this transformation had it not been for the status of domesticity at the time she began to write. The elevated view of the home and the housewife gave her both a touchstone of values and the self-confidence to tackle so ambitious a topic as slavery. This seems manifest because the novel is filled with domestic images and values. The status of the home in the culture then helped to give her the largest audience that any American author reached during the entire nineteenth century.

It is important to note at the outset all that was remarkable about the writing of *Uncle Tom's Cabin*. First, American novelists had been—almost to a person—silent on the subject of slavery up to 1851. Second, although women writers were tapping a vast market with the domestic novel, there were few attempting to write on public issues for a general audience. Margaret Fuller, who drowned at sea in 1850, had struck many of her contemporaries as an anomaly because of her wide-ranging intellectual claims. Female abolitionist lecturers stirred up storms of outrage when they dared to speak in public. Finally, Stowe, though the member of an accomplished family, had no reason to think of herself as destined for a public role. Her life had been difficult, as we have seen, because her husband Calvin was never able to provide more than the barest necessities for his family, and Stowe's own writing did not yet provide enough revenue to supply the lack. Indeed, just before *Uncle Tom's Cabin* made her a world-wide celebrity, she had written a letter to Sarah Josepha Hale, responding to Hale's request for her likeness and for biographical information, in which she specifically denied having any claim on the public's attention: "My sister Catherine has lived much more of a

life—and done more that can be told of than I whose course and employments have always been retired and domestic. . . . I have been
mother to seven children—six of whom are now living. . . ."[29]

Modest though this statement is, it provides the essential clue to
Stowe's motivation for writing her masterpiece: she had just suffered
the death of a much-loved infant son, and she could not bear to think
of the slave system or of a law that might visit the cruel fate of permanent separation from her child on a slave mother. Stowe's child
died approximately one year before the passage of the Fugitive Slave
Act. When a sister-in-law wrote this appeal to her in response to the
law's passage, "Hattie, if I could use a pen as you can I would write
something that will make this whole nation feel what an accursed
thing slavery is," she was ready.[30] Despite the birth of her last child
in 1850, her words poured onto the pages, and the first installment of
Uncle Tom's Cabin appeared in The National Era on June 5, 1851.
It would be hard to overstate the success of the serialized version and
then the novel. At long last, an American novelist had had the courage to break the silence about slavery. Henry Wadsworth Longfellow
recorded a typical reaction in his journal: "How she is shaking the
world with her Uncle Tom's Cabin! At one step she has reached the
top of the stair-case up which the rest of us climb on our knees year
after year. Never was there such a literary coup-de-main as this."[31]
Stowe began to receive an outpouring of letters in response to her
novel. To one correspondent, a member of the British aristocracy,
she replied as follows: "I wrote what I did because as a woman, as
a mother, I was oppressed and broken hearted with the sorrows and
injustice I saw."[32]

The novel is a stunning achievement because it combines moral
and religious passion with the realistic detail of a genre painting.
Stowe wanted to replace the sordid, unchristian, money-grubbing
values of the marketplace and the accommodationist politics of those
who voted for the Fugitive Slave Act with a new set of values based
on true Christianity and love. But rather than a utopian approach to
what could replace the status quo, she had a very practical vision,
which was the set of values and behavior to be found in a loving
Christian home presided over by a large-hearted woman. In the

words of Jane Tompkins, "the popular domestic novel of the nineteenth century represents a monumental effort to reorganize culture from the woman's point of view," and *Uncle Tom's Cabin* is the "summa theologica" of this effort.[33]

In his introduction to the 1962 Harvard edition of *Uncle Tom's Cabin*, Kenneth Lynn ponders what could have enabled the preacher's daughter, living on the edge of genteel poverty, to write the first masterpiece of American realism. It is unlikely that she had read Balzac, for example. All the evidence indicates that she was steeped in the Romantic tradition, with its view of the isolated self versus society, a genre she was to transcend in *Uncle Tom's Cabin*. "What was the force that propelled her to such creative audacity?" he queries. His answer is that her imagination was unleashed by the revolt against her father's Calvinism. No doubt this is part of the explanation, because each of Lyman Beecher's children had to chart his or her own religious course. But the other part of the explanation, unnoticed in 1962 because the cult of domesticity had not yet received a name, is that her creative imagination was also triggered by the necessity to provide homely details about domestic settings in order to render a convincing case for the saving grace of home.

In fact, if we were to examine Stowe's novels as a group we would find that the housewives constitute a veritable gallery of competent women, while the kitchens and the cookery receive careful attention, too. The Widow Scudder in *The Minister's Wooing* is a particularly accomplished example of the notable housewife because she is gifted with "faculty." As Stowe explains to her readers: "*Faculty* is Yankee for *savoir faire* and the opposite virtue to shiftlessness." She gives another character this speech explaining the Widow Scudder's achievements: "Cerinthy Ann, it's *faculty*—that's it; them that has it has it, and them that hasn't—why they've got to work hard and not do half so well, neither." As an example of the summit of housekeeping skill, we find the following description of a tea, prepared exclusively by the widow and her daughter:

> Meanwhile the tea-table had been silently gathering on its snowy plateau the delicate china, the golden butter, the loaf of

faultless cake, a plate of crullers or wonders, as a sort of sweet
fried cake was commonly called,—tea rusks, light as a puff, and
shining on top with a varnish of egg,—jellies of apple and
quince quivering in amber clearness,—whitest and purest honey
in the comb,—in short, everything that could go to the
getting-up of a most faultless tea.[34]

On the one hand, Stowe spoke out against slavery in *Uncle Tom's
Cabin* and analyzed the Calvinist heritage in her New England
novels. On the other hand, the religious, political, and ethical reflections in these novels are always interspersed with domestic descriptions, as if the latter reinforced her confidence for tackling the former. Writing an autobiography in the twentieth century, the novelist
and giver of domestic advice Marion Harland (Mary Virginia Terhune) recalled a helpful neighbor she had known as a girl: "She was
a 'capable' housewife, according to Mrs. Stowe's characterization of
the guild."[35] In other words, Stowe's housewives, in their vividly rendered settings, were so memorable as to constitute a category of their
own.

Yet despite her respect for "faculty," Stowe shows us in *Uncle
Tom's Cabin* that it is not enough. There are two skilled housewives
in this novel: Miss Ophelia St. Clare of Vermont and Mrs. Rachel
Halliday of Ohio. Only when Miss Ophelia learns to feel, like Rachel,
a generosity of spirit toward blacks, does she become a fully sympathetic character.

Rather than recapitulating the entire book, we can examine selected episodes in order to gain an appreciation of the extent to which
Uncle Tom's Cabin advanced an epic view of domesticity and of the
housewife. The first two episodes involve Eliza Harris, a young slave
mother who escapes across the frozen Ohio River to free territory
with her small son rather than permit him to be sold away from her.
By coincidence, Eliza and Harry seek refuge at the home of a senator
who has recently voted for the Fugitive Slave Act. He has just fin-
ished explaining to his gentle, submissive, but unconvinced wife why
reasons of state required him to support this legislation, when a servant announces the arrival of the fugitives. Eliza appeals to Mrs.
Bird for help by saying, "Ma'am, have you ever lost a child?" It so

happens that Mrs. Bird has buried a beloved child only a month earlier. Invoking the moral authority of the bereaved mother, she persuades her husband to spirit the fugitives to safety. This episode thus dramatically illustrates the kind of power women possess if only they will assert it.

A slightly later episode shows Eliza and her son under the sheltering wings of a Quaker family whose home embodies all of Stowe's most deeply felt values. The kitchen is bright and neat, the chairs themselves convey hospitality, but, above all, Rachel Halliday has "a heart as good and true as ever throbbed in woman's bosom." Far from envisioning their home as an enclave sacred to the family alone, these Quakers make a point of sharing their living quarters with fugitive slaves. Because their domestic activities form the moral center of the novel, Stowe describes the most mundane details such as fixing breakfast with the "joyous fizzle" of chicken and ham frying and the griddle cakes that reached the "true, exact, golden-brown tint of perfection."[36]

With his wife and child safe, at least momentarily, Eliza's husband George also finds his way to the Quaker settlement. He has been undergoing religious doubts because of the cruel stresses to which his family has been subjected. Nonetheless, in coming down to the Halliday's breakfast table, George has an experience of what we might call the domestic sublime:

> It was the first time that ever George had sat down on equal terms at any white man's table; and he sat down, at first, with some constraint and awkwardness; but they exhaled and went off like fog, in the genial morning rays of their simple, overflowing kindness.
>
> This, indeed was a home,—home, a word that George had never yet known a meaning for; and a belief in God, and trust in his providence, began to encircle his heart, as, with a golden cloud of protection and confidence. . . .[37]

For Stowe, thus, as for Horace Bushnell, home had a specifically religious function.[38]

In these terms, to be a good housekeeper is clearly fraught with moral significance. Stowe gives a complex depiction of Miss Ophelia, the New England cousin of a southern plantation owner, who is called upon to bring order to her cousin's household. Augustine St. Clare, the plantation owner, represents the way in which the slave system promotes moral decay even among decent people. He has abdicated from assuming moral and religious responsibility for his household, and his wife is similarly unwilling to exert herself to bring order out of chaos where the domestic sphere is concerned. Marie St. Clare is "indolent and childish, unsystematic and improvident." It is, therefore, necessary to send to Vermont to obtain the services of Miss Ophelia, "the absolute bond-servant of the 'ought.'"

Arriving in New Orleans, Miss Ophelia sets to work:

> The first morning of her regency, Miss Ophelia was up at four o'clock; and having attended to all the adjustments of her own chamber, as she had done ever since she came there, to the great amazement of the chambermaid, she prepared for a vigorous onslaught on the cupboards and closets of the establishment of which she had the keys.
>
> The store-room, the linen-presses, the china-closet, the kitchen and cellar, that day all went under an awful review. Hidden things of darkness were brought to light to an extent that alarmed all the principalities and powers of kitchen and chamber. . . .[39]

Despite her command of the domestic arts, however, this prototypical Yankee notable housewife is flawed because she is guilty of racism. Only when she overcomes her aversion to black skin and learns to love the slave child Topsy can she partake of the same moral qualities as Rachel Halliday. In other words, domesticity for its own sake is insufficient for Stowe. It must be wedded to a generous social vision.

If Miss Ophelia and Rachel Halliday represent different gradations of the notable housewife archetype and their homes reflect their capacities and moral qualities, then Simon Legree is the antithesis, and his home, an anti-home.[40] Cruel to his mother in his youth, Legree has grown up to repudiate all the values summed up in the cult of domesticity. His home is not only disorderly but filthy, "ragged," and "forlorn" in appearance because of Legree's "coarse neglect." Rather than a pleasant meal such as breakfast at the Quaker settlement, we are shown a scene of drunken carousal at Legree's plantation. Further, he has never married, preferring to exploit a series of slave mistresses. In effect, Legree has closed out the possibility of any refining female influence that might soften his brutality to his slaves. Having rejected Christianity, too, he confronts the powerless with the full force of unmitigated greed.

In offering us an anti-home as a counter to the home of the Hallidays, Stowe is trying to dramatize what is wrong with a society that does not pay sufficient heed to its mothers and to their values. Legree's home is an extreme, but it demonstrates the potential for evil in letting market-oriented values hold full sway. Lest the reader conclude that only women have access to the right values, however, Stowe makes her title character a man who is gentle and kind but who possesses the moral strength to stand up to Legree. Indeed, Stowe is clearly trying to create a new model of strength appropriate for both sexes. Uncle Tom gets the better of Legree—despite Legree's responsibility for his death—because he is true to his faith and to his principles. This is a victory achieved not with physical force but with moral courage aided by divine grace. As such, it is a gender-free ideal and fully commensurate with an epic style of domesticity.

A series of articles Stowe wrote during the darkest days of the Civil War reveal yet another facet of her approach to domesticity. In effect, she offered "household merriment" as an antidote to what the twentieth century has called existential despair, in this case, despair caused by the toll on the battlefield. Using the pen name of Christopher Crowfield—no doubt trying to appeal to male readers—she extolled the good housewife, the joys of lavishing care on house plants, and the brightness of sunny rooms, among other matters.[41] She explained to her publisher:

> I feel I need to write in these days to keep from thinking things that make me dizzy and blind, and fill my eyes with tears so that I cannot see the paper. I mean such things as are being done where our heroes are dying as Shaw died. It is not wise that all our literature should run in a rut cut through our

hearts and red with our blood. I feel the need of a little gentle
household merriment and talk of common things, to indulge
which I have devised the following.[42]

We can only assume that Stowe must have turned to nurturing activities herself prior to this as a way of finding solace for the loss of
two beloved sons (another son had died in 1857).

Finally, although Stowe held back from full-fledged participation
in the nascent feminist movement in her prime and evidently became
more conservative as she aged,[43] she did endorse suffrage—unlike her
sister Catharine—in the pages of *Hearth and Home*. Moreover, during the crisis years of the 1850s, she advocated a forceful public role
for women. In her recollections of Stowe, Annie Fields says that,
after the passage of the Kansas-Nebraska Act, the author of *Uncle
Tom's Cabin* engaged in "constant correspondence" with Charles
Sumner and other like-minded politicians so as to keep abreast of
events. She then issued an appeal to the women of America: "The
first duty of every American woman at this time is to thoroughly
understand the subject for herself and to feel that she is bound to
use her influence for the right." Stowe went on to enumerate ways
in which women could exert this influence such as circulating peti-
tions, hiring lecturers, and circulating congressional speeches.[44]

Thus, the larger political implications of Stowe's work and of her
life are manifest. She held up images of female competence and the
worth of the home while exhorting women to activity outside the
home during the years of the sectional crisis. Moreover, in the characters of Uncle Tom and the pseudonymous Christopher Crowfield,
she tried to show that men, too, could partake of the virtues engendered by home. And in describing the home of Rachel Halliday, always open to those in need of refuge, she gave a concrete demonstration of the redemptive capacity of a loving home. Like her sister,
Stowe possessed an epic vision of domesticity.

One contemporary who understood exactly what Stowe was about
was Theodore Parker. Home enlarges, he argued. "Its human or gen-
eralizing power may be seen in the character of woman, on whom
most of its cares, duties and pleasures, too, as things now are, seem to
devolve, as her sphere is home." Therefore it was not surprising to

Parker that a woman should have broken the silence of American literature—which had been "deaf as a cent to the outcry of humanity expiring in agonies"—on the subject of slavery. "Do you not hear the cry which, in New England, a woman is raising in the world's ears against the foul wrong which America is working in the world?"[45] Home is the center of love and kindness; women are closer to home than men are and are thus better able to sensitize themselves to the plight of the unfortunate. But there is a remedy for men: "Discharge lovingly the duties owed to wife and child, by and by you shall wonder how your heart beats with men afar off, for the wrongs of red men, black men, man everywhere."[46]

As in the 1770s when American homes and housewives made possible the successful boycott of British goods, thus putting pressure on the British to rescind unpopular legislation, American homes were being called upon to serve as a political resource, energizing men and women of good will to fight against slavery. That a militant abolitionist—as Parker clearly was[47]—endorsed this view of the matter is one more indication of the pervasiveness of the ideology of domesticity. It is also indicative of the fact that home and history were more firmly intertwined than ever. That is, the domestic sphere was not viewed as an ahistorical enclave where people could meet basic needs, as it had been in the colonial period, but rather as a dynamic scene of actions that could affect the outcome of history. Proof of the validity of this approach was the undeniable fact that one such action *had* been carried out at home and by a woman whose employments had "always been retired and domestic": the writing of *Uncle Tom's Cabin*. That Stowe's work had affected the outcome of history was attested to by the widely quoted remark Lincoln is supposed to have made to her when they met during the Civil War: "So this is the little woman who made this big war."

Emerson had enjoined hospitality to bridge the gap between home and the world. Stowe advocated remaking the world in the home's image, suggesting, too, that both sexes could participate in domesticity in some fashion, whether by creating it or by celebrating it. For both of these writers, however, the day-by-day running of the home belonged to women alone. This assignment of duties to each sex was so ingrained a cultural assumption that even visionaries rarely questioned it. Thus to encounter a woman who did question it is to encounter a most unusual human being—such as Antoinette Brown Blackwell, the first woman to be ordained as a Protestant minister in this country.[48]

Blackwell had a long and extraordinary life, from lecturing about abolition in the antebellum years to casting a vote in 1920. Born in 1825 and raised on a farm in upstate New York, she managed to make her way to Oberlin for a college education less than ten years after this institution had opened its doors to women. At Oberlin she received the theological training that enabled her to be ordained in 1853. (She served a parish only briefly, devoting most of her energies to guest sermons and to her lectures and writing.) At Oberlin she formed a friendship with Lucy Stone that would prove to be a lifelong one, enhanced by the fact that they eventually married brothers. After graduation and before the two women married, however, they both launched careers as feminist-abolitionist lecturers. As she traveled to advance her causes, Blackwell evidently pondered how someone with her values and unusual style of life would ever be able to enjoy any of the domestic comforts of a home, assuming as she then did that she would never meet a man who would share her values. She wrote a letter to Stone outlining her plan to adopt some "ragged, outcast" children and thereby establish a home:

> Then again I can't go wandering up and down the earth without any home. Not can't because it would require too much self-denial, but because I should get to [sic] excited and too down hearted from reaction to accomplish anything. . . . I need a pleasant happy home to rest in and some pleasant happy children there to keep me from being a misanthrope. Dear Lucy I do think we are in danger of this; it is my greatest temptation and sometimes I almost feel it did no good to try to make people better. . . . But give me a quiet home surrounded by trees and flowers and there I can worship God and love the world and can make as many and as long lecturing tours as seems best and go when and where Providence makes an opening.[49]

She thought that her father would be able to subsidize such an undertaking, and that her own role would be that of an executive, directing the work of a housekeeper and servants.

Significantly, Blackwell did not assume that there was any contradiction between activism and devotion to the home. Rather, she recognized that anyone subjected to the emotional stresses attendant on the life of the reformer would need to have a loving home as a place of emotional refreshment. Her proposed solution may have been unrealistic and elitist inasmuch as it would have required that a woman have a certain family wealth. Nonetheless it is further evidence of the consonance of reform and domesticity at mid-century.

Antoinette Brown was fortunate enough to meet and marry a man, Samuel Blackwell, who not only shared her values but also devoted a substantial portion of his time to sharing the household responsibilities.[50] Giving birth to seven children, she sometimes found herself discouraged by the volume of work, though, even with her husband's cooperation. She wrote a rare complaining letter to Susan B. Anthony in 1859 when her oldest child was three years old. Enumerating her chores, she exclaimed, "This, Susan, is woman's sphere!"[51] Another letter she wrote that year, in this instance to Lucy Stone, expressed near despair about married women's prospects for activism: "No one has faith enough in me to lend a finger's worth of help. . . ."[52] But as time went on, as a household routine was established, and after Sam developed a business that could be carried on at home, her mood lightened. In 1879 Blackwell wrote in a letter to Stone that she wanted to organize her life so as to "give and take some home comfort."[53] In fact, this phrase is very reminiscent of the tone of the letter she had written to Stone nearly thirty years earlier in which she had set forth what she wanted from a home.

That she herself experienced domestic comfort as something one both gives and receives may be a part of the explanation for the fact that Blackwell went further than any other thinker of her day in envisioning a symmetrical gender system. In books, in articles in the feminist periodical, the *Woman's Journal,* and at woman's congresses attended by leading feminists of the immediate postwar period, she enunciated her views. Both sexes should have a domestic role, and both sexes should have a public role:

> Wife and husband could be mutual helpers with admirable effect. Let her take his place in garden or field or workshop an hour or two daily, learning to breathe more strongly, and exercising a fresh set of muscles in soul and body. To him baby tending and bread making would be most humanizing in their influence, all parties gaining an assured benefit. . . . We need a general reconstruction in the division of labor. Let no women give all their time to household duties, but require nearly all women, and all men also, since they belong to the household, to bear some share of the common household burdens.[54]

Even though her appeals for a more egalitarian division of household labor were aimed at a middle-class audience, she was astute enough to understand that there were class as well as gender implications appertaining to asymmetrical sex roles. She referred to these implications as follows:

> . . . [It is] a false theory that because women are to be the mothers of the race, therefore they are not to be the thinkers or the pioneers in enterprise. This ancient dogma enfeebles one class of women and degrades the other. We believe in a fairly equal division of duties between men and women. . . . If woman's sole responsibility is of the domestic type, one class will be crushed by it and the other throw it off as a badge of poverty.[55]

Implicit in this passage is the idea that it would be unfortunate should domesticity be devalued in this fashion. In short, both women and the home will be better off if women have opportunities outside the home.

Blackwell believed that all human beings need to cultivate both intimate ties and large social sympathies. While love for the multitude may be "more broadly godlike" than home sympathies, it is in the home that people learn to transcend self-interest in an immediate fashion. To give women exercise for their brains and a larger public role will not prove antithetical to the home because women will move from "bound to rebound" between home and work: "A home-nest, with the young birdlings in it, has warmth enough to shed its influence outward upon the maternal heart, go where it may; and the active womanly brain, which has sufficient breadth to appreciate the widest human interests, and to work to promote the welfare of the race, stimulated by its deeper affections can have no difficulty in applying itself also to the loving details of the home regimen."[56]

All this did not necessarily add up to perfect symmetry. Women might still bear somewhat more of the household responsibilities than men, Blackwell conceded, and men more of those in the public realm.[57] Moreover, as we shall learn when we talk about the feminist response to Charles Darwin, Blackwell was also willing to concede that there might be biological differences between the sexes other than merely in the reproductive systems. On balance, however, her work represented a bold attempt to combine more flexible sex roles with a deeply felt respect for the home. In effect, Blackwell linked home and the world by calling for opportunities and responsibilities for both sexes in both spheres.

The reformer and Unitarian clergyman, Samuel May, added yet another dimension to the subject of allocating domestic chores. He had what might be called a life-cycle approach to balancing private and public duties. While the children are young, "the family . . . ought never to be neglected for the service of the state, by the father any more than the mother." When the children are raised, both sexes should strive to contribute to the "common weal." He thought that in general men were far likelier than women to be the disrupters of families. Therefore, he saw no danger to the home in enfranchising women, a development that would give women an important public role.[58]

It was his unusual view of the human personality that underlay this vision of the domestic sphere as something for which both sexes need to accept responsibility: "A perfect character in either a man or a woman, is a compound of the virtues and graces of each. . . . In Jesus, the dearly beloved of God, we see as much feminine as masculine grace."[59] If the individual character requires this balance, so, too, should the home and ultimately the state. In fact, the state needs mothers as well as fathers.

May thus had a remarkably egalitarian and flexible view of gender roles; in addition, he had the personal habit of extending hospitality to all who needed it. After his death a friend recalled: "The home was always a place of refuge for passing unfortunates, and was familiar with the tread of almost every man or woman who has contributed conspicuously to American reform."[60] In other words, for May domestic sharing was of two varieties. On the one hand, it extended to the realm of responsibility, and on the other hand, it meant making one's home freely available to outsiders. In a sense, May took Emerson's prescription for the just household and made it democratic with respect to gender, too.

If a whole range of Americans from domestic novelists, most notably Harriet Beecher Stowe, to male "creators of culture" to reformers were arguing for the redemptive power of domestic values and therefore, by implication, for the crucial importance of female influence on society, what were women themselves doing? The answer, of course, is that American women had been organizing for charitable purposes since the early nineteenth century and thereby struggling to achieve that influence. It is beyond the scope of this work to go into detail about the history of women's voluntary associations. Nonetheless, it is important to review the outlines briefly, because activism began when Republican Motherhood gave women an excuse for involvement in affairs outside the home. That activism accelerated as the cult of domesticity gained increasing stature and credibility. By the late nineteenth century, women were routinely using the home to justify their claims for influence, in particular, their demands to control male drinking behavior.

In fact, a number of religious, social, and educational factors—in addition to the new political role for mothers—were conducive to female organization beginning in the late eighteenth and early nineteenth century. Several historians have pointed to the role of the Second Great Awakening in creating a context for such activity. In conjunction with the disestablishment of the churches, this outburst of institution building around the new nation was so demanding that it opened up opportunities for talented women. Although women were not performing the clerical functions itself, they were the mainstays of their congregations in other respects. In the words of Mary Beth Norton:

> The disestablishment of American churches in the 1780s and 1790s opened new pathways for the women who numerically dominated the Protestant denominations. As the churches lost their politically privileged positions and access to tax revenues, they needed to generate new sources of funds, support, and loyalty. That need helped promote the formation of voluntary associations tied to individual churches; the earliest of these were denominationally sponsored sewing circles or female charitable societies organized in New England in the last two decades of the century. After the Second Great Awakening (1790–1840), which brought even larger numbers of female converts into Protestant churches, women's charitable and reform associations burgeoned, creating what historians of the nineteenth century called "the benevolent empire."[61]

By the 1830s, voluntary associations, male and female, had proliferated to such an extent that Tocqueville dilated at some length on the American propensity for forming them: "The Americans make associations to give entertainments, to found seminaries, to build inns, to construct churches, to diffuse books, to send missionaries to the antipodes; in this manner they found hospitals, prisons and schools. If it is proposed to inculcate some truth or to foster some feeling by the encouragement of a great example, they form a society."[62] The extraordinary geographic mobility of American society in these years, a condition that promoted the home as a source of social cohesion, also made Americans of both sexes feel compelled to come together in groups outside the home. Yet women had a special role to play because they were defined as uniquely capable of larger social sympathies in a society dedicated in the main to individual self-betterment. Thus it was entirely appropriate for beings previously lacking an extra-domestic role to organize for the relief of social problems.[63]

Linda Kerber has argued that the ideology of Republican Motherhood was most consequential for women in the way that it fostered improved education. Suzanne Lebsock, in her recent study of the women in one small town in Virginia, goes on to link improved female education with the founding of the first charitable institution to be established by female effort, an asylum for orphaned girls that came into being in 1812: "The best guess is that education made the difference; the founding of the asylum marked the coming of age of Petersburg's first generation of educated women."[64]

Thus Republican Motherhood enhanced the likelihood of female activism outside the home both indirectly—improved education for women—and directly—giving women a role in the civic culture. The high status of the home also suggested that those closest to it would be the most capable of generosity toward the unfortunate. These developments, together with the changes precipitated by the Second Great Awakening and the diminution of the drudgery of housework for middle-class housewives, created a new pattern of daily life for thousands of women. Mary Ryan found that in Utica in the 1840s, for example, there were more than a dozen women's groups in a small city of only 12,000 people.[65] Although men were creating associations, too, the women were the ones who were creating the benevolent empire. This, in turn, gave women a new political role:

> During the nineteenth century, women expanded their ascribed sphere into community service and care of dependents, areas not fully within men's or women's politics. These tasks combined public roles and administration with nurturance and compassion. They were not fully part of either male electoral politics and formal governmental institutions or the female world of the home and family. Women made their most visible public contributions as founders, workers, and volunteers in social service organizations. Together with the social separation of the sexes and women's informal methods of influencing politics, political domesticity provided the basis for a distinct nineteenth-century women's political culture.[66]

That the ideology of domesticity also fostered social and political activism by women because it enhanced female self-confidence is clear. The domestic novel, with its images of the competent housewife, presented the female craft tradition in such a way as to promote a sense of efficacy on the part of its women readers. That efficacy was also promoted by the ringing endorsement of the value of women and home from the pulpit. Political scientists consider the sense of personal efficacy to be one of the most important variables explaining levels of political integration.[67] Thus it is not surprising to find the newly self-confident women using the home, a home then representing the height of cultural value, to explain and justify their assumption of an extra-domestic role. The women under discussion in this chapter certainly fit this pattern. Finally, as early as the antebellum period, Theodore Parker used the argument that the state needs the involvement of housekeepers to justify woman suffrage. This foreshadowed a refrain that would be heard from many suffragists in the late nineteenth and early twentieth century, culminating in Jane Addams's famous "municipal housekeeping" article in the *Ladies Home Journal* in 1910.

Simply put, the epic style of domesticity empowered women both inside and outside the home. Yet to speak of empowerment suggests a corollary to this generalization: domesticity would become more controversial as the century wore on because power won by one group may well entail the loss of power and privilege by another. Furthermore, after the sectional crisis ended, some of the political issues galvanizing the nation resolved themselves into the politics of gender, pitting men against women. In short, the interaction of domestic feminism with the world outside the home generated a remarkable history that has been insufficiently understood because domesticity has been underestimated by most historians. That history is the subject of the next chapter.

THREE

Domestic Feminism and the World Outside the Home

OMESTIC FEMINISM, whether confined to the home or embodied in female activism outside the home, always contained within it the potential for engendering a strong sexual politics. In the first place, some husbands no doubt resented a new self-confidence and assertiveness on the part of their wives. What is more, at mid-century the women's magazines propounded their own style of barely disguised sexual politics. For example, even though Sarah Josepha Hale refused to endorse woman suffrage, she was hardly apolitical. The pages of *Godey's* frequently contained denunciations of male behavior together with characterizations of female behavior as "sublime." If one examines the themes of the best-selling novels of the domestic writers, one again encounters, at least in some books, polarized values, with the female characters representing all that is positive and the male characters all that is negative. Nonetheless, it was not until after the Civil War that the publicly expressed sexual politics reached the level of adversary relations. With the ending of the sectional crisis as well as the emancipation of the slaves, male and female reformers were no longer working together for the same cause in the same way. Indeed, many women understandably felt betrayed by their former male allies' refusal to link suffrage for women to the cause of suffrage for freedmen.[1] Furthermore, in the late nineteenth century women formed their own temperance society. This also promoted polarization along gender lines because women claimed the moral authority to control male drinking behavior—and did so on the basis of the female role in the home. As we shall learn, domestic feminism would survive into the twentieth century when it surfaced as the "municipal housekeeping" argument for woman suffrage. This chapter will examine the evolution of domestic feminism and assess its impact on the status of domesticity in the culture at large.

Domestic feminism became overtly political because women reformers began to launch attacks on aspects of male culture in the name of their own higher virtue.[2] In fact, attacks on male culture began to appear in some of the best-selling women's novels as early as the antebellum period.[3] By examining the themes of certain of these novels we can gain an insight into the sources of the sexual politics that would find full-blown expression in the temperance movement of the late nineteenth century.

Antebellum women novelists knew that the home provided their protagonists with the most secure basis for power in an insecure and male-dominated world. We have already become acquainted with the tyrannical Aunt Fortune in Susan Warner's *The Wide, Wide World*. Warner says of Aunt Fortune: "The ruling passion of this lady was thrift; her next, good housewifery. First, to gather to herself and heap up of what the world most esteems; after that to be known as the most thorough housekeeper and the smartest woman in Thirlwall."[4] Aunt Fortune has a house that is immaculate and over which she enjoys absolute control. When she falls ill and is temporarily bedridden, she tries to dictate the terms under which she can receive help, telling her niece Ellen, for example, to let no one else into the buttery. Sick though she is, Aunt Fortune insists that the sick room—which is the one room whose maintenance she can still directly supervise—be kept spotless: "Every rung of every chair must be gone over, though ever so clean; every article put up or put out of the way; Miss Fortune made the most of the little province of housekeeping that was left her."[5] Warner thus gives an excellent demonstration of why the nineteenth-century woman vested so much importance in her home: she could exert control over a physical environment and in so doing go a long way toward controlling the behavior of other people. The glorified home of the nineteenth century commanded a new respect, even from men, relative to earlier periods of American history, and this gave housewives the leverage to enforce their own standards.

In one of her Christopher Crowfield articles, articles that originally appeared in the *Atlantic Monthly*, Harriet Beecher Stowe sets forth a fictitious conversation between two men on the subject of an overly fussy housewife. A harassed husband describes his household to Crowfield in these terms: "Now, you see, Chris, my position is a delicate one, because Sophie's folks all agree that if there's anything in creation that is ignorant and dreadful and mustn't be allowed his way anywhere, it's a man."[6] Although Stowe was exaggerating for effect, there is a residue of truth to this passage. The cult of domesticity might well have given a woman power over her husband in just this fashion. As Mary Ryan puts it, "A father in a Victorian parlor was something of a bull in a China shop, somewhat ill at ease with the gentle virtues enshrined there."[7]

Emma D. E. N. Southworth was a novelist who well knew the value of the domestic sphere in enhancing female power, a cause in which she fervently believed. One of the most prolific and popular novelists of the nineteenth century, Southworth had been left to support herself and two small children because of her husband's abandonment, and thus wrote out of urgent necessity and with no great love for the male sex.[8] Given her own experiences and her insight into the value of home as a counterweight to male values, it is not surprising to find Southworth displaying sensitivity to the political uses of domesticity in her novel, *The Deserted Wife*.

The action begins in Maryland. Early in the proceedings we are introduced to Heath Hall, a cold, comfortless, and neglected mansion, as well as to a number of flamboyant characters who comprise the protagonists in a novel that clearly owes much to the Gothic tradition. Hagar, the orphaned heroine, is virtually as neglected as Heath Hall. Lacking the usual supervision a girl would have had in 1850, Hagar grows up untamed. Having fallen in love, she nonetheless marries reluctantly because she intuits that marriage will mean a loss of freedom:

> It was curious; her very name and title were gone, and the girl, two minutes since a wild, free maiden was now little better than a bondwoman; and the gentle youth who two minutes since might have sued humbly to raise the tips of her little dark fingers to his lips, was now invested with a life-long authority over her.[9]

Once married, Hagar accompanies her husband to his family home in the north. There, we see another perverted version of the domestic ideal. Her husband tells Hagar that he wants her to be merely an ornament—no pantry smells or household cares for her: "You have nothing to do with house, love, cultivate your beauty." Before long he is cruelly mistreating her. Eventually he sails off to Europe with another woman.

Abandoned, Hagar returns to Maryland with her twin daughters and newborn son. Immediately, she begins to feel a return of the vitality she had lost because of her husband's mistreatment. "She was at *home*, under her own roof; what if the house were half a ruin—it was HER OWN. She was upon her own land, and though it was only a desert heath, it was HER OWN."[10] But Heath Hall does not remain a ruin for long. Hagar becomes an internationally renowned singer and uses her new wealth to rebuild her ancestral home. Once she has accomplished this, renaming her home "Alto Rio," her husband returns—on her terms. The restored domestic sphere, restored by Hagar's own efforts and energy, is thus the direct means by which the heroine reestablishes her life. Moreover, it is the means by which she establishes control over her errant husband.[11]

This new openness about female striving for control, best evidenced by the appearance of the woman suffrage movement and the married woman's property movement in the same years, was bound to generate divided feelings for many women. A best-seller from the 1860s, Augusta Evans's *St. Elmo* reveals a profoundly ambivalent attitude toward the assertion of female power. Edna Earl, yet another orphaned heroine, is fortunate enough to be adopted by a wealthy widow whose son, St. Elmo, is one of the most extreme misogynists to be encountered in the domestic novels. As Edna matures and develops into an intellectual of formidable proportions, St. Elmo is attracted to her, but sneers constantly at women in general and at literary women in particular: "I should really enjoy seeing them tied down to their spinning wheels and gagged with their own books, magazines, and lectures."

It is Edna's combination of ferocious ambition with stubborn refusal to endorse suffrage that reveals Evans's own divided mind about female power. Edna aspires not merely to be a literary woman but also to be a philosopher. Toward that end she learns Greek and Hebrew. Yet there is one scene in which she is depicted as mending her mentor's clothes. Her first book is a philosophical treatise—which meets with a stunning success, naturally—but her second is entitled "Shining Thrones of the Hearth" and has as its aim "to discover the only true and allowable and womanly sphere of feminine work." On the one hand, Edna quotes John Stuart Mill approvingly. On the other hand, she voices her dismay about Mill's endorsement of woman suffrage, calling it "this most loathesome of political leprosies." Evans explains Edna's purpose as follows:

> Believing that the intelligent, refined, modest Christian women of the United States were the real custodians of national purity, and the sole agents who could successfully arrest the tide of demoralization breaking over the land, she addressed herself to the wives, mothers and daughters of America. . . . Jealously she contended for every woman's right which God and nature had decreed the sex. The right to be learned, wise, noble, useful, in women's divinely limited sphere; the right to influence and exalt the circle in which she moved . . . the right to modify and direct her husband's opinions.[12]

After achieving an international success as an author, while yet staying within carefully defined bounds, Edna retires to marry the now-reformed St. Elmo, presumably to live happily ever after and, if St. Elmo's directions are obeyed, never to write again. Evans thus tries to create a situation in which her heroine can have the best of both worlds.

But even while trying to set limits to Edna's achievements and to keep her grounded in domesticity, Evans manages to create a heroine who is so independent and autonomous that she would have been unthinkable a generation earlier. To compare Mrs. Barclay of *Home* with Edna Earl is instructive. Neither is agitating for suffrage, but, unlike Mrs. Barclay, who spends her time "directing domestic affections," Edna sets her own course, has intellectual aspirations the equal of a man's, and shows only a token interest in the activities centered in the home. The domestic novel thus changed in thirty years from a vehicle for exhortation and pious example to a genre whose heroines could barely be contained within conventional roles; in short, to a highly politicized genre—and this despite an individual novelist's misgivings about female striving for power.[13]

To read issues of *Godey's* from the 1850s and 1860s is to encounter similar attempts to chart a course for women, a course that would be independent and yet stop short of encroaching on the male sphere. In an "Editor's Table" of March 1852, for example, Sarah Josepha Hale said the following:

> Give women some pursuit which men esteem and see if their work is not well done, provided they are suitably trained. Now we do not desire to change the station of the sexes, or give to women the work of men. We only want our sex to become fitted for their own sphere. But we believe this comprises, besides household care and domestic duties, three important vocations. . . .

She then went on to enumerate not only teaching but also preserving and helping, under which rubric she included a call for women physicians. She went even further the following year, saying that any indoor employment would be akin to home and thus appropriate for a woman who has to support herself, and pointing out that Louis Godey employed eighty-eight female operatives in the different departments of the *Lady's Book*, not including the editor and the women contributors.[14]

In a book published in 1868, *Manners or Happy Homes and Good Society All the Year Round*, Hale gave an endorsement of female nature and a prescription for male responsibilities. Those who read and reflect on the Bible will soon realize that God put special care into the creation of woman, she argued. "Woman was the crown of all" because she is superior in spiritual qualities.[15] If the Bible says "Honor her as the weaker vessel," this means to take care of and appreciate her as one would fine porcelain rather than rough clay. A husband has an obligation to "bring home smiles and sunshine" if he is to be worthy of the woman he married.[16]

Thus the new roles for the home and the new female activism generated both a heady sense of possibilities and uneasiness, sometimes coexisting in the same person. Whether going so far as to advocate suffrage or not, many women were challenging the status quo and making wholly unprecedented claims for female influence. If we examine one reform-minded household in particular, that of Julia Ward Howe (1819–1910) and Samuel Gridley Howe (1801–1876), we can see the ramifying effects of the new situation on a marriage. In this instance each party understood full well what domesticity had to do with power. A man with a national reputation for his humanitarian undertakings, particularly in the area of the education of the deaf, Samuel Howe was reluctant to share power with his wife and jealous of the fame she achieved with "The Battle Hymn of the Republic." Early in their marriage he insisted on hiring the servants himself, once dismissing the entire staff while his wife was out of town. Moreover, he tried to achieve control over the education of both sons and daughters, in opposition to the claims by Catharine Beecher and others that education should properly be assigned to woman's sphere.[17]

For her part, Julia Howe, sensible of the utility of domesticity for justifying female claims, advised young girls in her autobiography to learn all they could about running a household before marriage so that they would not feel inadequate once married. It is easy to infer from her confession of her own inadequacy as a bride how much she was placed at a disadvantage vis-à-vis her husband by a combination of her ignorance and her youth.[18] But a growing competence inside the home and her achievements outside it changed all this, and she began to hold her own. Shortly before his death and after his wife had become nationally celebrated, Samuel Howe complained to a friend, "Mrs. Howe grows more and more absorbed in the public work of obtaining woman's suffrage; and, like most of her co-workers, shows more zeal than discretion; and, in my opinion, does more harm by subordinating domestic duties to supposed public ones."[19] That she continued to ground such public activities in the home as a power base for women is clear, however. She explained the dynamics of what the twentieth century has called "domestic feminism" as follows: "But surely, no love of intellectual pursuits should lead any of us to disparage and neglect the household gifts and graces. A house is a kingdom in little and its queen, if she is faithful, gentle and wise, is a sovereign indeed."[20]

If some women had reason to view the private relationship of marriage in adversarial terms, others were learning considerable distrust of men in the public realm, too, in the postbellum years. By mid-century a well-developed woman's movement had come into being, with suffrage and property rights for married women as the two most pressing issues. Although women no doubt outnumbered men in the movement, both sexes frequently worked together because of the pervasive and inclusive reform culture of the period, a culture that encompassed both abolition and rights for women. But the politics of Reconstruction produced a schism in the woman's movement, with almost all male abolitionists and some female ones taking the position that the vote for black men must take precedence over woman suffrage. Those women who disagreed with this position, Elizabeth Cady Stanton and Susan B. Anthony being the most prominent, did so strongly and were profoundly discouraged about the setback to their cause. Indeed, the exclusion of women from full citizenship was made even more explicit by the use of the word "male" in the Fourteenth Amendment, which granted citizenship to freedmen. As a result Stanton and Anthony formed a new suffrage organization, the National Woman Suffrage Association, a group that excluded men from participation.[21]

The new, women-only group was symptomatic of an important change in the United States. What happened in the years after the Civil War was a collision between antagonistic male and female cultures, with the temperance movement as the major battleground. Moreover, despite the schism, female culture held its own as effectively as at any preceding time in American history because of the general esteem for the home.[22] Even those men who wanted to dismiss female-centered values found this difficult to achieve. Indeed, if there was tension in the writings of some women between the assertion of autonomy and the assertion of conventional views of woman's sphere, this was echoed by tension in the writing of certain men between reverence for the home and rebellion against it.

No male writer of the period better demonstrates this tension than Mark Twain, and the tension is manifest in more than one novel. In fact, it is not too much to say that his complicated and ambivalent feelings about domesticity were a major theme of Twain's work. That Samuel Clemens was born in 1835 and came to maturity during the very years when the cult of domesticity was at its height may explain this phenomenon.

The family, genteel but poor, lived in a raw little village in Missouri when Samuel Clemens was born. Judge Clemens died in 1847, and young Sam's formal education came to a close the following year. After working at a variety of jobs which included journalism and piloting a boat on the Mississippi River, Clemens headed west for a stint as a journalist in Nevada and California. Much of his early writing, including "The Celebrated Jumping Frog of Calaveras County" and Roughing It, drew upon the experiences he had in the rough-and-tumble gold country. Further, he enjoyed cultivating the image of being anti-establishment and more than slightly outrageous in these years.

Yet when he fell in love in his early thirties, he fell in love with a woman who represented all the values he was flouting. While on a European trip, he met a young man from a prosperous, upstate New York family, who possessed an ivory miniature of his sister. Clemens subsequently sought the sister out, fell in love, and courted her assiduously. Olivia Langdon was young, beautiful, deeply conventional, and "pure as snow" in her lover's eyes. At one point during their engagement, he was horrified to learn that she was reading Don Quixote, which he regarded as too coarse for her pure mind, whose purity he was eager to preserve.[23] Says one of Clemens's biographers, Justin Kaplan, "He courted her by offering in all sincerity to make over his character and habits to suit her standards."[24] Shortly after their marriage, he wrote to a friend, "Before the gentle majesty of her purity all evil things and evil ways and evil deeds stand abashed,—then surrender."[25]

Not only did he marry a woman who represented the genteel culture at its most genteel, but also he demonstrated his affinity for domesticity by the house he built in Hartford when his writing success enabled him to construct a temple to his own prosperity. In his youth a wanderer whose adventures could and did furnish the material for a picaresque novel, he relished the palatial residence at Nook Farm, and even became involved in its design and decoration.[26] Although he grumbled about the effort required, he kept tight control of such matters. Moreover, the domestic side of Samuel Clemens is revealed by his fondness for his three daughters. The magnificent Hartford house clearly represented his desire to give them an idyllic childhood, in addition to being a monument to Mark Twain's ego.

Yet the chronicle of a rough westerner tamed and domesticated by his love for his wife and family is only part of the story. Clemens never lost his enjoyment of being outrageous, a trait that could manifest itself in diverse ways such as trying to sneak a dubious passage in his book past the censor (his wife) or playing the role of the perpetual bad boy in his own household—or even in the households of close friends. As Susan K. Harris argues in her book, *Mark Twain's Escape from Time*, "home" provided two functions for Clemens: it was at once his haven and his prison, thus giving him something to rebel against.[27] Another way of putting this might be that he voluntarily submitted to his wife's authority with respect to standards of behavior and then resented the yoke.

That resentment came quickly to the surface in his hymn to boyhood, *Tom Sawyer*, published in 1876. The book, set in a thinly disguised version of Clemens's hometown of Hannibal, opens with an assertion of female authority over a male: Aunt Polly is searching for her mischievous charge and calls out "Tom!" The reader soon learns that Tom and Aunt Polly love each other deeply, but that

Tom cannot forswear mischief for any length of time. Indeed, Clemens seems to be saying that it is a boy's nature to be mischievous, and that there is something suspect about one, such as Tom's younger brother Sid, who conforms to female standards.

Tom himself is far from impervious to the female sex, however. He reveals Aunt Polly's most powerful weapon in a conversation with a friend: "She! She never licks anybody—whacks 'em over the head with her thimble—and who cares for that I'd like to know. She talks awful, but talk don't hurt—anyways it don't if she don't cry."[28] If Aunt Polly's tears give Tom pause, he is completely disarmed by his love for Becky Thatcher, a love that motivates much of the action in the novel. When Becky temporarily rejects him, for example, he briefly runs away from home.

Tom, the naughty boy who is nonetheless the joy of his aunt's heart, is contrasted with Huckleberry Finn, the town outcast who need answer to no mother, aunt, or female guardian. Huck comes and goes as he pleases, never goes to school or to Sunday school and hence epitomizes freedom: "In a word, everything that goes to make life precious that boy had. So thought every harassed, hampered, respectable boy in St. Petersburg."[29] Both Tom and Huck enjoy adventure, but there are decided differences in their approaches to life because of Huck's inexperience with female standards. For example, during an episode involving Injun Joe, the villain, Tom "borrows" a towel from his aunt (to be used to muffle the light) and sneaks into a room where Injun Joe lies sleeping. Having to flee for his life, Tom later recounts the experience to Huck:

> "I just grabbed that towel and started!"
> "I'd never 'a' thought of the towel, I bet!"
> "Well, I would. My aunt would make me mighty sick if I
> lost it."[30]

Tom is brave enough to risk his life in order to defeat the evil Injun Joe but not so foolhardy as to push his aunt beyond her limits, at least on this occasion.

We also find out how much "home" means to Tom and his friends when they run away to Jackson Island to be pirates. They have a glorious time in the wild for a short period, but then all of them, even Huck, begin to long for St. Petersburg and all of their everyday comforts. After a few days they sneak back for their own funeral, are reassured to find out how much they are loved, and then reveal themselves to the startled congregation.

That Tom Sawyer is Clemens's persona is clear. Another episode in the book, Tom's brief tenure in the Cadets of Temperance, is clearly autobiographical and reveals the author's feelings about forbidden behavior. Having joined the cadets so as to be in a parade, "Tom soon found himself tormented with a desire to drink and swear." After this experiment ends, "Tom was a free boy again. . . . He could drink and swear, now—but found to his surprise that he did not want to. . . ."[31]

The book ends happily with Tom and Huck defeating Injun Joe and finding a lost treasure. But for Huck, this victory is not an unalloyed delight. He has redeemed himself from his outcast status and must suffer the consequences:

> Huck Finn's wealth and the fact that he was now under the widow Douglas's protection [he had prevented an attack on her] introduced him into society—no, dragged him into it, hurled him into it—and his sufferings were almost more than he could bear. The widow's servants kept him clean and neat. . . . He had to eat with knife and fork . . . whithersoever he turned the bars and shackles of civilization shut him in and bound him hand and foot.
>
> He bravely bore his miseries three weeks and then one day turned up missing.[32]

Tom tracks him down and talks him into going back to the widow's by promising that the boys will form a gang of robbers.

Because gender has been so neglected a category of scholarly analysis, most interpretations of Twain's work emphasize only the tension between the solitary individual and the society and, although this is surely an important element, they ignore what his work has to say about home and specifically female standards. The "domestic" interpretation is borne out by the fact that grown-up men who are not villains or buffoons are almost entirely lacking from *Tom Sawyer*. (Judge Thatcher is a sympathetic male character in the novel, but he lives outside of town.) Samuel Clemens was evidently trying to come to terms with female authority himself, and that is the crux of the matter for Tom and Huck. How much sacrifice of male independence is home comfort worth? If women give emotional content to life, what do they exact in return?

The answer to these questions is different in *Huckleberry Finn*. Published in 1885 but in gestation for a number of years, Clemens's masterpiece reflects a much more pessimistic view of the human condition than had the relatively sunny *Tom Sawyer*. There is no Becky Thatcher for Huck, no female figure to make the sacrifice of independence worthwhile. Huck, according to T. S. Eliot the most solitary figure in fiction, therefore rejects home and most of human society in his effort to be untrammeled.[33]

Written in the first person, the book begins with a paragraph explaining that Mark Twain wrote about Huck in *Tom Sawyer* and only lied a little: "I never seen anybody but lied, one time or another, without it was Aunt Polly, or the widow, or maybe Mary [Tom's cousin]." Here again we encounter women as the moral exemplars. And how successful they are at inculcating their values! Early on, Huck, Tom, and their friends are discussing the ground rules for the robbers' gang they hope to set up. One boy suggests that Sunday would be a good day for their operations since he can usually get out on Sundays, "but all the boys said it would be wicked to do it on Sunday, and that settled the thing."

The important female characters in *Tom Sawyer* are benign if troublesome. In *Huckleberry Finn* we are introduced to Miss Watson, of whom this cannot be said. Sister of the widow Douglas, she is a mean-spirited scold—unlike the widow, whose reaction to misbehavior is to look, according to Huck, "so sorry that I thought I would behave for a while if I could." Because Miss Watson represents entirely negative authority, as does Huck's cruel and drunken father, Huck sets off on a raft down the Mississippi in the company of Jim, an escaping slave. (It should be pointed out that Jim is escaping from Miss Watson, too, because she has talked of selling him down the river.)

In the context of this book the most significant of their many adventures is the encounter with the Grangerford family. Only a man who was thoroughly familiar with the "house beautiful" literature as epitomized in the book of that title by Clarence Cook could have written the passage about the Grangerford house.[34] Indeed the description of the house is so precise and so vivid that it recalls some of Stowe's descriptions of interiors and partakes of the same "genre" quality:

> It was a mighty nice family, and a mighty nice house, too. I hadn't seen no house out in the country before that was so nice and had so much style. . . . There was a big fireplace that was bricked on the bottom, and the bricks was kept clean and red by pouring water on them and scrubbing them with another brick. . . . There was a clock on the middle of the mantel-piece, with a picture of a town painted on the bottom half of the glass front, and a round place in the middle of it for the sun, and you could see the pendulum swing behind it. . . . Well, there was a big outlandish parrot on each side of the clock . . . [the] table had a cover made out of beautiful oil-cloth, with a red and blue spread-eagle painted on it, and a painted border all around. It come all the way from Philadelphia, they said.
>
> . . . And warn't the cooking good, and just bushels of it, too![35]

A few details, such as the parrot, tip the reader off to the satirical intent. We soon learn that the Grangerfords, who have created a beautiful and gracious home and who are the soul of hospitality to Huck, are engaged in a murderous feud with another family, the Shepherdsons. Even the women, with one exception, are bloodthirsty: "Miss Charlotte she held her head up like a queen while Buck was telling his tale [of an encounter with a Shepherdson] and her nostrils spread and her eyes snapped." After a massacre, Huck and Jim make their way back to the raft: "I was powerful glad to get away from the feuds, and so was Jim to get away from the swamp.

We said there warn't no home like a raft, after all. Other places do
seem cramped up and smothery, but a raft don't. You feel might free
and easy and comfortable on a raft."³⁶

In essence, Clemens is suggesting that home may be a fraud, that
the comfort may be merely on the surface. It is worth contrasting the
passage above with the climactic speech of Clifford Pyncheon in
The House of the Seven Gables, a speech similarly rejecting the
value of home. When Clifford rants that the railroad can free people
from the prison of home, Hawthorne clearly intends the reader to
apprehend that this is a personality on the verge of disintegration.
In the instance of Huck, Clemens gives tacit approval to the notion
that a raft makes the ideal home.

Tom Sawyer ends with Huck's captivity in the home of the
Widow Douglas. *Huckleberry Finn* ends with Huck's departure for
territories unknown: "But I reckon I got to light out for the Territory
ahead of the rest, because Aunt Sally she's going to adopt me and
sivilize me, and I can't stand it. I been there before." This passage
is an ironic echo of the plea from young Samuel Clemens to his
fiancée, "You will break up all my irregularities when we are married, and civilize me . . . won't you?"³⁷

Yet Huck's rejection of home and female standards is not Clemens's last word on the subject. Perhaps his most poignant tribute to
the value of wife and home appears in *A Connecticut Yankee in
King Arthur's Court*, published in 1889. Hank Morgan finds himself
in Camelot and quickly uses Yankee know-how and nineteenth-
century technology to win a place for himself in the kingdom. He is
nonetheless an outsider in the society. Only his marriage to Sandy, a
young woman with whom he has gone knight-erranting, and the
birth of their daughter relieve his loneliness. In the words of Susan
K. Harris, "A non-conformist in all societies, and constantly fighting
to master his situation in the public sphere, Hank finds repose only
in the figures of wife and child and the tiny community they represent."³⁸ Dying in the nineteenth century, Hank calls out "O, Sandy,
you are come at last—how I have longed for you!"

Evidently, Clemens never lost his reverence for feminine values
even while he chafed under the restrictions they placed on his free-

dom. He craved female affection and could occasionally display almost maudlin sentimentality with respect to women. Late in life, for example, he returned to Hannibal for a nostalgic voyage into the past. Speaking to a local club, he broke into tears when he touched on the subject of his mother.[39] What makes the corpus of his work so valuable for the study of the impact of domestic feminism is the fact that he felt and expressed both reverence for and resentment of the home and female standards with such intensity—to say nothing of literary artistry.

When we turn to the work of his contemporaries and imitators we see much less ambivalence about female standards as well as much less artistry. In fact, *Tom Sawyer* and *Huckleberry Finn* belonged to what has been called a "bad-boy sub-genre." Most of the authors who wrote in this vein displayed more crudely anti-woman and anti-domestic attitudes than did Clemens. At a time when the home empowered women to make large claims for cultural influence, male authors evidently found it difficult to attack domesticity using the persona of a full-grown man. Therefore many of them "acted out" their rebellion in descriptions of a rebellious, but lovable, boy.

The scholarly consensus holds that the sub-genre was invented by Benjamin P. Shillaber with his stories of the widowed Mrs. Partington and her mischievous nephew Ike. Shillaber's sketches had originally appeared in the *Boston Post* and then came out in book form in 1854. The book begins with a brief biography of Mrs. Partington, emphasizing her goodheartedness and her domestic skills in addition to her propensity for malapropisms. The reader is then introduced to eleven-year-old Ike: "He is as merry a boy as you will find any day, and though a little tricky and mischievous, the first beginning of malice doesn't abide with him."[40] The rest of the book consists of vignettes featuring Ike's pranks and Mrs. Partington's various torturings of the English language. Although we laugh at her, we are clearly meant to love her too, for her generosity and innocence.

The next significant development was the publication of Thomas Bailey Aldrich's *The Story of a Bad Boy* in 1869. "This is the story of a bad boy. Well, not such a very bad, but a pretty bad boy. . . ." Aldrich says that the young hero is not really vicious but that he deserves the title of bad boy because he is no story-book angel. Whether the author thinks that Tom Bailey is vicious or not, some of his pranks are cruel. For instance, he has an enemy at school, Bill Conway. Tom and his friends notice that Bill's widowed mother, a seamstress, is enamored of a young druggist whose mother she might have been: "The lady's fondness and the gentleman's blindness, were topics ably handled at every sewing-circle in the town. . . . We disliked the widow not so much for her sentimentality as for being the mother of Bill Conway; we disliked Mr. Meeks, not because he was insipid . . . but because the widow loved him. . . ." Late one night the boys sneak in and put a sign in the druggist's window, "Wanted, a Sempstress!" thereby rendering her the laughing-stock of the town.[41]

In the late 1870s and the 1880s the bad-boy books proliferated, and at the same time many of them descended to the level of burlesque. In *Ike Partington* (1879) Benjamin Shillaber dispenses with tributes to Mrs. Partington's good nature and gets right down to the business of making her look foolish. Moreover, he explains that Ike's mischief has won him a bad reputation in town but that Ike is heedless of this fact: "Who ever knew a boy that was morbidly sensitive or cared a continental copper what people said about him. He lives in a world of his own."[42] In truth, this passage has a certain "whistling past the graveyard" quality, as if Shillaber were trying to convince himself of a boy's fundamental imperviousness to community pressure. (Conversely, Clemens's genius consisted of being able to show how deeply sensitive his "bad boys" were to the opinion of the community while at the same time needing to make independent moral choices.)

With George Peck and Peck's Bad Boy, we come to a series of books that can only be called misogynist. One of the books opens with the bad boy explaining how he bedevils his father:

> "How do you and your Pa get along now?" asked the grocery-man of the bad boy. . . .
> "Oh, I don't know. He don't seem to appreciate me. What he ought to have is a deaf and dumb boy, with only one leg, and both arms broke—then he could enjoy a quiet life."

If Pa is infuriated by the bad boy, he is also intrigued by his tricks, however. When the boy squirts Pa in the face with his trick boutonniere, Pa borrows it to take to a church social:

> "I never seen Pa more kitteny than he was that night. He filled the bulb with ice water and the first one he got to smell of his button-hole bouquet was an old maid who thinks Pa is a heathen, but she likes to be made something of by anybody that wears pants, and when Pa sidled up to her and began talking about what a great work the Christian wimmen of the land were doing in educating the heathen, she felt real good, and then she noticed pa's posey in his button-hole and she touched it, and then she reached over her beak to smell of it. Pa he squeezed the bulb, and about half a teacupful of water struck her right in the nose, and some went into her strangle place, and *O, My* didn't she yell."[43]

The bad-boy books, then, present young males who not only defy female authority but also are depicted as virtually immune to it. "Boys will be boys," after all. Contemporary with these books were other depictions of boys, with a very different intent because they were written by women. Indeed, the behavior of the young males in books by women could not have been more dissimilar to the bad-boy pattern.

One of the most famous fictional boys of the late nineteenth century was Little Lord Fauntleroy in the book of the same name by Frances Hodgson Burnett, published in 1886. Cedric Errol calls his widowed mother "Dearest," and she calls him "my pretty little Ceddie." (He is seven years old.) Described as having long golden curls or "love-locks" and wearing black velvet with lace, Cedric might seem rather effete, although Burnett does call him "a handsome, cheerful, brave little fellow." His conduct is so selfless as to defy belief, however. An American who learns that he is heir to an earldom and vast property, he thinks only of what he can do for other people such as a family of twelve and an apple-woman. Arriving in England, he redeems his heretofore selfish grandfather, the Earl of Dorincourt, from his lonely, loveless existence. Indeed, Cedric plays the same redemptive role as had countless other children in earlier Victorian fiction—little Nell, little Eva—except they had usually been girls and had usually died.

A more realistic depiction of appropriate male behavior from a woman's point of view is contained in *Little Men* by Louisa May Alcott, a sequel to the much-loved *Little Women*. Published in 1871, *Little Men* again takes up the story of the March family, centering on tomboy Jo as a woman, her husband Professor Bhaer, and their boys' school. At Plumfield the boys have pillow fights, and one young scholar, Tommy Bangs, is the perpetrator of pranks that bear a resemblance to those of Tom Sawyer; in other words, he is no Cedric Errol. Nonetheless, one of the most important lessons the boys must learn at Plumfield is to respect women. When they come up short in this regard, they must suffer heavy consequences, as the following episode will demonstrate.

Aunt Jo, mother of two sons and with a school full of boys to care for, also has charge of her niece Daisy. When the boys tell Daisy that she cannot play football with them, Aunt Jo responds by buying a little cook stove for Daisy, described so lovingly that it has been the envy of generations of young readers. The stove gives Daisy status in two ways: the boys admire the shiny new toy, and they want the treats that Daisy turns out. Aunt Jo also invites another little girl, Nan, to the school so that Daisy will not be so isolated. Some of the boys misbehave at a "ball" given by the two girls, and the retaliation is swift: they are forbidden from playing with the girls. Tommy pretends not to miss the "stupid girls," but the others are bereft:

> The others gave in very soon, and longed to be friends, for now there was no Daisy to pet and cook for them, no Nan to amuse and doctor them; and worst of all, no Mrs. Jo to make home pleasant and life easy for them. To their affliction Mrs. Jo seemed to consider herself one of the offended girls, for she hardly spoke to the outcasts, looked as if she did not see them when they passed, and was always too busy to attend to their requests.[44]

What we have here is clearly a primer in sexual politics, with domesticity as the chief female weapon.

In fact, what seems to have been occurring—although much more research will be needed on what is, in effect, "men's history"—is that both sexes were beginning to display more adversarial attitudes toward one another than had been the case earlier in the century. A brief glance at the culture of middle-class men in the late nineteenth century reveals the following. A genre of fiction known as "bachelor books" became popular, the best-known exemplar of which was *Reveries of a Bachelor* by Donald Grant Mitchell (who wrote under the pseudonym of Ik Marvel).[45] These books extolled the pleasures of the celibate life—a life in which women could be distanced or controlled. In the 1870s a certain number of American men began to subscribe to a belief in Social Darwinism with its emphasis on the need for untrammeled and even brutal competition.[46] In the 1890s there appeared a cult of the "strenuous life" best exemplified by the writings of Theodore Roosevelt.[47] In short, a self-consciously masculine world was being created in which women played little or no role.

If male and female cultures were in collision in the late nineteenth century, no doubt the biggest single reason was the female attempt to control male drinking behavior. There had, of course, been a temperance movement in the antebellum period, but it had been under male leadership. What was new about the Woman's Christian Temperance Union that emerged in the 1870s was its all-female constituency and leadership, paralleling that of the NWSA but with a much larger membership. Those who founded the WCTU were determined to be free of male influence. A letter to Frances Willard in 1874 revealed the spirit of the group: "I send you today three numbers—all that have been published—of *The Golden Mean*, a journalistic *crusader* entirely originated and operated by—God over us to be sure—but otherwise only by women. Our corps is one girl printer and two lady editors and publishers, and we do everything ourselves, even our own press work."[48]

In addition to its women-only policy, the WCTU was characterized by a willingness to be confrontational. Originating in a series of crusades in the Midwest in which heretofore shy and retiring housewives marched to saloons and gave highly charged speeches to their proprietors, at its height this organization empowered thousands of American women to be more outspoken in the public sphere. Strong men quaked at the thought of an invasion of praying women because the women would be drawing on the most sacred concepts in the culture—"home" and "mother" to be exact—to justify their militancy.

Further, it must be noted that the WCTU organized women on a wholly unprecedented scale. Within three months of the first anti-liquor crusade with long-term consequences—that in Hillsboro, Ohio, in December 1873—women had mounted offensives in more than 250 towns and cities.[49] No less an observer than Mark Twain counted 3,000 victories in what he called the "rum sieges" within a year of the Hillsboro crusade.[50] So widespread was the involvement by women that the temperance crusade assumed the character of a true mass movement.[51] Most significantly, it represented the fullest flowering of domestic feminism: women used the home to justify extraordinary departures from the usual norms of appropriate female conduct—including the call for suffrage.

At first the WCTU refrained from endorsing suffrage and in fact did not do so until 1881. Nonetheless, with the earliest crusade a dynamic had been set in motion that would lead in that direction. Mark Twain made the connection immediately. Crusading women might or might not have a long-term impact on temperance, he contended. Of that, no one could be sure. But more importantly, the women's direct action, mounted in the absence of access to the ballot-box, demonstrated courage and the likelihood that they would use the ballot to advance public morality.[52] Men would therefore be forced to consider the potential benefits in granting women the vote.

Frances Willard, the WCTU's outstanding leader and the most famous woman in the United States in the late nineteenth century, defined her organization's goal succinctly: "Were I to define in a sentence the thought and purpose of the Woman's Christian Temperance Union, I would reply: It is to make the whole world Home-like."[53] Therefore it is not surprising that when the WCTU formally endorsed woman suffrage, the call was for the "Home Protection" ballot, a formulation that Willard had been urging for several years. This was a masterly tactic because it neutralized the most powerful weapon in the anti-suffrage arsenal—the idea that the public act of voting was a violation of the divinely appointed domestic sphere of woman—and suggested that women might be unable to defend their homes without political rights.

The WCTU, then, was a movement that forced itself on the public attention and similarly forced Americans to examine their assumptions about appropriate female behavior, given the fact that militants were often the wives of leading citizens in their respective communities. Although there is no way of proving such an argument conclusively, it seems likely that the bad-boy books constituted a covert way of dealing with the male anxieties and hostilities triggered by such a movement. Certainly, Mark Twain's presentation of the dilemma faced by Tom Sawyer and Huck Finn—How much loss of freedom is home worth?—must have resonated in the minds of many men. No doubt, the sexual politics of the late nineteenth century also fed male fantasies about bachelorhood as a way of life or about all-male activity in the great outdoors as preached most memorably by Theodore Roosevelt.

The charged sexual politics set off by the women's crusades can also be discerned in the temperance literature itself. One of the most prolific authors of the nineteenth century was Timothy Shay Arthur, a giver of domestic advice who today is known best for *Ten Nights in a Barroom*. Within a few months of the Hillsboro crusade, Arthur produced a fictionalized account of the event. Set in a small town in Ohio, *Woman to the Rescue* depicts the efforts of the Widow Green to rouse the other women in her community to combat the evils of alcohol. Before long a band of praying women has visited all the saloons in Delhi:

> Our women are complete masters of the situation. They have said to their husbands, fathers, sons, brothers and lovers, "Stand off and give us fair play. Don't, after your failure of years to limit or suppress a traffic the curse of which has driven us to desperation, put in your bungling hands now. . . ." So the women, for once in *their* lives, are to have their will in Delhi. The ballot is now virtually in their hands, and the first use of it will be to close the saloons.[54]

While the WCTU and its adherents were making perhaps the most effective linkage between the home and power for women in the public sphere, they were by no means alone in this endeavor. Because political rights for women represented such a radical innovation, it is not surprising that suffragists and their allies used whatever arguments they could muster to justify their plea. As early as the 1850s, Theodore Parker employed the "government as housekeeping" analogy in a call for woman suffrage: "I know men say woman cannot manage the great affairs of a nation. Very well. Government is political economy—national housekeeping. Does any respectable woman keep house so badly as the United States?"[55] Others would continue this line of reasoning. In an article in the *Woman's Journal* of February 5, 1870, for example, Uncle Sam is referred to as an "old bachelor" whose appearance reveals his celibate state. In fact, this is why "our national housekeeping is carried on in such a slipshod manner." Votes for women will remedy the matter.[56] Lucy Stone extended the analogy to the level of local government. In an article entitled "Extravagant Housekeeping," Stone deplored the widespread indebtedness among Massachusetts cities and asserted, "This is very bad housekeeping." Obviously, the solution would be to give women the municipal suffrage.[57]

By the turn of the century the chorus of voices using the housekeeping argument for suffrage had increased substantially. In addition to members of the WCTU and suffragist leaders, it included certain Socialists as well as representatives of the new discipline of home economics. Unless a mother takes an interest in such matters as the regulation of trusts, "she is sadly neglecting her duties towards her child, towards her husband, and towards her home," contended Meta Berger, wife of the prominent Socialist leader, Victor Berger.[58] Therefore the ballot is of prime importance for every mother. Such a woman "will appropriate the ballot as a domestic necessity," predicted two pioneering home economists.[59]

No doubt the most influential presentation of the housekeeping argument was made by Jane Addams in an article in the *Ladies Home Journal* in 1910. By this time Frances Willard was dead, and Addams, with her settlement house work at Hull House, had taken

Willard's place as the best-known woman in the country. What she said on any subject—before, that is, she had the temerity to oppose American entry into World War I—was taken seriously by hundreds of thousands of her fellow Americans. This was especially true when Addams addressed the subject of urban problems, the area of her greatest expertise.

Simply put, Addams contended that the American city was in a bad way precisely because it lacked "domesticity." The humblest farm dwelling is more presentable than an urban landscape because a woman is directly involved in its maintenance, she argued. In order to redeem the city, even the most traditional women must begin to understand their social responsibilities in the areas of hygiene, education, child-labor legislation, and the like, responsibilities that can only be met via political action.[60] In effect, Addams set forth an ambitious agenda for Progressive reform, and in subsequent years women would throw themselves into just these battles.

Thus domestic feminism was a vital part of the American political landscape for decades. Arising in the antebellum period because the valorization of home gave women a powerful new tool for legitimating their claims to cultural influence, it succeeded so well that it generated what can only be called a backlash among male authors in the late nineteenth century. These attacks notwithstanding, women continued to use the home to serve their political purposes until well into the twentieth century. One could argue that the settlement-house movement itself, with its creative reform legacy, was a working-out of domestic feminist visions because settlement women sought to carry the values of home to slum-dwellers.

What needs to be addressed next is the issue of the negative aspects of a movement that had so many positive consequences for women and for American society. The first point to be made in drawing up a balance sheet is that there was nothing naïve about using the home to justify female activism. Rather, using the home was a brilliant and hard-headed tactic. But domestic feminism was sounder as a tactic than as a long-term strategy because it necessarily employed arguments that took women away from the natural rights case for female participation in public life and toward asymmetrical sex roles.

Reformers themselves began to speak of the special qualities of woman's nature—as sublime or motherly or unselfish—and to make large claims for what those qualities could do to redeem American political life. Perforce women had less ammunition to use against those who claimed that women's special qualities might be negative—such as lesser intellectual ability.

As we have seen, a few writers at mid-century had grappled with a way of valuing the home without wedding this to asymmetrical sex roles. But they were a tiny minority, too insignificant to constitute a "movement" because the overwhelming majority of Americans clung to deeply ingrained, if wholly unproven, assumptions about biologically determined male-female differences in character and ability.[61] Hence, for all intents and purposes, valorization of the home was closely allied with sexual asymmetry in the minds of both men and women. As a corollary to the cult of domesticity, then, women were able to feel a special self-righteousness because of the worth of their divinely appointed sphere. It was this self-righteousness that gave so many women the courage to break with tradition in their public behavior.

Hence a balance sheet for domestic feminism must acknowledge both positive and negative components of the movement. In effect, it empowered women by enabling them to claim moral superiority. But as the home changed, as domesticity declined in cultural value, woman's moral nature, identified as different by women themselves, could once again be trivialized as it had been in earlier periods of American history.

In a speech entitled "The Province of Woman" (undated but clearly pre–Civil War from the mention of slaves) Lucy Stone had set forth a much different argument. Men and women are equal, she asserted, quoting Genesis to prove her point. Women have the same duty to speak out on public issues that men have. God gave woman intellectual capacity and that implies a concomitant responsibility. "Wherever there is a place to do good, there is woman's appropriate sphere."[62] It was this vision, a vision that neither invoked nor repudiated the value of home, that domestic feminism lost sight of.

Furthermore, there would be public issues of great moment, such as those in the area of foreign policy, that would lie outside the boundaries of the housekeeping argument no matter how ingeniously applied. By tying female participation in the polity to the home, women risked their exclusion from such decisions as a declaration of war, for example.

Finally, it is difficult to prove exactly how much the male writers' attacks on home and female standards had to do with the eventual devaluation of domesticity. That the two were related seems likely, however. If Tom Sawyer, Huck Finn, and their kindred chafed so memorably against the tyranny of the domestic ideal in the world of fiction, they must surely have influenced their counterparts in the real world—who were probably already feeling resentment about the same thing. Politicizing the home and then turning this to female advantage inevitably made enemies for domestic values, enemies who would welcome a diminution in the sanctity of home.

FOUR

Toward an Industrialized Home

$\mathscr{B}$ECAUSE THE HOME had gained an array of new functions by the early nineteenth century, a cult of domesticity came into being. Because the home represented values antithetical to those of market capitalism, domesticity fueled reform energies in the antebellum years. Because the home enjoyed such esteem in the culture, women could use it to justify their activism in the public sphere. But even as the word "home" was being invoked by both men and women in their pleas for various reforms in the late nineteenth century, its capacity to play this overarching role was being undermined: the institution of the American home itself was in rapid flux, and the society that came into being during the Gilded Age made much of the context for the ideology of domesticity obsolete. No doubt these changes ultimately did more damage to the high esteem for domesticity than did all the attacks by disaffected men that we read about in the last chapter, although these attacks made the sanctity of the home less of a social given.

Fundamental to the high status of domesticity in Jacksonian America had been a tissue of assumptions that scholars have called republicanism, a blend of religious and political precepts. To subscribe to this world-view meant believing in the individual's efficacy, not only to direct his or her own life but also to contribute to the national well-being by being a good citizen. Of course, there were many Americans for whom this was myth, pure and simple, because their lives were directed by economic forces beyond their control. But in the absence of powerful organizations—such as the corporation—the myth held enough reality to command allegiance from hundreds of thousands of Americans. According to republican ideals, sturdy, independent male citizens were the backbone of the country, but so, too, were Republican Mothers because they socialized the next generation to the duties of good citizenship. As we have seen, each home became an essential unit in the larger pattern of the national community.[1]

By the late nineteenth century an ideology that rested on the individual's capacity to direct his or her own fate was a bitter joke to many Americans. If they still subscribed to republican ideas, it was a greatly transformed republicanism, relative to that which had existed in the antebellum years. Big railroads, big steel, big oil, big finance all changed the scale of doing business in the United States. Entrepreneurs scrambled to find new ways of consolidating their industries so as to avoid ruinous competition. In response, workers joined groups based on class interests. Farmers came together in various alliances and eventually in the Populist party. Professionals, too, formed organizations to defend their interests. What many of the new groups had in common was fear: fear of the rapacious economic order, fear of social unrest unleashed by those who were the victims of rapid change. To cling to the redemptive power of home under these circumstances would have seemed like a sentimental evasion.

The pervasive middle-class anxiety about the new urban-industrial society found its most significant expression in Edward Bellamy's *Looking Backward,* a book that spawned a short-lived movement called Nationalism and inspired numerous imitations. One of the best-selling novels of its era, *Looking Backward* deals with the adventures of Julian West, a man born in 1857, who wakes up one day to find that he is in the year 2000. This plot device then allows Bellamy to criticize his own world of the late 1880s as well as to describe an ideal society. The tone alternates between sunny optimism when Julian West learns about the future and nightmarish horror when he deals with the Boston of 1887, with its entrenched inequalities, cutthroat competition, and widespread strikes.

For our purposes, *Looking Backward* is valuable as a means of documenting the fact that many Americans were interested in rethinking the nature of the household in response to changes in their world. The individual householder and his wife could no longer be held up as the saving element in society; hence the good home could not readily play the role envisioned by Emerson, Catharine Beecher, and others in an earlier day. Given this, the problem became one of determining how the home could be organized to promote the maximum efficiency and productivity of each of its inhabitants, a very different matter indeed from seeing it as the source of transcendent values. Bellamy clearly spoke to the interests of many when he described a new set of arrangements.

To Julian West's wondering amazement, he learns that the twentieth-century United States is organized into industrial armies, one of men and one of women. People serve for a set number of years, and each adult has a credit card, thereby eliminating the need for a circulating medium or for wages. Homes are simple and modest, and housework has all but disappeared, thereby eliminating the need for domestic servants. Clothes are washed in public laundries, and meals are cooked in public kitchens. In short, a woman is free from household drudgery. The imagination and care lavished on the private household in the nineteenth century have been diverted to spaces and buildings dedicated to public life.

One of the most telling conversations between Julian West and his twentieth-century host, Dr. Leete, concerns the arrangements for social welfare in the new society. Julian queries his host about those who are too weak or infirm to make any genuine contribution to the industrial army. Dr. Leete explains that there is no such concept as charity because there is no such concept as self-support:

> "Who is capable of self support?" he demanded. "There is no
> such thing in a civilized society as self support. . . . As men
> grow more civilized, and the subdivision of occupations and

services is carried out, a complex mutual dependence becomes
the universal rule. Every man, however solitary may seem his
occupation, is a member of a vast industrial partnership, as
large as the nation, as large as humanity."[2]

Clearly, this view of society is a long way from that of early
nineteenth-century republicanism. Bellamy is still profoundly influenced by the Protestant tradition, still seeking redemption, but he
finds it only in the nature of social arrangements and not in the
hearts of individual men and women or in the homes they create.

By the late nineteenth century, then, the home was losing its
transcendent role. It still attracted the attention of thoughtful Americans of both sexes, but for more purely material and practical reasons
than had been the case in the antebellum years. And indeed the
institution of the home itself was changing so rapidly that it is not
surprising to find that people were trying to rethink the nature of
household organization.[3]

At the top of the agenda for change, the "servant problem" was
absorbing an unprecedented amount of time and attention in the
late nineteenth century, principally because by this time domestics
tended to be drawn from the ranks of despised immigrant groups,
especially the Irish (except in the South, where servants were black).
A brief overview of the history of domestic service would show the
following stages. In the colonial period servants were usually indentured; hence there was a wide social chasm between mistress and
maid. Between the American Revolution—by which time indentured
servitude was moribund—and the rise of mass immigration, the chasm
diminished in size, although the work of Faye Dudden would indicate that there were marked class differences as early as the 1820s.[4]
In Jacksonian America domestics were frequently farm girls who
came to the city to find work. With the flood of desperately poor
people from Ireland and later from southern and eastern Europe, the
supply of domestics shifted to groups that had had very little prior
experience with American standards of domestic practice, unlike the
farm girls of an earlier period.

The changing nature of domestic service created problems in more
than one way. In the first place, middle-class Americans' expectations

about domestic comfort had risen when the supply of servants had increased in the early nineteenth century.[5] As we have seen, housewives began to devote more time to housework of a ceremonial nature such as fancy needlework or holiday baking, secure in their ability to turn over the more mundane tasks to servants. But when the supply of servants shifted from native-born to immigrant, housewives began to confront domestics who had scarcely any idea of how to approach their work. Backgrounds of poverty and deprivation had provided little preparation for the performance of domestic duties according to American standards. The volume of complaints about servants swelled, with women typically blaming "green Erin" for all their difficulties.

Moreover, the relationship between mistress and maid shifted dramatically when ethnic and religious differences became so much more marked. Lucy Salmon, an outstanding student of domestic service at the turn of the century, was the first to identify this phenomenon. Salmon pointed out that in the early nineteenth century European travelers had always remarked on the absence of livery in this country, livery representing a clear badge of inferior status for servants in the Old World. Moreover, she quoted a New England woman of the same period who asserted that the "help" had always been married from the family parlor with her sisters for bridesmaids.[6] "Help" routinely took meals with the family. Other evidence exists to suggest that there could be an affectionate personal relationship between mistress and maid in those years. For example, surviving letters to Harriet Beecher Stowe from the family's nurse show that the nurse called Stowe "My Dear Mama."[7] Finally, the Barclays' faithful domestic in *Home* is "help" and not a "servant." Sedgwick calls her a "republican independent dependent."[8]

Clearly, no one was going to call "Bridget," as she was frequently so personified, a republican independent dependent. She was Catholic, poorly educated, and highly vulnerable. By no stretch of the imagination could she be considered a member of the family. As household size shrank because the average number of children declined (from 7.04 per married white woman in 1800 to 3.56 in 1900), she was an increasingly intrusive presence. Beginning around

1850, back stairs began to show up in American houses so that there could be more physical distance between servants and family.[9] Furthermore, and not surprisingly, a plethora of reformers directed their attention toward solving the servant problem. Between the Civil War and World War I, no other issue engaged so much attention in the pages of the women's magazines.[10]

There were three main attempts at reform in the late nineteenth century where domestic service was concerned. First, middle- and upper-class women formed schools for the proper training of potential domestics. For instance, one was founded in 1877 under the auspices of the Women's Educational and Industrial Union in Boston. There young women received practical instruction in cookery and related matters. Schools for servants grew out of many of the same impulses as did the domestic science movement, another late nineteenth-century development, to be discussed in Chapter Six. In particular, the impulse to train both mistress and maid frequently reflected invidious assumptions about the Irish. Harriet Beecher Stowe thought, for example, that the more the housewife herself might know about domestic procedures, the less likely she would be "the slave of a coarse, vulgar Irishwoman."[11]

Another possibility, explored more seriously in this period than at any time before or since, was that of cooperative housekeeping. Mary Peabody Mann explained the reasons for considering this approach in an article in *Hearth and Home* in 1869. Asserting that "Bridget has become demoralized," she went on to note that it was unlikely that enough black women would move north to supply the region's needs and saw only two possible solutions: cooperative housekeeping or Chinese servants, who would probably become Americanized all too soon.[12] In 1869 a group of forty households in Cambridge, Massachusetts, including most prominently that of Charles and Melusina Fay Peirce, experimented with cooperative housekeeping, an experiment that lasted about one year. A disappointed Melusina Peirce subsequently explained to Frances Willard that most of the women were unprepared to work hard enough to ensure the group's success.[13] Nonetheless, speakers at women's meetings such as the Congress of the Association for the Advancement of Women, and authors in periodicals such as *The Revolution* (the organ of the NWSA), the *Woman's Journal,* and *Godey's* called for this approach.[14]

If cooperative housekeeping attracted attention but not many adherents, a third approach to the servant problem, that of professionalizing housework, garnered much more attention because it seemed more practical. No less a figure than Harriet Beecher Stowe wrote an article advocating professionalized housework for *The Revolution.* She envisioned a model village with a town laundry, a town bakery (American housewives did not turn in large numbers to baker's bread until after 1900), and a town cook shop where soups and meats could be purchased.[15] In another context, "Christopher Crowfield" remarked, "Whoever sets neighborhood laundries on foot will do much to solve the American housekeeper's hardest problem." Stowe believed that if soap and candles could make the transition from home to commercial production with no loss of quality, then so could other components of the housewife's job.[16]

It is worth reminding ourselves of just how onerous that job could be in the absence of a level of household help beyond the reach of many Americans. An article in *Hearth and Home* describes a "simplified" method for doing laundry that offers us a gauge of energy expenditure that housewives needed to make on a regular basis. First, the housewife was to soak the clothes in cold water for six hours after rubbing the seams with soap. Then she was supposed to wash them in tepid water and wring them out. Then bring them to a slow boil. Then, fresh tepid water. Then wring them out and put them in a cold rinse with a light bluing. The writer called this procedure "a very moderate amount of hard labor."[17] It was this sort of backbreaking toil that made women interested in reform.

Another way of judging the nature of the housewife's job in the late nineteenth century is to examine a list made up by Abby Diaz in 1875. In discussing "A Domestic Problem," she tried to enumerate the more frequently recurring tasks:

> Setting tables; clearing them off; keeping lamps or gas-fixtures in order; polishing stoves, knives, silverware, tinware, faucets, knobs, &c.; washing and wiping dishes; taking care of food left at meals; sweeping including the grand Friday sweep, the lim-

ited daily sweep, and the oft-recurring dust-pan sweep; cleaning paint; washing looking-glasses, windows, window-curtains; canning and preserving fruit; making sauces and jellies, and catchups and pickles; making and baking bread, cake, pies, puddings; cooking meats and vegetables; keeping in nice order beds, bedding, and bedchambers; arranging furniture, dusting, and "picking up"; setting forth, at their due times and in due order, the three meals; washing the clothes; ironing, including doing up shirts and other "starched things"; taking care of the baby, night and day; washing and dressing children, and regulating their behavior, and making or getting made, their clothing, and seeing that the same is in good repair, in good taste, spotless from dirt, and suited both to the weather and the occasion; doing for herself what her own personal needs require; arranging flowers; entertaining company; nursing the sick; "letting down" and "letting out" to suit the growing ones; patching, darning, knitting, crocheting, braiding, quilting,—but let us remember the warning of the old saying ["If you count the stars, you'll drop down dead"], and forebear in time.[18]

Her list is daunting. No wonder women were interested in Edward Bellamy's ideas about the future.

Of course, Bellamy's utopia fit right into discussions of professionalized housework. He went further than merely the discussion in the novel, however, by writing an article with an agenda for change in *Good Housekeeping* in 1889. Servants are on the way out, he proclaimed. They are anachronistic in a democratic society. What, then, can be done to take their place? His analysis of the problem was better than his proposed solution. In addition to calling for cooperation—a reform that had been more discussed than implemented—and predicting technological breakthroughs, he advocated the consumption of bakery bread and called for a "scientific cuisine." This evidently relied on food prepared elsewhere than in the home kitchen.[19]

No writer went further in advocating professionalized housework than Charlotte Perkins Gilman, one of the most important feminists of the late nineteenth and early twentieth century. So thoroughgoing was Gilman's rejection of the domestic ideal, however, that it represented a much more fundamental break with the past—ironically she was the niece of Catharine Beecher and Harriet Beecher Stowe—than the ideas of those who merely wanted to save housewives from overwork. For that reason, Gilman's ideas will be discussed in the context of the feminist response to evolutionary theory, the subject of the next chapter.

Indeed, there were so many reformers with so many ideas that they added up to a "Grand Domestic Revolution," in the words of *Woodhull and Claflin's Weekly* in 1871, as quoted by Dolores Hayden in her book of that title. Hayden argues that the "material feminists"—that is, those who wanted to change the material foundations of domesticity—understood in a way that was subsequently lost sight of that it would be necessary to rethink the nature of the household in order to free women to live richer lives. "For six decades the material feminists expounded one powerful idea: that women must create feminist homes with socialized housework and child care before they could become truly equal members of society."[20]

Not surprisingly, many looked to technology for answers, and in the late nineteenth century there were indications that technology might indeed offer the housewife some relief. Although the home cannot be considered to have been fully industrialized until the 1920s, there were important developments in the latter years of the nineteenth century that were indicative of the character that housework would assume in the twentieth century.

As we have learned, woodstoves had replaced open hearths in post–Civil War cookery. This development did not necessarily lighten the housewife's load a great deal—a store of fuel still had to be kept on hand and the fire still had to be tended—but it did create the possibility of carrying on a greater variety of cooking operations at the same time. As the century wore on, stoves became increasingly elaborate. For example, in their *American Woman's Home* of 1869, Catharine Beecher and Harriet Beecher Stowe furnished the drawing of a stove that had a roaster on the side, so as to approximate spit-roasting, and a reservoir for hot water, as well as burners and a bake oven. By the 1890s, stoves were being manufactured with temperature gauges in the oven door.[21] In short, the nineteenth century witnessed revolutionary changes in the cooking process. Before 1830 a housewife bent over an open hearth and tended a heavy iron pot; in 1900 she stood at a stove, the temperature of which could be "scientifically" regulated, and used a pan that was made out of an alloy and hence was much lighter.[22]

Another invention that also lightened the load for women was the sewing machine, a device that came into widespread use in the 1860s. As one reads the diaries and letters of an earlier period one is impressed by the constant need for women to be sewing. Even on pioneering journeys, women spent time daily with their needles. In a recent book on "westering" women, Sandra Myres reproduces diaries of two such pioneers, one who took the overland trail and one who went by sea, and both of whom left records of what they sewed while en route.[23] As a further example, Lydia Maria Child complained to a friend about the heavy demands on her time occasioned by her sewing:

> Being so taken up with house-work all summer, my winter sewing has crowded very hard upon me. No comfortables or quilts for the beds, stout woolen trousers and frocks for Mr. Child and the man, various quiddities to keep father warm. . . . Ever since my girl came I have sewed diligently every hour not employed in cooking, Sundays excepted.[24]

What must be remembered is that Child's sewing burden was this great even in the absence of children. When growing children needed to be provided with clothing, too, the burden increased substantially. Therefore, the sewing machine was welcomed by *Godey's* as "the Queen of Inventions": "No wasting application, stooping over the needle, without time for outdoor exercise, wearying for want of change will be felt by women who have in their possession a good sewing machine."[25] As with stoves, sewing machines were being rapidly improved and refined in the late nineteenth century. A catalogue from the World's Columbian Exposition of 1893 listed the improvements in design since the Philadelphia Exposition of 1876: there was better tension, the stitch was firmer and more even, and the "lock" (to prevent unraveling) was more secure.[26]

Yet another area of innovation in household technology lay in refrigeration. Before the appearance of the "icebox," housewives had preserved food by a variety of means. Meat might be smoked, cured in brine, or salted down. The buttery was kept as cool as possible for dairy products. The root cellar stored fruits and vegetables. And, of course, in snowy climates the weather might produce the same effect as the modern freezer. There is, for example, a wonderful description in a memoir of Harriet Beecher Stowe by Annie Fields of how the Beecher family—children, help, and all—would throw themselves into the work of preparing apples for cider. They would then have a frozen barrel of cider in the milk room during winter from which were cut "red glaciers, which when duly thawed, supplied the table."[27] By the 1850s ice vendors with carts were selling ice harvested from frozen ponds to housewives in northern cities. This, in turn, led to the development of chests or boxes in which the ice could be placed. As in the instance of stoves and sewing machines, the catalogue of the World's Columbian Exposition of 1893 listed a number of improvements that had recently been made in the technology of refrigeration, such as improving the circulation of air inside the device.[28] An advertising circular for the Whitson Refrigerator circa 1880 suggested that the housewife could garner favor with the maid by buying the new product. "Shure an I'll lave the place if they take it out," says an Irish maid. "After going in dat box eberyting comes out right," according to a black maid.[29]

Thus even before electricity reached middle-class homes, there had been the development of new appliances. After homes were routinely electrified—by the first decades of the twentieth century—the possibilities for household technology expanded. The Electrical Building at the World's Columbian Exposition had suggested some of these possibilities: electric stoves, electrified pans, washing machines, and ironing machines, to name only a few.[30] Fascination with technology was so widespread as to be shared by feminists: in 1891 the Massachusetts Woman Suffrage Association staged a fair at which new products and gadgets were displayed, such as the "Little Wonder Ice Cream Freezer."[31]

Another development with liberating potential for women was

the implementation of municipal water systems that eventually brought running water into the average home. As with electricity, indoor plumbing was not diffused throughout the society until the early twentieth century. Therefore in the late nineteenth century, most women had to haul inside all the water for laundry, dishwashing, personal hygiene, and cooking, a truly onerous task. More unpleasant still was the necessity for disposing of slops, including the contents of chamber pots.

As late as the turn of the century laundry remained a remarkably burdensome task. A pamphlet written in 1906 presumes that the reader will have a mechanical wringer, but nonetheless sets forth a procedure that was an all-day undertaking (and more difficult still if the housewife lacked access to running water).[32] Despite the lapse of nearly forty years between the article in *Hearth and Home* cited earlier and this pamphlet, and despite a number of technological innovations, women still needed relief from this burden, hiring laundresses, for example, if they could not afford full-time domestic service.

Homes were changing, then, in many ways. The average size of the household declined steadily throughout the nineteenth century. For this reason, that is, because the family was becoming an increasingly tight and private unit, and because of the type of servants available, there was widespread dismay over the "servant problem." This dismay fueled a sense of urgency about the possibility of technological breakthroughs for the home. Despite the introduction of a number of new appliances, however, in 1900 housework was still hard work for both the housewife and her maid. Reformers sought a variety of means to lighten the load.

While these developments were taking place, there were other changes occurring, too, that would have important long-term consequences for the housewife. With the explosive economic growth of the post–Civil War period, the food-processing industry was one of a number of new industries to come into being and develop within the space of a few years. A combination of improved rail transportation and the growth of American cities created a national urban market, and this, in turn, made national brands and national advertising feasible.[33] The technology to preserve food in hermetically sealed cans had existed for decades, and in the 1870s and 1880s commercial canneries began to appear, especially in California. As with so many industries, ferocious competition led to a merger in the California canning industry in 1899, a merger that ultimately resulted in the creation of the giant multinational corporation Del Monte.[34] Before long, advertising copywriters would be telling housewives that food in cans was inherently superior to what the housewives could prepare on their own.

Even before the advent of canned foods, however, American cuisine was changing, and the consensus of culinary historians is that it was changing for the worse. As we have learned, there had been a proliferation of cookbooks in the second quarter of the nineteenth century, cookbooks which suggested that middle-class Americans were developing relatively sophisticated palates and had an appetite for baked goods made with sumptuous ingredients. Under the tutelage of authors like Eliza Leslie and Mary Randolph, housewives were perfecting their culinary skills. In the words of John and Karen Hess: "American cookery reached its highest level in the second quarter of the nineteenth century with Miss Leslie as its guide. From then on, it was downhill all the way."[35] They adduce such factors as additives, poorer quality flour owing to factory milling methods, and the increasing use of sugar to explain the decline. By the late nineteenth century the decline had become precipitous. Again quoting Karen Hess:

> By the end of the century with Fannie Farmer, there were no more questions because she, and those who followed, had lost touch with the fragrances, tastes, and textures of the past. Succeeding editions of her Boston Cooking-School Cook Book (1896) saw ever-increasing amounts of sugar in bread and salad dressings, and the inevitable substitution of sugary lemon gelatine full of artificial flavoring and coloring for traditional aspic mixtures; Jell-O was introduced in 1897 and swept the country and Fannie Farmer, a remarkably imperceptive cook

possessed of a raging sweet tooth, was to become the patron
saint of the American kitchen.[36]

Hess contends that by the end of the century, most cookbook writers
had become "handmaidens of industry, wittingly or no."

It was in the area of baking that the most noticeable deterioration
took place. Chemical leavening came into increasing use, and cooks
could thereby substitute pearlash, soda, cream of tartar, and eventually baking powder for natural leavenings such as beaten eggs. As
early as 1869 this was lamented in *Hearth and Home*. The anonymous author of "Housekeeping Experiences" recalled that her mother
had been one of the best cooks in their town. The sponge cakes of
bygone days had been made only of flour, sugar, and eggs, the latter
beaten until the arm ached: "In the time referred to, cream of tartar,
in its relation to cookery, was a thing unheard of. The arrangement
of making things sour with one chemical in order to make them sweet
with another, had not yet entered into the practice or imagination of
our mothers." The sponge cakes of 1869 were "dry and choky," the
author complained.[37] Certainly, chemical leavening permitted the
cook to economize on the other ingredients while requiring the cook
to possess less judgment and skill than one who used no such magic
shortcuts.

Thus when we examine the history of American cuisine, a striking pattern emerges, a pattern that may enable us to gain insight into
the impact of economic and technological change upon the home
more generally. We can discern two very distinct stages in the impact
of industrialization on cookery. The first stage produced more abundance and more time for the housewife, without any noticeable de-
skilling of the cooking process. In fact, the cuisine of the average
household improved inasmuch as the housewife could devote more
time to it as well as having access to more ingredients than she had in
the eighteenth century. But as the century wore on—scholars identify
the Gilded Age as the watershed—industrialization began to have the
opposite effect, and a de-skilling process began, along with the concomitant deterioration of the cuisine. This process would accelerate

in the twentieth century. It is perhaps more than coincidence that the high-water mark of the cuisine occurred at the same time as the high-water mark of the cult of domesticity, although which was cause and which was effect would be difficult to determine.

The overlap of the zenith of cookery with the Golden Age of Domesticity in the antebellum years reminds us that it is important to refer to the realm of culture when we try to assess the impact of economic and technological change in the Gilded Age. We must first take note of the fact that the domestic novel was dead, having played itself out sometime in the 1860s.[38] No longer were women writers rushing into print with their descriptions of housewifely prowess. The energy was going rather into children's literature (it must be acknowledged that some of the children's books were suffused with domestic imagery) and historical romances. Only in the area of regional or local-color literature were writers regularly presenting images of domestic competence, and this genre never enjoyed the best-seller status of the domestic novel.

A novella that also never enjoyed the status of best-seller but is nonetheless important for our purposes because it belongs to the literary canon and embodies so negative a view of domesticity is Stephen Crane's *Maggie: A Girl of the Streets,* published in 1893. More than most, this is a work that exemplifies the way in which the society of the Gilded Age seemed to some sensitive observers to be making domesticity irrelevant. Indeed, in *Maggie,* set in a New York slum, it is her chaotic, unloving home that drives the title character Maggie Johnson to ruin.

The first member of the Johnson family to whom we are introduced is young Jimmie, who is engaged in a fight with another street urchin. The fight having ended, he goes home to a ragged, dirty sister and two drunken parents. Crane describes the filthy tenement, using homely domestic details to underline the horror, indeed the hellishness of the environment: the doorways are "gruesome," the stove is "seething" rather than cheery, and the food is "grease-enveloped." Mrs. Johnson flies into a rage when she learns that Jimmie has been fighting. Settling down, at least temporarily, she prepares the evening meal:

"Git outa deh way," she persistently bawled, waving feet with
their disheveled shoes near the heads of her children. She
shrouded herself, puffing and snorting, in a cloud of steam at
the stove, and eventually extracted a frying-pan full of potatoes
that hissed.[39]

This is a grotesque caricature of the usual description of a mother
cooking for her family. Indeed, the Johnson's apartment is as much
an anti-home as the dwelling of Simon Legree. The difference between the approaches of Crane and Stowe lies in the fact that Stowe
made it obvious that Legree had created his house of horrors by
freezing out the softening influence of woman, except in the capacity
of mistress. In *Maggie*, the mother, with her fondness for breaking
furniture when in a rage, is the chief source of chaos. Her husband
explains his predilection for alcohol in this fashion: "My home reg'lar
livin' hell! Damndes' place! Reg'lar hell! Why do I come an' drin'
whisk' here this way? Cause home reg'lar livin' hell!"[40] Crane makes
it plain that if the home is hell, Mrs. Johnson is the culprit—along
with the underlying social and economic forces that create a slum in
the first place. Moreover, in *Maggie* there is no home that is an oasis
of love and comfort—the role of the Quaker home in *Uncle Tom's
Cabin*.

As we have seen, *Looking Backward*, which did enjoy best-seller
status, dealt at length with home, but only from a technocratic viewpoint. Nowhere in Bellamy's book is there any notion that traditional
skills might be valuable and hence worthy of being preserved. On
the one hand, he professes to value women highly and makes them
part of an "Industrial Army." On the other hand, women have a
highly distinct sphere, albeit not the home, and have what seems to
be second-class status.

Another best-seller of these years was the Reverend Charles Sheldon's *In His Steps*, written in 1896. Because it sold millions of copies,
it is a valuable document for the historian who is trying to understand the popular culture of the late nineteenth century, as well as
being valuable for insights into the evolution of American Protestantism. Sheldon's book posed the question "What would Jesus do?"
and then set the standard for Christians of trying to follow as closely

as possible "in His steps." If Henry Ward Beecher's *Norwood* is one of the central documents of Romantic Evangelicalism, then clearly *In His Steps* is one of the central documents of the Social Gospel that captured mainstream Protestantism at a time of widespread concern about the impact of industrialization. This is because all of Sheldon's characters wrestle with their responses to the social dislocations caused by urbanization and industrialization.[41] Saving their own souls is not enough for them.

As the book opens, Henry Maxwell, prosperous minister of an established church for the well-to-do, comes face-to-face with urban poverty when an unemployed man staggers into the sanctuary on a Sunday morning. Interrupting the sermon, the stranger challenges the congregation to consider what they really mean when they sing hymns about taking up the cross and following Jesus. The episode is a catalyst for Maxwell, who accepts the challenge, pledging himself and asking for volunteers to join him in throwing aside a conventional life and trying to live a committed Christian life. Those who join him must make a variety of sacrifices with respect to family life, business success, and career choice. When anyone wavers, he or she is made to confront the terrible suffering of those in poverty and despair and to realize how the past comfortable life had been built on social injustice.

Significantly, home and domestic values are largely irrelevant to Sheldon's purpose. The home provides no sanctuary for the urban poor because economic fluctuations make it so vulnerable. Indeed, the possession of a wife and children is seen as greatly increasing the suffering of the man who cannot find work. At one point during a discussion of the plight of such a man, a discussion taking place in a settlement house, a Socialist makes an impassioned speech denouncing the irresponsibility of most Christians. What he says about home is telling: "I thank God, if there is a God, which I very much doubt, that I, for one, have never dared to marry and try to have a home. Home! Talk of hell! Is there any bigger one than this man with his three children has on his hands right this minute?"[42]

If home offers no hope of redemption, neither does the love between a husband and wife, a love Beecher had presented as a major source of sanctification in *Norwood*. Several of the male characters who take the pledge in *In His Steps* do so without sympathy from their wives. Sheldon comments: "Truly 'a man's foes are of his own household,' when the rule of Jesus is the great divider of life."[43] Not only is this a departure from Beecher, it is a departure, too, from the thought of Horace Bushnell, with his emphasis on the saving role of Christian nurture in the household.

The one way in which a vestige of the domestic ideal is presented in *In His Steps* is in the character of Felicia Sterling, the "Angel Cook" of the slums. Forced to support herself after the death of her parents, the once-wealthy Felicia decides to devote her life to the poor: "I have had a dream of opening an ideal cook shop in Chicago or some large city and going around to the poor families in the slum district . . . teaching the mothers how to prepare food properly."[44] Armed with this ambition, she opens her shop and shortly thereafter can claim, "I know already that the pure food is working a revolution in many families." While these passages grant food an important role, they show little respect for the capacities of the housewife. In this, Sheldon reflected what was becoming conventional wisdom in the late nineteenth century: the American housewife was seen as needing help from outside experts in order to perform her work adequately.

The vulnerability of the home to economic forces was a special concern of other Social Gospel Christians. In 1886, Washington Gladden, one of the leading spokesmen for socially concerned Christianity, listed a number of ways in which he saw the home being weakened by industrialization. Most fundamental was the uprooting of the young people who had to leave home to find employment and often found themselves living in boarding-houses with little or no supervision. Moreover, there was the instability of industrial life owing to strikes and business failures. Gladden feared that these conditions militated against the possibility and the desirability of setting up a home in the eyes of many young men.[45]

Twenty years later, another outstanding Protestant leader, Walter Rauschenbusch, addressed many of the same difficulties. He argued that the "industrial machine has absorbed the functions which women

formerly fulfilled in the home and has drawn them into its hopper."
This diminishes their chances of marriage, he contended, and creates
a worrisome social problem: "The health of society rests on the welfare of the home. What, then, will be the outcome if the unmarried
multiply; if homes remain childless; if families are homeless; if girls
do not know housework; and if men come to distrust the purity of
women?"[46]

Both the mid-nineteenth century Protestants and the Social Gospel
Protestants agreed that the home was an institution of fundamental
importance to society. Where they differed was in extent of belief in
the independent power of the home. Using the language of modern
social science, we could say that Beecher, Bushnell, and Theodore
Parker saw the home as an independent variable, whereas Sheldon,
Gladden, and Rauschenbusch saw it as a dependent variable. For the
first group, the home acted upon society; for the second group, the
home was the passive object around which more potent social forces
swirled and upon which those forces acted.

The late nineteenth-century version of domesticity was, of course,
at variance with the militant vision of the home set forth by Catharine Beecher in her *Treatise on Domestic Economy* of 1841. Beecher
had seen the home as a virtual battering ram for benevolent social
purposes. One wonders whether Beecher herself changed her mind
as she grew older, and the country entered so different a phase. Her
last book, *American Woman's Home,* which came out in 1869, was,
in fact, a revision of the 1841 volume that listed Harriet Beecher
Stowe as co-author. Much of the content was similar as far as the
specifics of advice were concerned. One difference in the books, however, lay in their introductions: in 1841 Beecher had begun with extensive quotations from Tocqueville and had then given her own
thoughts on the political ramifications of domesticity: in 1869 this sec-
tion had been dropped. It may be that Beecher thought her points
were too well known to require repetition. In any event, *American
Woman's Home* is much less political in tone than the earlier book.

That the domestic advice literature continued to depict the home
in elevated terms until well into the Gilded Age is suggested by
Julia M. Wright's *The Complete Home,* which appeared in 1879.

"For national and social disasters, for moral and financial evils, the cure begins in the Household," Wright asserted in the preface. Each household should be "gladsome in itself" but also a "spring of strength and safety to the country at large." Her vision was a throwback to the republican ideal because she insisted that each member of the household, boys included, should contribute his or her labor to home activities so as to spare not only the mother but also the servants. If all labor willingly, then there will be time for beauty and social life, she contended.[47]

The changes in the home and the domestic ideal in the Gilded Age, then, can be summarized as follows. The ideal survived in advice literature and in the discussions of reformers. It no longer animated writers as it had a generation earlier and no longer afforded much hope to Protestant spokesmen. Industrialization had already led to a de-skilling of cookery, while new inventions proliferated that would ultimately transform the nature of housework. Given the problematic aspects of domestic service and the onerous burden of work that still existed in the average household, reformers sought means of relief for the middle-class housewife.

Men and women of goodwill struggled with the problem; technology provided increasingly elaborate devices to save the housewife from overwork; and yet the relief never really came. This seems manifest when one examines the studies that suggest that time spent in housework declined little if at all in the first two-thirds of the twentieth century.[48] An important reason that women's domestic responsibilities stayed so heavy was the widespread diffusion of the private automobile by the 1920s. The very decade in which household technology created an industrialized home saw the housewife's job turn into a post-industrial one; that is, the focus of her day began to shift from production—of meals, of baked goods—to providing the service of chauffeur. As Ruth Schwartz Cowan puts it, writing of the mid-twentieth century, "The automobile had become, to the American housewife of the middle classes, what the cast-iron stove in the kitchen would have been to her counterpart of 1850—the vehicle through which she did much of her most significant work, and the work locale where she could most often be found."[49]

Yet unless we are willing to accept a technological determinism and say that the automobile inevitably sealed the fate of the housewife, we must return to the late nineteenth century for an explanation of her fate. When one examines the evidence regarding the quantity of work that had to be done in the average home as late as 1900, it is clear that women still needed relief from overwork, especially if the home were to become genuinely democratic and nonexploitative. Technology could have played a much more benign role than it did. What went wrong?

It goes without saying that the interests of corporate America were served by the commodifying of the home that would take place by the 1920s. This was a development that greatly enhanced the deskilling process without giving women any new skills instead. Moreover, new and less skilled tasks took the place of the old, about which more will be said in subsequent chapters. But beyond blaming the forces of advanced industrial capitalism, we can scrutinize the ideas of those late-nineteenth-century reformers who tried to provide a direction for their society. They can, in fact, be held responsible for a number of errors in judgment, despite their good intentions.

In the first place, in common with most human beings in the late nineteenth century (except perhaps, Henry Adams), they embraced technology in an entirely uncritical fashion, making no attempt to differentiate between household drudgery and work drawing on valuable skills. They were confident that machines could do any job well. Yet if one examines the tasks of the housewife, one finds some, like laundry, that are akin to the traditionally male job of ditch-digging, and some, like cookery, that are more akin to cabinet-making. The point is that, if anyone had tried seriously to analyze which household tasks belonged to a valuable craft tradition and which could be eliminated from the home with no loss in skills, the housewife would have benefited greatly.

Edward Bellamy was particularly blind to such nuances. The department store in his utopia provides a good case in point. Dr. Leete's beautiful daughter Edith conducts Julian West to the twentieth-century emporium where people (mostly women) make all their purchases. Julian looks around for a clerk to question about his proposed purchase. Edith explains that there is no need for such interaction, as all goods are clearly labeled and the clerk has no stake in a sale. What Bellamy fails to understand is that he has envisioned a type of clerical employment in which any possibility of personal satisfaction in a job well done would be gone. Similarly, he fails to understand that by removing most of the work from the home and giving women a second-class status in the work force, he is not really improving their position. Edith herself is little more than a consuming drone, however beautiful.

Bellamy's estimate of the importance of home cooking was best revealed in his *Good Housekeeping* article. In this, he argued that there was less predisposition in favor of home cooking than had existed twenty-five years earlier: "Mothers have long [since] ceased to make pies." Further, mothers and aunts were unlikely to return to the kitchen because they could not count on the appearance of their menfolk at the dinner table: "The club and the restaurant now bid successfully against the family table for the patronage of father, son and husband, while the reproaches of the ladies too evidently derive their edge from envy." The obvious solution to the problem in Bellamy's eyes would be the removal of cooking from the province of the home.

If reformers uncritically accepted "improvements," regardless of which tasks were being displaced, this owed, too, to a lack of appreciation for emotional intimacy and the ways in which the opportunity for sharing emotion can be institutionalized at home. As we have learned, Antoinette Brown Blackwell had written of her desire to "give and take some home comfort," coining a memorable phrase. There was precious little home comfort in Bellamy's utopia, however. In dispensing with the family dinner table, he eliminated the single most likely means of providing for communion or any other emotional interchange in a household.[50]

Yet another failure among reformers in the late nineteenth century, especially among the "material feminists," to use Dolores Hayden's phrase, was their assumption that the problem of overwork for the housewife could be solved without relying on men to do their fair share of the housework. A few thought that women should cooperate among themselves to lighten the burden. Technology would provide the answer in the minds of many. Others thought a new source of household labor was the answer; still others thought removing most work from the home was the solution. The latter two approaches drew upon entrenched class and ethnic biases and assumed that there would be a permanent class of menials whether inside or outside the home. Yet in the words of Dolores Hayden:

> Women can never gain their own liberation from stereotypes of gender at the expense of other women of a lower economic class or another race whom they exploit by paying them low wages to do sex-stereotyped work. Black women and white women, Yankee women and immigrant women, housewives and servants, had to break out of woman's sphere together, or else not at all. Any exceptional woman who escaped unpaid or low paid domestic work could always be sent back to woman's sphere again by men, unless the grand domestic revolution touched all women and all domestic work.[51]

In the last analysis, all of the proposed solutions were retrograde insofar as achieving full sexual symmetry, because they were steps away from the vision articulated by Samuel May and Antoinette Brown Blackwell.

Moreover, those reformers who failed to appreciate the importance of a home's capacity to provide intimacy were unlikely to solve the problem of mediating between public and private spheres. Many of them—Bellamy, in particular, and Charlotte Perkins Gilman, as we shall learn—wrote as if the public sphere should absorb all of society's energy. They thus gave little or no attention to the issue of how to create the virtuous home and how to link such a home to the larger society, a problem that had engaged Emerson, for example. Ironically, the long-term consequence of ignoring this issue was not to liberate women, who were still ascribed to the home, but to trivialize the home, thereby rendering it a much less satisfactory work environment.

Thus, material factors conduced to diminish the status of the home, both in its capacity to play a transcendent role in the culture and in its capacity to serve as an arena for the display of female prowess. Yet industrialization was not the only means by which domesticity was being devalued in the late nineteenth century. Contemporary with the rapid economic changes of the Gilded Age was the crystallization of a new world-view—Darwinian evolution—that ascribed the creative role in human development to male activity outside the home. That "material feminists" and other reformers gave so little thought to what could and should be preserved of the traditional home doubtless owed much to the new world-view. To the impact of evolutionary theory on the status of the home, we now turn.

FIVE

Darwinism and Domesticity:
The Impact of Evolutionary Theory
on the Status of the Home

Periodically in modern history scientists have set forth new theories whose consequences go far beyond the internal development of science as a system of knowledge and far beyond such practical applications as they may happen to have. Discoveries of this magnitude shatter old beliefs and philosophies; they suggest (indeed often impose) the necessity of building new ones. They raise the promise—to some men infinitely alluring—of new and more complete systemizations of knowledge. They command so much interest and acquire so much prestige within the literate community that almost everyone feels obliged at the very least to bring his world outlook into harmony with their findings, while some thinkers eagerly seize upon and enlist them in the formulation and propagation of their own views on subjects quite remote from science.

—Richard Hofstadter

WITH THIS STATEMENT, Richard Hofstadter opened his seminal work about Darwinism in the United States, *Social Darwinism in American Thought*, published more than forty years ago.[1] Although scholars in succeeding decades have explored many facets of Charles Darwin's impact on American society, only in the last dozen years have they turned their attention to Darwinism and women.[2] The impact of Darwinism on the status of domesticity has received no attention at all. Yet the sweeping changes effected by a truly revolutionary theory such as that attributed to Darwin should lead us to expect that the theory must have had a profound impact on gender constructs as well as on the status of the home. Briefly, the impact can be summarized as follows. Darwinism tended to be reductionist with respect to women, making reproductive capacity the chief criterion of female excellence. Hence the whole complex of moral, social, and religious values associated with Republican Motherhood was cast in shadow. Moreover, Darwin and many of his followers explicitly stated that women are biologically inferior to men. This, too, had a negative impact on the status of the home. Perhaps most damaging to the home was the fact that Darwin's theory of sexual selection located the source of evolutionary change in male struggle for mates, making men and male activity the "vanguard of evolution." Finally, Darwinism helped promote the secularization of American society, and thus served further to undermine the religious role of the home. All of this eroded the interest of American intellectuals, including women, in domesticity.

The orthodox Christian world-view was being undermined from early in the nineteenth century onward. Even before Darwin published *On the Origin of Species* in 1859, there were a number of individuals who were beginning to accept the idea that species are changeable rather than fixed for eternity by God, which was the orthodox view. The most important pre-Darwin theorist of evolution was the French scientist, Jean-Baptiste Lamarck (1744–1829), who thought the engine of evolutionary change to be the heritability of acquired characteristics. In other words, Lamarckianism allowed for a dynamic interaction between an organism and its environment such that the organism could pass on to its offspring what it "learned" about adaptation to the environment. Inasmuch as the precise understanding of genetics has been a twentieth-century development, this argument had a certain plausibility in the nineteenth century.

Another important predecessor to Darwin in creating a new worldview was Sir Charles Lyell, the British geologist. Before the theory of evolution could capture the allegiance of the majority, our very understanding of time needed to be altered. In the early nineteenth century, prevailing religious opinion set strict limits to the lifespan of the earth. In the 1830s—while Darwin was on his epochal voyage on the *Beagle*—Lyell published his multi-volume *Principles of Geology*, which convincingly argued that the earth was many hundreds of millennia old, thus providing the time necessary for species to evolve from one into another.

It is important to understand some of the groundwork for Darwinism lest we fall into the error of attributing every aspect of the new world-view to Darwin himself. Of course, Darwin must receive the credit for working out in enormous detail the most widely accepted theory of the mechanism by which evolution is thought to take place—natural selection. While serving on a five-year voyage of discovery sponsored by the British government, he was struck by the close resemblance of species on isolated islands that shared a similar environment—close resemblance but *not* identity. This led him to speculate about evolution. By his own account, it was while reading Malthus on population problems that he was further struck by the fact that far more organisms are born than can survive. Common sense suggests that only the fittest can survive to breed and create a new generation. Given long periods of time and random changes in organisms, a new species could evolve. Darwin's logic rested not on genetics, unknown at the time, but rather on how breeders of domestic animals can breed for desirable characteristics with a measure of success.

Darwin in fact published the *Origin* some twenty years after this insight came to him. He spent years of hard work laying the empirical groundwork for his edifice, paying close attention to selected species. Clearly aware that his views would be controversial, he was determined to protect himself against attack as best he could. In fact, only the realization that another scientist, Alfred Russel Wallace, was also on the track of natural selection galvanized him into publishing as soon as he did. He appears to have been both consumed by anxiety about the anticipated attacks and equally determined to tell the truth according to his best lights. So wearing was this tension that he spent the better part of his adult life as a semi-invalid.

The *Origin* appeared, and so did the attacks. Nonetheless, important adherents on both sides of the Atlantic soon joined the cause. Darwin continued to work diligently, and in 1871 *The Descent of Man* appeared. In this book he made up for the omission of his own species from the earlier work; specifically, he included humans in the evolutionary process. Moreover, the *Descent* propounded the theory of sexual selection as an addendum to—perhaps a modification of—natural selection. Darwin was struck by the existence of secondary sexual characteristics, such as the brilliant feathers on a male peacock, that seem to have no obvious role in natural selection. He concluded that some characteristics must have evolved in order to increase success in mating, rather than success in obtaining food or in defense. He further thought that there are two kinds of sexual selection, one having to do with male struggle for mates and one having to do with choice exercised by females.[3] It was here that he dealt explicitly with human females and revealed the extent to which he was the prisoner of his own culture's sexual norms.

We know from a number of sources that Darwin was not especially enlightened about women. Perhaps most telling was his attitude toward marriage. Returning to England from the voyage of the *Beagle*, he resolved that he must quickly come to a decision about whether or not to marry. His journal records some of his thoughts about the pluses and minuses of matrimony:

> Children—(if it please God)—constant companion, (friend in old age) who will feel interested in one, object to be beloved and played with—better than a dog anyhow—Home and someone to take care of house—charms of music and female chitchat. These things good for one's health. Forced to visit and receive relations *but terrible loss of time.*[4]

A recent (and largely admiring) biographer, Peter Brent, says of this passage, "It would be hard to conceive of a more self-indulgent, almost contemptuous, view of the subservience of women to men; in this, as in so much else, Darwin was a true and conventional son of his time and class."[5] Having convinced himself that his interests would best be served by marriage, he soon proposed to his cousin, Emma Wedgwood, and was accepted. She bore him ten children, to whom he was an affectionate father. Brent concludes that, on balance, Darwin was a considerate husband, too. He was too much the duty-bound Victorian to be otherwise. Moreover, he was sensitive to the suffering of others, whether slaves, mistreated animals, or exhausted wives.

What he lacked and possibly feared was depth of feeling. His mother had died when he was a boy of eight, and Brent speculates that this loss "rendered his deepest emotions inaccessible to him." Over the years, he lost the capacity to enjoy art except in the most superficial fashion—by having light novels read aloud by the women of the family. This meant that he avoided contact with that area of nineteenth-century English culture in which women were most likely to excel. Indeed, his brother Erasmus was friendly with women of accomplishment like Harriet Martineau and Jane Carlyle, but Charles Darwin sequestered himself in his rural retreat and had no contact with important literary intellectuals of either sex. He has been called an "anaesthetic man" because of the crippled way he dealt with the realms of art and profound emotion.[6]

This then, was the man who set forth his view of inherent female capabilities in 1871. The tragedy is that one so limited in his contacts and stunted in his emotional capacity was taken as guide on the subject by millions of educated people around the globe. Sexual selection as presented by Darwin took the status quo of Victorian society—as he experienced it—and read it into nature, proclaiming it to have "the force of natural law."

In dealing with the differences between the sexes, Darwin used the work of Sir Francis Galton as a starting point. Galton had concluded that "men are capable of a decided pre-eminence over women in many subjects" and possess greater variability than do women. Said Darwin, "The chief distinction in the intellectual powers of the two sexes is shown by man's attaining to a higher eminence, in whatever he takes up, than can woman—whether requiring deep thought, reason, or imagination, or merely the use of the senses and hands."[7] He suggested that lists of eminent men and women be drawn up and a comparison made in order to verify his and Galton's contention.

If "man is more courageous, pugnacious, and energetic than woman, and has a more inventive genius," how did his superiority arise? The answer lies in the struggle among savages for women: "With social animals, the young males have to pass through many a contest before they win a female, and the older males have to retain their females by renewed battles." It takes more than brute strength to prevail, said Darwin, and over time both sexual selection and natural selection will favor the passing on of traits of courage and perseverance more fully to the male than to the female. "Thus man has ultimately become superior to woman."[8] (It should be remembered that no one understood the mechanism of inheritance, and most assumed that males passed on more of their traits to their sons, and females, to their daughters.)

For Darwin, the only way to address the inequality of the sexes is by biological means:

> In order that woman should reach the same standard as man, she ought, when nearly adult, to be trained to energy and perseverance and to have her reason and imagination exercised to the highest point, and then she would probably transmit these qualities chiefly to her adult daughters. All women, however, could not be thus raised, unless during many generations those who excelled in the above robust virtues were married and produced offspring in larger numbers than other women.[9]

While civilized man does not struggle for a mate as did savage man, he does struggle to maintain himself and his family, and this will keep up or even increase man's mental powers and, "as a consequence, the present inequality of the sexes." It should be noted that this analysis is rooted in a tacitly Lamarckian view of evolution whereby training women will not only educate the current generation, but also improve the stock.

What is most important is the fact that this formulation makes the home utterly irrelevant to human progress. Male struggle outside the home is the engine of change. Of necessity confined to the home and to nurturing activities, women necessarily carry a biological taint.

Thus, disdain for the home, because of its inability to promote change that could improve the species, and disdain for female abilities reinforced one another.

Darwin was not the only influential evolutionary thinker of the late nineteenth century. His compeer in propagating the new worldview, especially in the United States, was the British writer Herbert Spencer. Spencer was converted to evolution after reading Lyell and before Darwin published his *Origin*. Of course, the appearance of that magisterial tome furnished a would-be evolutionist with much useful ammunition. For decades, Spencer worked out his interpretation of the social implications of evolution in a series of influential books. Hofstadter says that by December 1903 the number of copies of Spencer's books sold in America was 368,755—apparently a record for books of such difficulty.

A great popularizer of science, Spencer was deeply influenced by contemporary work in physics as well as in biology, especially by the First Law of Thermodynamics, which posits the conservation of energy. Transferring both the "persistence of force," as he called it, and evolution to the discussion of gender, Spencer developed his view of women and their capacities. In *The Study of Sociology* he wrote, "The first set of differences [between the sexes] is that which results from a somewhat earlier arrest of individual evolution in women than in men, necessitated by the reservation of vital power to meet the cost of reproduction." The fact, then, that women mature earlier than men—the point of Spencer's remarks—creates "a perceptible falling short in those two faculties, intellectual and emotional, which are the latest products of human evolution—the power of abstract reasoning and that most abstract of the emotions, the sentiment of justice. . . ."[10] Trying to change this given of nature by overeducating a woman may serve to hamper her ability to reproduce because, since energy is finite, that which goes to the brain in the process of education will have been ineluctably drained from her demanding reproductive system.

This explains the quantitative difference between the sexes in mental capacity. As for the qualitative difference, it can be explained by natural selection:

In the course of the struggles for existence among wild tribes, those tribes survived in which the men were not only powerful and courageous, but aggressive, unscrupulous, intensely ego- istic. Necessarily, then, the men of the conquering races which gave origin to the civilized races, were men in whom the brutal characteristics were dominant; and necessarily the women of such races, having to deal with brutal men, prospered in pro- portion as they possessed, or acquired, fit adjustments of na- ture. How were women, unable by strength to hold their own, otherwise enabled to hold their own? Several mental traits helped them to do this. We may set down, first, the ability to please, and the concomitant love of approbation. . . . And (recognizing the predominant descent of qualities on the same side) this, acting on successive generations, tended to establish, as a feminine trait, a special solicitude to be approved, and an aptitude of manner to this end.[11]

It would be absurd to suggest that Darwin and Spencer created the view of women as biologically inferior to men. All too many, even friends of womankind such as Theodore Parker, were willing to con- cede that women on the average have lesser intellectual capacity than do men. Rather, what Darwinism did was to ratify pre-existing preju- dices and give them greater validity by linking female inferiority to a specific evolutionary argument about the virtue of male struggle. In this regard, there were parallel developments in racial thought. Racism certainly existed before the *Origin*. But after its publication, "the potentialities of Darwinism as a rationale for American racist at- titudes were soon apparent."[12] Before long, evolution or the survival of the fittest were being routinely invoked to justify a variety of racist attitudes and policies.

What must be clearly understood is that evolution is fact, and nat- ural selection is theory.[13] Scientists still only imperfectly comprehend how natural selection operates, let alone sexual selection. Nonethe- less, the view of men as the vanguard of evolution penetrated widely throughout American society in the late nineteenth century. Thus, an arbitrary focus on male struggle as the engine of change was taken as fundamental scientific truth. Says the Harvard biologist Ruth Hubbard in her essay, "Have Only Men Evolved?":

It is likely that the evolution of speech has been one of the most powerful forces directing our biological, cultural, and social evolution, and it is surprising that its significance has been largely ignored by biologists. But, of course, it does not fit into the androcentric paradigm. No one has ever claimed that women cannot talk; so if men are the vanguard of evolution, humans must have evolved through the stereotypically male behaviors of competition, tool use, and hunting.[14]

Clearly, the new world-view, which greatly enhanced the human capacity to understand the natural world, also contained a core of contempt for what were taken to be female nature, the female environment, i.e., the home, and the female contribution to human progress, based not so much on "science" as on cultural assumptions.

What, then, of the reception of Darwinism in the United States? That general question can be divided into two parts—the reception among scientists and the reception in the larger society—both of which we must address because in this instance biological theory and social and cultural change had a high degree of interaction. As for scientists, Darwin obtained a remarkably smooth victory in this country. His great antagonist, Louis Agassiz, the Swiss-born naturalist, found that even his own students were defecting shortly before his death in 1873.[15] But though evolution enjoyed such an easy conquest, this was not tantamount to a complete victory for Darwinian orthodoxy. A number of American scientists began to subscribe to a view they identified as "neo-Lamarckian," in which they downplayed the importance of natural selection and emphasized the significance of change through the heritability of acquired characteristics. In the 1890s there were probably more neo-Lamarckians than Darwinians in American science.[16] Only the work of August Weismann in that decade and the rediscovery of Gregor Mendel's work on genes around 1900 permanently discredited Lamarckianism.

Well before the arrival of Darwinism on these shores, science had begun to enjoy remarkable esteem in American culture. It has been suggested that, with the erosion of traditional Christian belief, science offered Americans a new orthodoxy, a new source of authority, and even a new set of values. In a penetrating analysis of the impact of science on American social thought, Charles Rosenberg argues that the nineteenth century saw "a constantly shifting equilibrium between secular and religious imperatives. The similarity between scientific and religious values made it natural for most Americans to move fluidly from one intellectual and emotional realm to another."[17]

Nonetheless, Darwinism offered a considerable challenge to traditional Christian belief, a challenge that required hard thought and difficult decisions for those Christians who wanted to be up-to-date in their opinions. If Lyell and Darwin were right, what happened to the literal truth of the Bible and its depiction of creation? Darwin offered a rigorously materialistic view of the universe—so much so that he wrote a book, *Expression of Emotion in Man and Animals*, in which he treated the emotions in the light of their evolutionary role. What, then, happened to the role of the human spirit? These were troubling questions, but most liberal Christians were able to resolve them, at least for a time, in such a way as to cling simultaneously to Darwinism and to their religion.[18]

By the 1890s, belief in evolution if not in the entire Darwinian approach had captured the citadel of American thought. Yet so protean were its uses that one has to be very careful in dealing with the topic. For example, for most people, evolution conduced toward a view of the universe as highly deterministic and mechanistic. In the case of the philosopher Charles Peirce, on the other hand, an adherence to Darwinism convinced him of the role of chance in life. He therefore coined the term "tychism," after the Greek word for chance, to describe his own view of the importance of randomness.[19] One generalization that seems secure, however, is that Darwinism focused attention on biology rather than on culture.

Not surprisingly, it did not take long before the heightened attention to biology showed up in work dealing with women. A particularly clear example of biological reductionism was the statement by a physician in 1870: "It was as if the Almighty in creating the female sex, had taken the uterus and built up a woman around it."[20] The most notorious example of such thinking—and one that evoked a strong response from contemporary feminists—was Dr. Edward Clarke's *Sex in Education; or a Fair Chance for the Girls*, published in 1873. In some ways, Dr. Clarke was willing to place a higher value on women than had either Spencer or Darwin. Indeed, he began his book—which had originated as an address to the New England Women's Club—with a strong denial that one sex is superior to the other. Nonetheless, he proffered the argument, reminiscent of Spencer, that girls must receive an altogether different education than boys, lest their reproductive systems be damaged: "There have been instances, and I have seen such, of females in whom the special mechanism we are speaking of [the reproductive system] remained germinal,—undeveloped. It seemed to have aborted. They graduated from school or college excellent scholars, but with undeveloped ovaries. Later they married, and were sterile."[21] According to Clarke, because American girls were in general better educated than their European counterparts, their health had suffered accordingly. All too often, American girls were required to study even while menstruating, and this did them irreparable harm. Hence, coeducation was ill-advised. What made the book so damaging to women was the fact that it set up the reproductive capacity as central in evaluating a woman's life and worth. An educated woman who opted for a small family was not exercising rational choice but instead demonstrating her biological impairment. Interestingly, Clarke argued that factory girls were not at the same risk as school girls because physical labor does not tax the nervous system in the same way that brain work does.

Particularly infuriating to feminists was Dr. Clarke's use of the term "agene" (Greek, meaning "without sex") to characterize those women who had "arrested development of the reproductive system." Women suspected that he was really maligning single women as a group when he spoke of "Amazonian coarseness and force" in his subjects and called them "analogous to the sexless class of termites."

So threatening was Dr. Clarke's book to the cause of higher education for women, to say nothing of coeducation, that it provoked a series of articles in the leading feminist publication of the day, *Woman's Journal*, that were subsequently collected into a book. The authors wanted to refute Dr. Clarke, yet were limited in their ability to do so by their clinging to the same view of woman's special nature that he postulated—although they placed a higher value on it. Julia

Ward Howe edited the volume, and her essay is a particularly striking example of this dilemma. She fully agreed with the view that menstruation places extraordinary demands on the female system: "I have known of repeated instances of incurable disease and even of death arising from rides on horseback taken at the critical period."[22] Where she took issue with Dr. Clarke was in his indictment of education as the sole cause of the problem. Indeed, the respondents in the volume all took the doctor with the utmost seriousness and shared many of the same premises.

A more systematic and hence more effective response came from Antoinette Brown Blackwell in her remarkable book, *The Sexes Throughout Nature,* published in 1875. In this work, she took on not only Dr. Clarke but Charles Darwin and Herbert Spencer as well. While Blackwell, too, accepted the premise that there are significant differences between the sexes, she rejected out of hand the idea that women need to be treated as semi-invalids during a portion of their lives. Rather, hard and meaningful work will promote good health: "It is one of my firmest convictions that if overwork has slain its thousands of women, underwork has slain its tens of thousands, who have perished more miserably." Given the fact that she had no training as a scientist, she tried to take on the male scientific establishment with logic, a formidable tool in her hands.

It has taken the better part of the twentieth century for the understanding to coalesce that science is a human activity, subject to the prejudices of its practitioners as are all human activities, and not a purely objective reading of the book of the universe. Nonetheless, Blackwell began her book by making this very point:

> Any positive thinker is compelled to see everything in the light of his own convictions. The more active and dominant one's opinions, the more liable they must be to modify his rendering of related facts—roping them inadvertently into the undue service of his theories. . . . When, therefore, Mr. Spencer argues that women are inferior to men because their development must be earlier arrested by reproductive functions, and Mr. Darwin claims that males have evolved muscle and brains much superior to females, and entailed their pre-eminent qual-

ities chiefly on their male descendents, these conclusions need not be accepted without question, even by their own school of evolutionists.[23]

Having begun with the insight that those who accept the truth of evolution need not accept as gospel everything that Spencer and Darwin said about gender, Blackwell goes on to make a series of telling points. For example, if Darwin and Spencer were correct about the differential evolution of the two sexes, how much longer will men and women belong to the same species? "These philosophers both believe that inheritance is limited in a large degree to the same sex and both believe in mathematical progression. Where, then, is male superiority to end?" Given the long time span required for evolution to take place, even small differences could become gross differences over the millennia, if Darwin and Spencer were right.

Again congruent with her original insight, she argues that Darwin fixed his attention only on masculine characteristics and could thus conclude that there is a decided imbalance in the capacities of the two sexes in favor of the male. If one takes seriously the contribution of the female to the species, whatever the species may be, a balance will be restored:

> It requires a great amount of male surplus activity to be expended physically in motion and psychically in emotion, as well as a good deal of extra ornamentation and brilliancy of coloring, to balance the extra direct and indirect nurture, the love, and the ingenuity which the mother birds, and even the insects, bestow upon their young.[24]

In other words, nurture, like struggle, is an activity that must be taken seriously in the evolutionary process. In making this point, Blackwell was, in effect, offering a brief for the significance of the home.

The key to Blackwell's argument is the contention that the two sexes must of necessity be roughly equal in overall contributions to the survival of a species because small differences, over time, could add up to something other than small differences. She even made a diagram to show how the contributions of men and women are in a state of equilibrium. So eager was she to have her approach validated that she called for scientific research in the area: "By all means, let the sexes be studied mathematically."

What she both believed in so strongly and hoped for so fervently—the equality of the two sexes—led her into those speculations about the division of household labor with which we are already acquainted. Only if woman has every opportunity to excel will the world know what she is capable of, and that opportunity will not come if she carries the complete responsibility for housework:

> Whatever her hand finds to do let her do it with her might, in demonstration of her capacity.
>
> Morally certain it is that she will neither forego, nor desire to forego, her domestic relations; nor will the average woman seek to evade an equitable share of the burdens and disabilities of her station, or shrink from sharing honorably all the many duties which arise within the home-life. Evolution has given and is still giving to woman an increasing complexity of development which cannot find a legitimate field for the exercise of all its powers within the household. There is a broader, not a higher, life outside, which she is impelled to enter, taking some share also in its responsibilities.
>
> This need in no wise interfere with the everyday comforts, the fostering mental influences, and the moral sanctities of the home. . . .[25]

It was a brave attempt, but she was overmatched, not in intellectual ability, but in credentials and hence in access to an audience. Because she lacked an aura of authority and had no mass social movement to take up her claims—indeed, it served the purposes of domestic feminism to emphasize male-female differences—knowledge of her writing died out. Only in the last fifteen years or so has it been rediscovered.[26]

It is useful to examine current responses to biological reductionism by way of contrast. In 1975 a new intellectual formulation, sociobiology, emerged, a formulation that once again emphasizes biology at the expense of culture. While it has captured its adherents and garnered predictable media attention, it has also encountered powerful opposition from feminist scientists, male and female. Many scientists who oppose sociobiology possess the very credentials of scientific training and tenure in a prestigious university that Blackwell lacked. Further, important scientific developments of the twentieth century make possible a more effective response to biological reductionism than could be made in the nineteenth century. A brief discussion of some of the ideas put forward by contemporary scientific opponents of sociobiology will underline the difficulties feminists faced one hundred years ago in trying to defend female nature against the evolutionary onslaught.

Neurophysiologist Ruth Bleier contends that the methodology of sociobiology "consists essentially of flipping through the encyclopedic catalogue of animal behaviors and selecting particular behaviors of fishes, birds, insects or mammals that can be readily made to exemplify the various categories of human 'traits' and social arrangements that Sociobiologists claim to be universal and genetically based." She then summarizes the modus operandi of sociobiologists as follows:

> Sociobiologists attempt to reconstruct evolutionary history by inventing plausible stories that attempt to show how a particular behavior or social interaction in humans or other species *could* have or *would* have been adaptive and therefore favored by natural selection and genetically carried through subsequent generations.[27]

Since the nature of genetic encoding was not established until the 1950s, this line of argument—one that suggests that sociobiologists are guilty of a certain circularity of argument wedded to an imperfect understanding of genetics—was unavailable to those who might desire to oppose biological reductionism one hundred years ago. Another line of argument that was not available has to do with the current understanding of the stability of the human species. Modern science has demonstrated that "Homo sapiens arose at least 50,000 years ago, and we have not a shred of evidence for any genetic improvement since then."[28] Of course, Darwin and Spencer assumed otherwise and rested much of the argument for male superiority on the supposition

that male struggle continues to promote male evolution at a disproportionate rate compared to that of the female.

Finally, Ruth Hubbard offers an astute observation about the
similarity in context in which both sexual selection and sociobiology
arose: "The recent resurrection of the theory of sexual selection and
the ascription of asymmetry to the 'parental investments' of males
and females are probably not unrelated to the rebirth of the women's
movement. We should remember that Darwin's theory of sexual selection was put forward in the midst of the first wave of feminism."[29]
In this instance, history has given a twentieth-century scientist an
insight impossible to achieve in the Gilded Age.

Given the intellectual tools that were unavailable, how *did* the
friends of womankind deal with evolutionary theory in the late
nineteenth century? The two most important defenders of woman
after Blackwell were Lester Frank Ward and Charlotte Perkins Gilman. In defending female humanity against the charges of biological
inferiority, Ward and Gilman used the home as an explanation for
woman's alleged underdevelopment. This they could do because they
both steadfastly adhered to Lamarckianism and saw the home as an
environment that stunted the development of those who spent time
in it. Hence, in addition to the devaluation of domesticity suggested
by evolutionary theory itself, there was a further attack on the home
by two of woman's champions.

Lester Frank Ward was one of the truly remarkable individuals of
the late nineteenth century. Born in 1841, one of ten children, he
worked as an agricultural laborer and fought in the Civil War before
obtaining a college degree at night school. His professional experience
eventually included legal training, botanical publications, work with
the U.S. Geological Survey, and the publication of outstanding works
in the field of sociology. One of the founders of the latter discipline,
he became a professor of sociology at Brown University in 1906 and
was elected to be the first president of the American Sociology Society that same year.

Ward's *Dynamic Sociology* was the first important treatise in the
field to be published in the United States. For Hofstadter, Ward was
the American who, while adhering to the truth of evolution, tried

hardest to reclaim it from those such as Spencer and William Graham Sumner, the latter of whom used Darwinism to justify laissez-faire. Thus Ward was a pioneering advocate of positive state action to achieve benevolent social purposes. This stance rested on the distinction he made between blind, natural forces and social phenomena that can be governed by human intervention. In effect, he was trying to reestablish teleology, since belief in a purposive universe had fallen victim to Darwinism. In the words of Hofstadter, "If there is no cosmic purpose, there is at least human purpose, which has already given man a special place in nature and may yet, if he wills it, give organization and direction to his social life. Purposeful activity must henceforth be recognized as a proper function not only of the individual but of a whole society."[30]

A genuine democrat with much faith in the power of education to ameliorate social ills, Ward recoiled in dismay from established inequalities, including those between the sexes. Accepting natural selection—with an admixture of Lamarckianism—and praising Charles Darwin for his pioneering role, Ward nonetheless adhered to premises quite unlike those of Darwin in his own discussion of male-female differences. Ward began with the understanding that, for the purposes of nature, "the fertile sex is of by far the greater importance and this increased importance is abundantly shown throughout all the lower forms of life where these purposes are predominant." If nature favors the female sex in myriad ways among plant and animal species, what, then, created the obverse condition among humans? Ward speculated that since, according to contemporary belief, males have stronger sexual appetites than do females, males wrested the power to choose a mate away from the sex to whom this power belongs throughout most of the natural world. Male passion conquered female virtue—in the old-fashioned sense of the word "virtue" meaning prowess. Women then became property and were often chosen for their beauty rather than for intellectual qualities. "And the inferior position of woman, maintained through so many ages, has actually resulted in rendering her both physically and mentally inferior to man."[31]

Ward thus agreed with Darwin and Spencer that modern women

are inferior to men. Where he differed was in his estimate of the relative position of the sexes in the rest of the natural world, in his understanding of how women became inferior, and in his prognosis for humanity. Indeed, the prognosis to be inferred from Darwin and Spencer had been grim. Darwin had offered the slight hope that both the education of women and the greater fecundity of those who were well educated might help women catch up with men over a number of generations. But Spencer dashed that hope with his theory, which generated a great deal of attention, that educating women would make them *less* fertile. Ward had an easier solution—get women out of the kitchen:

> It is often remarked that women are, as a rule, more frivolous and trifling than men. Being the truth, it may as well be spoken, and the explanation will prove a sufficient vindication of the sex; for it will be found that their ideas are exactly as much less important than those of men as their experiences are less useful. Where the only objects with which woman comes in contact are those of the kitchen, the nursery, the drawing-room, and the wardrobe, how shall she be expected to have broad ideas of life, the world, and the universe? Her ideas are perfectly natural and legitimate. She has seen and handled culinary utensils, china, and silver-ware, and she has idea of them. In the absence of other ideas, she will think about them, talk about them, have her whole mind absorbed with them. The mind must act, and this is all the material it has to act upon. It is the same of dress; her soul is engrossed in dress, since it is her most important object of experience. If you wish to make her forsake it, you must give her something else to think of. Give woman an interest in great subjects, and she will soon abandon small ones. If she knew as much about the great men of history or of her own age as she does about her neighbors, she would cease to talk about the latter and talk about the former. Teach her science, philosophy, law, politics, and you will do much to put an end to gossip, slander, and fashion-worship.[32]

While Ward's desire to give women a broader sphere of activity and an improved education was positive for women, less positive

was his summary dismissal of women's culture and his apparent
blindness to the female energy that had gone into a number of reforms throughout the nineteenth century. Only one who accepts as
true by definition the idea that female small-talk is trivial while male
small-talk is not, could have written this paragraph. Furthermore, one
as committed to humane reform as Ward was might have been expected to have noticed the existence of the "benevolent empire" of
female charitable activity. Finally, unlike Blackwell, Ward offered
no suggestion as to how domestic tasks might be performed so as to
free women. So unimportant did they seem to him as to be unworthy
of attention. Ward's attitude should be contrasted with that of
Theodore Parker, who, in an earlier period, argued that home duties
enlarge the social sympathies.[33]

Over the centuries, woman's confinement to the home has had a
physical impact on her brain, Ward thought. "Brain can only develop by use. It must languish from disuse. The causal faculty of
woman has had no exercise, therefore it has not developed."[34] In the
antebellum years, when domesticity had enjoyed its greatest esteem,
the givers of domestic advice had been emphasizing the contrary—
that running a household and kitchen as well as setting the moral
tone of the home required both intelligence and character. How
much the emergent attitude owed to evolutionary theory per se and
how much to the economic forces unleashed in the late nineteenth
century is difficult to judge with certainty. What is certain is that the
new attitude boded ill for those who, by reason of gender, class, or
race, might still be consigned to perform the housework.

An even more forceful attack on the home was launched by Charlotte Perkins Gilman in a number of important books written in the
late nineteenth and early twentieth century. A student of Ward's
work and an evolutionist, Gilman was a brilliant systematizer who
tried to go beyond political rights for woman to such matters as
woman's economic dependence and her sexual role. A dedicated
iconoclast, she argued that confinement to the home is the chief
reason for woman's inferiority.

So thoroughgoing was Gilman's rejection of her culture's prescriptions for women that she lived her iconoclasm as well as writing

about it. As a child, Charlotte Perkins had had little reason to see her home in any very favorable light. Writing her autobiography near the end of her life, she recalled a chaotic and unloving household owing to her father's irresponsibility and her mother's coldness. Gilman's mother, a woman whose best hopes had been blighted by her unhappy marriage and subsequent divorce, and the life of genteel poverty to which the family was then condemned, withheld affection from her daughter so as to toughen her for the vicissitudes of life. The mother was "passionately domestic" but had not been able to enjoy even that activity because of the family's circumscribed existence. A brother fourteen months older than she was the source of teasing rather than companionship for Gilman. For all these reasons, as an old woman, she could still recall vividly her first encounter with a loving home. Visiting some cousins, she said, "I saw how lovely family life could be. Instead of teasing and ridicule here was courtesy and kindness."[35] Another vivid childhood memory was the visit to her great aunt, Harriet Beecher Stowe. (Gilman's paternal grandmother was Mary Beecher Perkins.)

Not surprisingly, when she became an adult, she had profoundly mixed feelings about marriage. She had striven for years to achieve control over her emotions and distrusted the powerful feelings, sexual attraction among them, that were evoked in her by Charles Stetson, a young painter who wanted to marry her. She took months before reaching an affirmative decision and suffered "periods of bitter revulsion, of desperate efforts to regain the dispassionate poise, the balanced judgment I was used to."

As a young married woman and then a mother, Gilman suffered an emotional decline and eventually a breakdown. Her mother came to help, her husband undertook to perform more than the usual allotment of husbandly duties, but nothing relieved her despair: "Here was a charming home; a loving and devoted husband; an exquisite baby, healthy, intelligent and good; a highly competent mother to run things; a wholly satisfactory servant—and I lay all day on the lounge and cried."[36] Domesticity was literally driving her to madness, or so it seemed to her at the time. Consultation with a leading physician, Dr. S. Weir Mitchell, who specialized in nervous disorders and had obviously taken Herbert Spencer's ideas to heart, only made things worse. Gilman recalled his advice as follows: " 'Live as domestic a life as possible. Have your child with you all the time.' (Be it remarked that if I did but dress the baby it left me shaking and crying—certainly far from a healthy companionship for her, to say nothing of the effect on me.) 'Lie down an hour after each meal. Have but two hours' intellectual life a day. And never touch pen, brush or pencil as long as you live.' "[37]

In her short story "The Yellow Wallpaper," Gilman uses homely domestic details to evoke the horror of her own breakdown. Written in the first person, the story describes a young housewife's descent into madness. Deprived of meaningful work by her husband's sinister overprotectiveness, she lies in her room and follows the pattern of the wallpaper, becoming increasingly obsessed by it. Eventually she loses the ability to distinguish between real life and her fantasies about the wallpaper.[38]

Happily for her emotional well-being, Gilman rejected Dr. Mitchell's advice and asserted her autonomy by leaving her husband. She then transgressed a sacrosanct cultural norm by allowing him and his second wife to do a major share of the rearing of young Katharine Stetson—for which she received a great deal of criticism. Having established a national and eventually an international reputation as a writer and lecturer and thus an identity distinct from domesticity, Gilman was able to remarry, happily, at the age of thirty-nine. Yet she never fully recovered from the breakdown, being subject to periodic depressions for the rest of her life. Despite this self-confessed emotional flatness, however, her boldness and her prolific writings gave her a high status among her contemporaries. The *Nation* praised *Women and Economics* (1898) as "the most significant utterance" about women since John Stuart Mill's *The Subjection of Women*, and the suffrage leader Carrie Chapman Catt placed Gilman at the top of her personal list of outstanding American women.[39]

The extent to which Gilman departed from earlier discussions of domesticity by feminists can best be gauged if we survey, in brief, the history of feminist thought with respect to the home. In her *Vindication of the Rights of Woman* (1792), the founding mother of Anglo-American feminism, Mary Wollstonecraft, had insisted that women needed a broader education than they then received in order to perform their domestic duties adequately. Too often, she charged, a woman was expected to take the role of frivolous plaything, a role for which ignorance was seen as a desirable attribute. This then militated against the optimal performance of domestic duties because, trained from birth as a being who could be "the weathercock of its own sensations," she could never develop the requisite "austerity of behavior" in later life. Wollstonecraft concluded, "It is plain from the history of all nations, that women cannot be confined to merely domestic pursuits, for they will not fulfil family duties unless their minds take a wider range."[40] This bears a certain resemblance to Blackwell's contention that both woman and the home would benefit if she were to move from "bound to rebound" between public and private spheres. In any event, Wollstonecraft certainly dignified the importance of the home.

The great generation of antebellum feminist-abolitionists dignified the importance of the home, too—although some of them uttered heartfelt complaints about their own heavy domestic burdens. What is most striking is the fact that many of the women who married found like-minded men who were willing to rearrange their own lives for reform purposes, and thus these women had far less reason to be angry about domestic responsibilities than did the average middle-class woman of the day. In her study of feminist-abolitionists, Blanche Glassman Hersh contends that her subjects thought it was important to be good at both roles—reformer *and* housewife. For example, Elizabeth Smith Miller wrote for the *Revolution* as well as publishing a book with recipes and advice on entertaining.[41] Hersh quotes Lucy Stone as follows: "I think that any woman who stands on the throne of her own house, dispensing there the virtues of love, charity, and peace . . . occupies a higher position than any crowned head. . . . However, woman could do more."[42] After her death, her widower Henry Blackwell wrote a tribute to the suffrage women in the *Woman's Journal:* "Never have I known more affectionate wives, more tender mothers, more accomplished housekeepers, more satisfied husbands and children, more refined and happy homes."[43] In

short, the suffrage movement exhibited pride in all the accomplish-
ments, including the domestic, of its leaders.

A woman who had more to complain of than many of her sister
suffragists was Elizabeth Cady Stanton. Henry Stanton tended to be
thoughtless and unhelpful. As Elizabeth struggled under the domestic
load occasioned by her large family, she turned to her close friend
Susan B. Anthony for relief, rather than to her husband. At one
point she wrote to Anthony, "I pace up and down these two cham-
bers of mine like a caged lion, longing to bring to a close childrearing
and housekeeping cares. I have other work at hand." And again, "Oh,
how I long for a few hours of leisure each day. How rebellious it
makes me feel when I see Henry going about where and how he
pleases. He can walk at will through the whole wide world or shut
himself up alone, if he pleases, within four walls. As I contrast his
freedom with my bondage, and feel that because of the false position
of women, I have been compelled to hold all my noblest aspirations
in abeyance in order to be a wife, a mother, a nurse, a cook, a household drudge, I am fired anew and long to pour forth from my own
experience the whole long story of woman's wrongs."[44]

Despite her resentment, however, Stanton also prided herself on
her skills as a housewife. At one point, writing in the *Revolution,* she
engaged in a war of words with "Mrs. Kate Hunnibee," who wrote
a pseudonymous column in *Hearth and Home.* Stanton suggested
that there seemed to be considerable sickness in the "Hunnibee"
household and attributed this to "Mrs. Hunnibee's" being too little
engaged outside the home. Asserting her own domestic credentials,
Stanton pointed out "Why, Kate, it is only ten years since that we
dandled our last. . . ."[45] A year later an anonymous article in the
Revolution entitled "Homes of the Strong-Minded," gave a glowing
description of the Stanton household. "Mrs. Stanton is a scientific
cook. . . . Better bread, and more savory *goodies,* one could find
nowhere, strange as it may seem."[46]

One of the most interesting commentaries on the value of the
home in feminist eyes came from Susan B. Anthony, a woman who
never married and who spent much of her life traveling to promote
the suffrage cause. Nonetheless, she understood that most women

would not like to be placed in the position of having to choose between access to opportunity or the possession of a home. Rejecting invidious stereotypes of the old maid, Anthony also rejected the idea that an unmarried woman must perforce live with married relatives. Realistically, she acknowledged that there might be a period of transition during which more women than men would have outgrown "the Blackstone coverture" view of marriage whereby a married woman gave up her autonomous legal identity. Therefore, she thought it important that women be informed of the various "Homes of Single Women" that she herself had visited so that they might have a positive image of the single state, and be less tempted to marry someone unsuitable out of desperation. She described homes in Massachusetts and in Colorado—homes that were cozy, comfortable, and hospitable.[47]

At the age of seventy-one Anthony took her own advice, moved to Rochester, and set up housekeeping. A letter to her brother reveals her amused delight about the new venture: "Now can't you and May come down and visit us—visit sister Susan in her first attempt at a house all by herself alone!! . . . I feel that I am going to take lots of comfort being in my own house and entertaining my friends at my very own table—Of course sister Mary laughs and doesn't believe I shall succeed—but at least she seems happy to let me prove I can't do it—and that is a good deal."[48]

Convinced that domesticity was important even if the full responsibility for it oppressed women, the nineteenth-century advocates of woman's rights wrestled with the issue. Who *would* do the domestic work? We have seen that some of them came to positions that can be called "material feminist." A few adopted openly elitist positions. For example, a letter to the *Woman's Journal* in 1870 contended that only those who have no vision beyond the kitchen should be doing the housework. Bright women should aspire and drudges should keep the home fires burning.[49] In the 1870s there was an efflorescence of serious discussion about how to achieve what we now call a two-career household with Blackwell as "the most remarkable and creative figure in the making of the new marital program."[50] While some may have held positions that were not rigorously thought-out, in general, many of these women were asking the right questions.

When we come to Gilman, however, we come to one whose loathing for the home limited her ability to envision how domesticity and justice for women could be compatible. Moreover, she shared Darwin's low estimation of the female contribution to human progress. Indeed, the two attitudes were not unrelated. It was because she saw so little positive in "home-making," insisting that what traditionally have been women's tasks are not truly productive, that she could dismiss female contributions so readily.

Gilman took from Ward the insight that in most of nature, except for humankind, females are the more consequential gender, and built on it. She cites an article in which he makes this argument that appeared in the November 1888 issue of *The Forum* as being central in the development of her own thought. "We are the only animal species in which the female depends on the male for food, the only animal species in which the sex-relation is also an economic relation."[51] In becoming economically dependent on man, woman then forfeited her ability to contribute to progress. "Back of history, at the bottom of civilisation, untouched by a thousand whirling centuries, the primitive woman, in the primitive home, still toils at her primitive tasks."[52]

Like Ward a Lamarckian, Gilman assumed that the domestic environment endowed women with a hereditary taint. By this time, it was known that both sexes inherit from both parents so that neither she nor Ward made the same mistake as that made by Darwin and Spencer, who argued that male struggle continues to upgrade men alone. Rather, Gilman saw a kind of evolutionary see-saw operating in which male activity tends toward human progress and enforced female passivity toward retardation of the species: "This [the fact that daughters inherit from fathers] has saved us from such a female as the gypsy moth. It has set iron bounds to our absurd effort to make a race with one sex a million years behind the other. . . . Each woman born re-humanized by the current of race activity carried on by her father and re-womanized by her traditional position, has had to live over again in her own person the same process of restriction, repression, denial. . . . All this human progress has been accomplished by men. Women have been left behind, outside, below, having no social relation whatever, merely the sex-relation by which they lived."[53]

Of course, the principal objection to this categorical denunciation of woman's work would have to do with the importance of motherhood. Gilman acknowledged the possibility of such an objection and then dismissed it by denigrating the value of a human mother's nurture. She asserted that because the human female neither personally obtains the food nor builds the shelter for her offspring she does less for her young "than any other kind of mother on earth." Furthermore, human young need more than "primitive," instinctual mothering: they need instruction by qualified teachers. "So largely is this true that it may be said in extreme terms that it would be better for a child today to be left absolutely without mother or family of any sort, in the city of Boston, for instance, than to be supplied with a large and affectionate family and to be planted with them in Darkest Africa."[54] What a mother does for her family is to cater to their personal needs and tastes, and this is inherently a lesser undertaking than one which is social in nature. "The 'sacred duties of maternity' reproduce the race, but they do nothing to improve it."

Gilman's attack on the home extended even to the physical nature of the structure itself: "Sewer gas invades the home; microbes, destructive insects, all diseases invade it also; so far as civilized life is open to danger, the home is defenceless." Moreover, "modern therapeutics is now learning how many of our disorders of the throat and lungs may be classified as house diseases."[55] In short, she suggests that staying too much at home may make a person sick.

Not only did Darwinism help to shape her estimate of woman's work, but evolution also explained the primitive nature of the home in her view. Rather than equating antiquity with value, she equated it with datedness: the home is our oldest institution and perforce the lowest and most out-of-date. To revere the home is as irrational an act as ancestor-worship would be. If the home has improved at all, this is only because men, with all of their restless energy, have been at least slightly involved with it as it has changed, slightly, over time.

In her prescriptions for how to deal with housework, she owed a great deal to Bellamy and *Looking Backward*. Like Bellamy she had little appreciation of the way in which family meals can provide an opportunity for emotional intimacy. Therefore she was more than eager to remove as many of the remaining functions from the home as possible, including cooking and dining. Further, in her strong desire to get women out of the house, she went beyond what any of her predecessors had said by attacking housewifely competence. Women are not good cooks, she claimed, and never can be as long as they are working merely to please their families, "with no incentive for high achievement." Home cooking is predicated on ignorance, "the habits of a dark, untutored past." There are no "aunties of high repute" in this scenario, nor is there any respect for female domestic prowess. Rather, Gilman darkly hints that home cooking may bear part of the responsibility for "the diseases incidental to childhood."[56] Even if the cooking makes no one ill, it will always be mediocre as long as women consult their families' palates instead of the latest scientific findings. Professional cooks would display no such sentimental weakness, she maintained. In the antebellum period, home had been seen as valuable because it represented a counterweight to the market. Fifty years later Gilman depicted it as hopelessly flawed because it lacked market incentives and "business methods."

What are we to make of Gilman's analysis? That she had insights of great power and originality respecting the consequences of woman's economic dependence is incontrovertible. But, building on evolutionary theory, she probably did more to separate the home from history, that is, to make the home seem to be a retrograde and irrelevant institution, than any individual. It was not that Gilman herself had large numbers of adherents for her program. Educated people were acquainted with her ideas, however, as well as with the Darwinian view of sexual selection, and the home began to seem like a sentimental embarrassment, not to be taken seriously. If educated men reflected about the home at all, there was the reassuring thought that a new discipline, home economics, had come into being to solve domestic difficulties.

More than one scholar dealing with the Progressive period, when Gilman's reputation was at its height, has used the word "rationalization" to characterize the direction of change in the early twentieth century. In many instances the term seems vague or empty. In this instance, however, the term can be used with precision. Gilman saw the responsibility for maintaining personal life as an important cause of women's oppression. Therefore, she subjected the realm of the domestic emotional life to her most rational scrutiny, paying lip service to the idea that the home represents love and nurture but demonstrating little appreciation for ways in which that role can be fostered. In this regard she had much in common with other creators of the "culture of professionalism." Work began to be valued most when it was most abstract, most devoid of emotional content, most male-oriented.[57]

Because the reconciliation of domesticity with justice for women requires so much imagination and intelligence, we still lack all the answers to how this may be accomplished. Indeed this reconciliation, which also involves the relationship between personal life and social obligations in a complex, technologically sophisticated society, will require the best efforts of our best brains. It is regrettable that there was a large gap in American history between the 1870s and the 1970s, when almost no one gave the issue any thought. There were those who cared about domesticity—the home economists—but they had little claim to feminist credentials after the initial period. The few feminists often proved that they were serious intellectuals by the extent of their disdain for traditional female pursuits.

One who made an interesting, if unsuccessful, attempt at such a reconciliation was Carrie Chapman Catt, in an article published in 1928. Catt begins by confidently predicting, in evolutionary terms, "In another generation the woman who knows how to make bread or an apple pie will be as extinct as a dodo." She points to the increasing number of women in the work force and the unfair double burden they have in carrying all the domestic responsibilities. Yet she wonders, "Will the home disappear in the impending ruin of the old order?" On the one hand, she thinks that even if many women can successfully juggle marriage and career, it is wrong that they should have the functional equivalent of a baby on the back as in the old days. On the other hand, clearly concerned about the disintegrative forces at work in American society, she says that the "need of our time" is "to preserve the home as long as possible." The best she can do in mediating between these two priorities is to suggest that the housewife limit her domestic activities to an eight-hour day.[58] As long as Catt was under the influence of the idea that evolution could make the home virtually obsolete, she was unlikely to come up with a more creative solution.

Men and women living in a modern secular society are under a handicap in dealing with transcendent values. Darwinism helped create a secular and materialist outlook. As a consequence, reflective people now lack a vocabulary for talking about love, nurture, or the social importance of home without sounding sentimental and faintly ridiculous, a liability that did not affect our nineteenth-century forebears.[59] When Blackwell, for example, spoke of the "moral sanctities" of home, she drew upon the tradition of Christian nurture, many of the spokespeople for which belonged to the socially concerned wing of American Protestantism. Conversely, the only people likely to use the term in the 1980s would be the religious right. Thus the epic style of domesticity, with its linkage of the home and the world through the redemptive power of love, perished in the late nineteenth century under the dual impact of economic upheaval and evolutionary theory. Rather than attracting the attention of creative and socially engaged intellectuals of both sexes, the home increasingly became the domain of technocrats and advertisers.

SIX

The Housewife and
the Home Economist

ON SEPTEMBER 19, 1899, eleven people gathered in Lake Placid, New York, to set a formal seal on a development that had been proceeding informally for several decades—the emergence of a new discipline variously called domestic economy, domestic science, and eventually home economics. No doubt the leading spirit at that conference and, for the rest of her life, in the discipline itself, was Ellen Swallow Richards. The only man in attendance was Melvil Dewey, developer of the Dewey Decimal System. Another well-known name was that of Maria Parloa, author of a popular cookbook. Although their numbers were few, those in attendance had an ambitious agenda. They chose the name "home economics" for the new discipline. They then discussed how to publicize and popularize it and how to include it in curricula at all levels of education. It is noteworthy that this conference coincided almost exactly with the birth of the Progressive Era, a period when Americans throughout the country and at all levels of government sought reform that would enable their society to deal with the new urban-industrial order. Thoroughly imbued with the Progressive ethos and full of good intentions with respect to the home, those who attended the Lake Placid conference nonetheless set a process in motion by which the devaluation of the female craft tradition, an important component of the ideology of domesticity, was greatly accelerated. This was because, in order to establish their own profession as worthy, they perforce needed to denigrate the quality of housewifely competence. In this way, what Harry Braverman has called the "division of hand and brain" was carried forward in the home as well as in the male-oriented workplace.

Usually recognized as the founding mother of home economics—unless that title should go to Catharine Beecher—Ellen Richards had a career that demonstrates just how circumscribed the choices available to women were in the late nineteenth century. Born in 1842, she entered Vassar College at the age of twenty-five, where she studied astronomy with Maria Mitchell, the leading American woman scientist of the nineteenth century. After graduating from Vassar, Richards entered the Massachusetts Institute of Technology as a special student in chemistry, the only woman student to be enrolled. Clearly, her presence was uncomfortable for the administration because they admitted her without charge so as to camouflage the fact that she was studying there. In 1873 she obtained both a baccalaureate of science from MIT and a master of arts degree from Vassar. Despite the fact that she studied another two years at MIT—and did distinguished work—she was never deemed to be an appropriate candidate for a doctorate.

When she developed an interest in applied chemistry, such as studying sources of pollution in the home, it was easier for the scientific world to deal with her. Whereas a woman scientist was almost unthinkable, a woman devoted to cleaning up the domestic environment was not violating any norms respecting the two spheres. The young Ellen Swallow had already shown a willingness to accommodate cultural norms by keeping needles and pins on hand so as to mend for various professors at MIT. On February 11, 1871, she wrote, "I am winning a way which others will keep open. Perhaps the fact that I am not a Radical or a believer in the all-powerful ballot for woman to right her wrongs and that I do not scorn womanly duties, but claim it as a privilege to clean up and sort of supervise the room and sew things, etc. is winning me stronger allies than anything else."[1] Happily for her, in 1875 she married Robert Hallowell Richards, a metallurgist who was sympathetic to her scientific ambitions, and with whom she collaborated early in the marriage. In 1884, MIT established a chemical laboratory for the study of sanitation, and Ellen Richards received the position of instructor in sanitary chemistry, a post she held until her death in 1911. During that period she published a number of important books on the subject of sanitation and the home.

Other pioneer home economists took a similar route. Of a slightly later generation than Richards, Isabel Bevier (b. 1860) studied chemistry at a number of the leading institutions in the country, including MIT, where she worked with Richards. With these credentials, Bevier spent a brief time as a professor of chemistry at Lake Erie College for women, where she was expected to plan the menus. She was to spend more than two decades at the University of Illinois and to become one of the best-known home economists in the country, perhaps *the* best known after Richards's death. Nonetheless, she came to the field because Professor Albert W. Smith of Case School of Applied Science told her that "the place for women in chemistry was in food chemistry." After receiving the appointment at Illinois, she had to make it clear to the administration that "fine cooking was not in my repertoire."[2]

Another home economist was Marion Talbot (1858–1948). Like Bevier, she studied with Richards at MIT. Obtaining her baccalaureate of science in 1888, she briefly taught domestic science at Wellesley. For most of her distinguished career, however, she was associated with the University of Chicago, as dean of undergraduate women between 1899 and 1905 and then as head of the department of household administration. What is especially remarkable is that Talbot, a fighter against sexual segregation in higher education, nonetheless found herself administering a sex-specific department. She had originally hoped that sanitary science and public health would be at the center of the agenda for reforming American cities. By 1912 she had given up this hope and asked William Rainey Harper, president of the university, to create a department devoted to the study of the household and to put her in charge. Sanitary science had been part of the department of sociology and the subject of study by both men and women. Household administration was, for all intents and purposes, for women only. In a sense she was yielding to the inevitable because she was already receiving a steady stream of letters from state universities asking that she recommend women as teachers of home economics.[3]

The early home economists, then, including Richards, Bevier, and Talbot, thought they were establishing a beachhead for women in science in the American university system. In a sense they were, but they created little opportunity for women outside of home economics, except in the women's colleges. Says the most distinguished student of women scientists, Margaret Rossiter, "[Home economics] was the only field where a woman scientist could hope to be a full professor, department chairman, or even a dean in the 1920s or 1930s."[4]

Thus an important component, perhaps the most important, of the new discipline was the pool of talented and college-educated women who wanted to be scientists but were only allowed the opportunity to pursue this career if they applied science to the domestic sphere. Another important component was the birth of the land grant college. In 1862 Congress passed the Morrill Act, designed to encourage the study of the agricultural and mechanical arts. As the institutions set up under the Morrill Act began to introduce coeducation, it was not surprising that administrators set up domestic science courses for their women students. In the 1870s such courses appeared in Iowa, Kansas, and Illinois. By 1900 there were thirty departments in the country, chiefly associated with land grant colleges. Indeed, *Godey's* had launched a campaign to achieve this goal soon after the passage of the Morrill Act and had called for "National Normal Schools and Seminaries of Household Science for young women." Sarah Josepha Hale contended, "Every young woman there trained would learn to serve God and her country, to love her home and the duties that make the beauty, the happiness, and the glory of home."[5]

Yet another component of the new discipline was the growing popularity of the urban cooking school. In March 1867, *Godey's* noted that Professor Blot of Paris was currently lecturing to women in the largest American cities. By the following decade there were regularly established cooking schools in New York, Boston, and Philadelphia. Maria Parloa, in attendance at the first Lake Placid conference, was associated with the Boston Cooking School. In the 1890s Ellen Richards and others founded the New England Kitchen, designed both to provide nutritious and reasonably priced meals for working-class families and to give cooking lessons. This particular experiment failed because the families, largely immigrant, proved resistant to Yankee cuisine. Nonetheless, there were enough middle-class women who either wanted to study cooking themselves or to hire servants so trained that the cooking schools became successful, and a similar success was ensured for the cookbooks that came out of these ventures.

Finally, the late nineteenth-century fairs, in particular the Centennial Exposition of 1876 in Philadelphia and the World's Columbian Exposition of 1893 in Chicago, provided excellent opportunities to demonstrate the developments in domestic science. Richards herself singled out the Philadelphia Exposition as an occasion "when America was awakened to its own deficiencies in the culinary art, and in home furnishing and decoration among other things."[6] Two decades later the New England Kitchen, a failure in its immediate purpose, led directly to the Rumford Kitchen at the World's Columbian Exposition. Administered by Richards as part of the Massachusetts exhibit, the Rumford Kitchen featured lunches whose food values had been carefully calculated and specified on a menu. "The Rumford Kitchen was the first attempt to demonstrate by simple methods to the people in general the meaning of the terms proteids, carbohydrates, calories, and the fact there are scientific principles underlying nutrition."[7]

Most of these developments can in a sense be traced to the influence of Catharine Beecher's *Treatise on Domestic Economy*. Lacking the access to higher education enjoyed by those born fifty and more years later than she (Beecher had been born in 1800), she nonetheless attempted to give the most up-to-date information possible, based on her understanding of chemistry, horticulture, and other technical matters. Inasmuch as she firmly believed that well-trained women teachers should instruct other women in the household arts, the urban cooking schools and the programs at state universities would doubtless have met with her approval.

Nonetheless, when one studies Beecher's work in conjunction with the writings of the pioneer home economists, one may well be more struck by the differences than by the similarities. This phenomenon can be explained by the changes in American society, many of which we have already discussed, that had taken place between 1841 and 1899, the year of the first Lake Placid conference. Briefly stated, by 1900 the authority of science had gone a long way toward replacing the authority of religion. Therefore, although the home economists at the turn of the century nodded in the direction of the "value" of home, for most of them the real interest lay in technique. It should be recalled that Beecher, for all her interest in technique, had begun her *Treatise* with lengthy extracts from Tocqueville and a philosophically oriented discussion of what home could and should do for the larger society. Moreover, even if Beecher wanted to improve the practice of housewifery, she cast relatively few aspersions on contemporary housewives. Many of the turn-of-the-century home economists, on the other hand, launched attacks on housewifely competence that bore a strong resemblance to those of Charlotte Perkins Gilman.

In fact, the birth of home economics as a discipline can only be understood as part of the larger pattern of the development of the culture of professionalism in the late nineteenth century. Clearly, the home economists faced a challenge because professions were upgrading themselves by excluding amateurs, by defining themselves as "manly" in a variety of ways, and by emphasizing the abstract over the concrete. If their discipline were to be a profession at all, they would do best to emulate existing male professions. The most important step was to distance themselves from that lowly amateur, the housewife. Another was to attempt to rationalize as many household processes as possible as well as to set standards against which actual practice could be measured. Hence the differences in tone between Beecher and her successors.[8] Hence, too, the deleterious impact of the home economists on the female craft tradition.

An examination of the proceedings of the Lake Placid conferences—there were ten in all, culminating with the founding of the

American Home Economics Association in 1908—will demonstrate how the pioneers set about their task. One of the most clear-cut themes to emerge is the importance of overruling the palate—what the family likes—in favor of nutrition—what experts deem to be good for people. A favorite device was to imply that there was something suspiciously sensual—and not at all scientific!—about a too-enthusiastic enjoyment of food. "The 'breaking of bread' is a universal sacrament and it is given to men primarily for the strengthening of their bodies, not for the gratification of their palates." Choosing food on the basis of whim or habit or because it tastes good will lead people away from the "higher life," according to another author.[9] Yet another set a most unusual standard for good food: the less memorable the better. "It is a great waste of time to spend several hours preparing an elaborate dish which will be eaten in fifteen minutes, and after that time will not make the partaker any happier. The test of good food is to have no reminder of it after eating."[10]

Of course, personal preferences are inherently anarchic. If the goal was to set standards, then people had to be taught not to trust their own tastes. Further, if people were to follow the advice of experts, they had to be taught to despise tradition and the advice of older women. Both of these themes emerge in the Lake Placid proceedings. One author complained, "There is absolutely no standard existing." Yet her committee had concluded that there was "willingness to accept a standard from an authority on the subject," especially among younger housewives.[11] Ellen Richards herself was frequently given to attacking the weight of tradition. She worried that "the traditions of the past bind us with bands of steel." Summing up ten years of these conferences, she said, "Tradition has held longer sway over home life than over even religious life. . . . Knowledge to make the necessary changes could come only from the outside where investigations were being carried on, and tradition forebade the house mother to go outside to learn."[12] Therefore, the only way that beneficent change could come to the home was through the instrumentality of the outside expert.

Faith in the capacities of the expert was one characteristic of the Progressive generation; another was a reforming zeal dedicated to overhauling a broad range of institutions and practices. That the pioneering home economists were imbued with the spirit that under- lay Progressive reform is clear from the sheer scope of what they were trying to accomplish. They wanted to help the housewife by simplifying housekeeping. They wanted to train teachers. They wanted to prepare brochures for dissemination by the federal gov- ernment. They wanted to establish an outreach to farmers' wives. They wanted to study the ways in which standards of living are affected by sanitary science. Yet the scope of what they were attempt- ing also betrays the confusion that underlay the founding of the dis- cipline: was its primary purpose to provide manual training for women or was it to study nutrition and sanitation in a non-sex-specific fashion? Both of these objectives showed up at the Lake Placid con- ferences.[13] In 1902, Marion Talbot tried to resolve the confusion by arguing that manual training for girls should take place in trade schools, and college courses should be open to both men and women. Nothing came of this suggestion at the time, however.

Thus, the best way to understand home economics is to see it as a combination of elements derived from Catharine Beecher along with elements of the nascent professional ethos and elements of Pro- gressivism. Despite the focus on technique, for example, some of the pioneers did try to draw on broad general culture and to invest the housewife role with a social dimension. A course syllabus from 1895 prepared by Helen Campbell includes references to works by Lester Frank Ward, William Morris, John Ruskin, Ellen Richards, Have- lock Ellis, and many more. Yet most of the topics listed really fall into the area of technique: The Building of the House, Decoration, Furnishing, Food and Its Preparation, and Cleaning and Its Pro- cesses. We may note parenthetically that Campbell's career pattern provides further evidence for the contention that the discipline of home economics came into being in large part because talented women were invariably ascribed to studying the home. Campbell received graduate training in economics from Richard Ely at Wiscon- sin yet received no doctorate and never had a stable academic job.[14] She then turned to domestic science or home economics and wrote extensively.

Of the pioneering generation, Marion Talbot had perhaps the clearest vision of what home economics could and should be and what it should not be. In a book co-authored with Sophonisba Breckinridge, an important member of the Chicago reform community, the two women argued forcefully for the social potential of the housewife's role as consumer. They began by pointing out that many prophets were predicting that the home and family would not endure as then constituted. Yet while some tasks had already left the home, a new one had crept in that was of overweening importance—intelligent consumption: "The woman who administers the affairs of a household may well regard herself as placed at the real heart of things. . . ." As an example of how she might function, she could look for the union label when buying clothes for the family. "And so the duty of selecting wearing apparel for the members of her group becomes an opportunity of the richest kind."[15] The home economist's task thus became that of alerting her to these ramifications.

At a time when the model of scientific management captured the imagination of many middle-class Americans, Talbot and Breckinridge rejected this model as inappropriate for the home. They argued that "the household is not a form of organization whose purpose is pecuniary profit."[16] It is, therefore and of necessity, less efficient than a business enterprise. The clear message of the book became one of trying to direct the discipline away from technique for its own sake and toward the study of the home in relationship to the larger society.

As it happened, however, most members of the Progressive generation, including home economists, were uncritically infatuated with scientific management. Says Samuel Haber, one of the leading students of the subject:

> The progressive era is almost made to order for the study of Americans in love with efficiency. For the progressive era gave rise to an efficiency craze—a secular Great Awakening, an outpouring of ideas and emotions in which a gospel of efficiency was preached without embarrassment to businessmen, workers, doctors, housewives, and teachers, and yes, preached even to preachers. Men as disparate as William Jennings Bryan and Walter Lippmann discoursed enthusiastically on efficiency. Ef-

ficient and good came closer to meaning the same thing in these years than in any other period of American history. . . . An efficient person was an effective person, and that characterization brought with it a long shadow of latent associations and pre-dispositions; a turning toward hard work and away from feeling, toward discipline and away from sympathy, toward masculinity and away from femininity.[17]

Fundamental to scientific management was the capture by efficiency experts of expertise that had previously been part of the workers' own craft tradition. Another student of scientific management, Harry Braverman, documents the way in which these experts set about their work. Quoting long extracts from Frederick Taylor, the father of scientific management, Braverman demonstrates that the first such experts to be employed in factories set out to destroy a worker's faith in his or her own judgment. The expert or the manager should do the brain work, according to this theory, and the worker's job should be as fully rationalized and programmed as possible. The fewer the wasted motions, the greater the worker's productivity, and ultimately the greater the employer's profit. According to Braverman, the key issue is control. The more fully rationalized the work in any given workplace, the less autonomy each worker has, and the more manipulable he or she becomes.[18]

Although the same motives could not have inspired the pioneer home economists, who dealt with isolated workers outside the cash nexus (the use made of their work is another matter and will be discussed in the next chapter), it is striking to see the extent to which their methods paralleled those of the Taylorites. If Taylor hammered away at the intelligence and judgment of Schmidt, the pig-iron handler he was retraining,[19] the home economists frequently did the same to the housewife. Helen Campbell, for example, shared Charlotte Perkins Gilman's critique of the abilities of the average housewife. (The two were, in fact, close friends.) Like Gilman, she had an evolutionary perspective. Women, isolated in the home, were isolated, too, from human progress. Those advances that have been made in the home have come through the instrumentality of men. Speaking of cookery, she contended, "The main reason that our household cuisine shows any advance over that of the primitive savage is, that some men have become cooks, and developed the function and its essential machinery." If women were to have their way, there would never be any improvement. "There are many of these domestic industries still almost as rude and primitive as in the beginning. . . . Even the intelligent housekeeper still talks about 'luck with her sponge cake!' *Luck!* There is no such word in science, and to make sponge cake is a scientific process!" So severe are women's deficiencies, thought Campbell, that there is a "blank wall between women and true progress erected chiefly by their own hands and bearing at intervals such mottoes as Blessed be Drudgery!"[20]

As if all this were not enough, Campbell also disparaged a housewife's competence with respect to the physical care of the house itself. In the first place, whatever innate taste she might have possessed had been blighted: "The average woman's life is so spent in conflicting interests and industries that she cannot develop any true taste for large truths of relation." In the second place the home was potentially so filthy that she was likely to be fighting a losing battle just to keep it clean. Campbell cited research conducted by Ellen Richards in which a pinpoint of dust was taken from the top of a dining-room door: "Out of this pin-point of dust grew three thousand living organisms, not all malignant, but all enemies of health." All one had to do was to compare hospitals with the average home and one would soon realize how primitive was the approach to cleanliness. For every spotless New England home, there were all too many less desirable examples, as instanced in "the frowsy shiftlessness of the poor white in the South or in the workman's home of the North."[21]

Campbell's approach was far from unique. Gilman had argued that housewifely backwardness might contribute to the infant mortality rate. While not going that far, Isabel Bevier did hint that the family's health could suffer from a mother's ignorance:

> Happily the days are passing when the feeling prevails that "anyone can keep house." We have been a long time in learning that housekeeping is a profession for which intelligent preparation is demanded. The woman who attempts to usurp the authority of the trained nurse in charge of the patient does

so at the risk of the patient's life. Results quite as disastrous to the life of the household may be expected from the woman ignorant of the first principles of household management and care.[22]

In this view, the authority belongs by right to the scientifically trained expert. The housewife who ignores that expert's advice and "usurps the authority" can be held responsible for any mishaps that may occur—perhaps occasioned by one of Richards's three thousand microbes. Only a very brave woman could ignore this onslaught and adhere to a belief in her own methods. Moreover, even those who escaped home economics courses per se were unlikely to escape the onslaught entirely because it pervaded the women's magazines, too.

Another influential treatise of the Progressive Era, tellingly titled *Increasing Home Efficiency,* was written by Martha and Robert Bruere. In this book the Brueres espoused what might be called a New Nationalist approach to home economics, because they clearly had been influenced by Walter Lippmann and Herbert Croly's theories about the value of large-scale enterprise. For example, in a chapter entitled "A Housekeeper's Defense of the Trusts," they argued that breaking up the trusts might impede the growth in abundance for all Americans and therefore that housewives should oppose trust-busting. Above all they emphasized the value of the expert, in this case a domestic science teacher who became a "housekeeper":

> It is a desirable condition based on knowledge of housekeeping—ordered knowledge gained from experts in school, and in startling contrast to the wisdom of "mother," who was equipped for the business of teaching with nothing better than tradition, devotion to her home, humility as to what she had a right to demand in the way of mechanical assistance or financial compensation, and especially with a firm and disastrous conviction that her own experience, however limited, was an infallible guide.[23]

Indeed, the housewife had an obligation to be as well trained as possible because she owed her family and her society the utmost in efficiency: "In a word the one answer to many questions is that the middle-class mother must stop soldiering on the job."[24] This is a revealing turn of phrase because "soldiering" was the term used to characterize the activities of the deliberately unproductive factory worker. Thus we see a very clear manifestation of the linkages between scientific management and home economics.

Perhaps the clearest linkage was manifested in the collaboration between Frank and Lillian Gilbreth. Frank, with Taylor, was one of the leading industrial engineers of the early twentieth century. His wife Lillian shared his work and then carried it on by herself after his death. Their collaboration extended to the domestic realm, too, where they tried to run their household of twelve children according to the best scientific principles. Frank had carried out motion studies of factory workers. In a book published after his death, Lillian suggested that family members collaborate to determine how best and most efficiently to perform domestic tasks. With careful study, procedures could be evolved in such a way as to be used even by a guest who might be helping out.[25] Lillian Gilbreth's earnest exposition of such matters might lead one to envision a rather joyless household. Happily, we know from the memoir, Cheaper by the Dozen, written by two of their twelve children, that the Gilbreths' devotion to efficiency was leavened by a certain amount of humor. In any event the Gilbreths' research has had long-lasting consequences. In a subsequent memoir written in 1970, Frank, Jr., spoke of his mother's enormous influence on the design of household appliances: "every washing machine, kitchen stove, and refrigerator that rolls off the assembly lines today bears the imprint of her research."[26]

Thus, home economics was a quintessential Progressive program, especially in its faith in the power of experts. By the second decade of the twentieth century it had gained legitimacy as a discipline well suited for women in the opinion of most Americans. It was taught at all levels of education; it had a professional association; a publication, the Journal of Home Economics, devoted to disseminating research; and a growing body of literature. In 1916, 17,778 students were enrolled in home economics courses in 195 institutions of higher education.[27] Moreover, certain developments of these years heightened the popularity of the field. The passage of the Smith-

Lever Act of 1914 was especially significant. Using the land grant colleges, this act set up a network of cooperative extension courses for those women who were not regularly enrolled in a college or university. As early as 1917 some 27,000 students attended 450 extension courses.[28] Finally, the First World War, brief as American participation might have been, made many housewives receptive to expert advice. Owing to wartime exigencies, patriotic households were being urged to forgo meat on specified days and, therefore, families needed to alter their diets. According to an early historian of home economics, the result was an enormous popularity for such government pamphlets, published by the Department of Agriculture, as "Do You Know Corn Meal?," "Save Sugar," "A Whole Dinner in One Dish," "Choose Your Food Wisely," and "Wheatless Bread and Cakes," each of which was sent to one million homes.[29]

As a consequence of all these changes, in July 1923 the federal government established the Bureau of Home Economics as a part of the Department of Agriculture. Something of the broad-based support for this undertaking is indicated by the range of women's groups that participated in the preliminary planning conference. Among the participants were representatives from the newly established League of Women Voters, the General Federation of Women's Clubs, the PTA (Parent-Teachers Association), the WCTU, the American Association of University Women, and the American Home Economics Association.[30] Nonetheless, as with the Lake Placid conferences, the early history of the Bureau indicates a certain confusion of goals. Its announced functions were twofold: "to study practical home problems and in this manner aid in improving and bettering living conditions," and "to study the relative utility and economy of agricultural products for food, clothing, and other uses in the home. . . ."[31] Purpose number one implied that the Bureau was assuming a responsibility for all housewives as consumers. Purpose number two, on the other hand, implied that the Bureau was going to look out for the interests of the agricultural producers. It was, after all, part of the Department of Agriculture. That the two purposes might have been fundamentally in conflict seems not to have troubled people at the time. Another potential conflict soon surfaced concerning the approach to values. At the planning conference, the Secretary of Agriculture reported on the scope of what the new Bureau hoped to accomplish, and the women responded that they would like to see more emphasis on the spiritual aspects of home life. Shortly thereafter, a paper presented to the Association of Land Grant Colleges argued that with the new bureau, home economics could become just as empirically based as any other science.[32]

The establishment of a federal agency devoted to home economics was the culmination of decades of struggle for acceptance and legitimacy by partisans of the new discipline. The Bureau of Home Economics, established nearly forty years before John F. Kennedy created his precedent-setting Commission on the Status of Women, was a welcome indication that the federal government was planning to continue to take an interest in women after the passage of the Nineteenth Amendment in 1920. Yet the new field never came close to fulfilling the high hopes of its founders, let alone the expectations of many women's groups, that had reached an apogee in the early twenties after the founding of the Bureau.

In evaluating the impact of home economics and attempting to comprehend why people with so much goodwill failed to raise the status of the home, we must first acknowledge that there were important positive components of the discipline. It must be clearly understood that home economics represented one of the ways by which women attempted to carve out a place for themselves in the male-dominated world of work. Had men been more willing to accept women in the academy, especially in the sciences, there would have been less need for pioneer home economists to denigrate housewives in order to set themselves apart from their sisters and thereby define themselves as worthy of inclusion among male professionals. Let it be remembered, further, that the pioneers were working and writing in the shadow of Darwin. If they attempted to advance themselves by attacking housewifely competence, they were drawing upon the most widely held scientific tenets of the day about the impossibility of progress coming to the home through the efforts of house-bound women.

Moreover, there were many who hoped that the consumer function possessed enough importance that it would provide an entering wedge enabling women to advance the cause of social justice. It is easy to see how this could be congruent with domestic feminism, that is, with the idea that their domestic duties give women special moral qualities and a special claim to influence in American society. Most of the important home economists of the first generation had ties to reformers in other sectors of Amercan society, men and women who were wrestling with the problem of how to humanize an industrial society, many of whom firmly believed that women had a special role to play. An extant program for the first public meeting of the Chicago Household Economic Society, for example, shows that the speakers included Helen Campbell, Marion Talbot, Jane Addams, and Charlotte Perkins Gilman.[33] The later image of the home economist as "Betty Crocker," telling housewives what to buy, distorts the picture of the profession when it first emerged.

A brief examination of the career of Caroline Hunt will give an especially clear example of how closely home economics was related to the larger reform community in the early twentieth century. A professor of home economics at the University of Wisconsin between 1903 and 1908 (after having done graduate work in chemistry at the University of Chicago), Hunt became well acquainted with members of the leading Progressive family in the state, the La Follettes. For four years she wrote a regular column, "Home and Education," for *La Follette's* magazine. That she seasoned her domestic advice with a concern for social justice is revealed in the table blessing she wrote for the January 30, 1909, issue: "Humbly Recognizing as one of the Mysteries of Life the fact that we have Food and in Abundance while others worthier far than we, and even Little Children, Starve or Go Hungry, we would learn to use effectively the Strength of Mind and Body obtained from this food in the effort to secure a Fairer Distribution of Life's Material Blessings." After Ellen Richards died in 1911, Hunt wrote what has been the standard biography of Richards. Later, when the Bureau of Home Economics came into being, Hunt went to work there and became one of the key staff members for Louise Stanley, the first director of the Bureau. Finally, when Hunt died in 1927, Belle La Follette wrote the eulogy, and the funeral took place at Jane Addams's Hull House.[34] Hunt's life and work demonstrate how misleading it would be to emphasize only the scientific management aspect of home economics.

Whether the profession helped the urban woman very much is debatable. That the profession was genuinely helpful for rural women seems evident, however. By the first decades of the twentieth century, the nature of the housewife's job in the countryside was vastly different from what it was in a city. For example, a farmer's wife might find herself cooking for a dozen threshers at certain times of the year. She was much less likely than her city sister to have modern conveniences such as a gas stove or running water. Because the job was so demanding, the advice to farm women given by Nellie Kedzie Jones in her column in *The Country Gentleman* between 1912 and 1916 was very different in tone from that directed to an urban audience—more practical and less patronizing. Where Lillian Gilbreth was to suggest that a child follow his mother around with thread so that she could eliminate wasted motion, Jones had much less esoteric goals in mind:

> With hired men at your table, make up your mind to three hearty meals every day in the year. [The columns were directed to an imaginary niece.] I know the prospect is appalling to one who is doing her own work, as you are; but face the fact, prepare for the worst, and any respite you may get later count as pure gain. Most of the writing of recipes, the estimates of quantities for families of various sizes, and marketing directions, have been done by Home-Economics experts who have gotten their data from colleges, public institutions, city homes and city eating places, but not from farms. They are too small for farm conditions. Add about fifty per cent to the usual standard recipe, or even double it and you will not be far off. From the hired man's point of view a short ration is the unpardonable sin. He believes that a pie ought not to be cut into more than four pieces. I get round that difficulty, though, by often serving easy puddings.[35]

It is not difficult to understand why a woman faced with work as demanding as Jones posits would be grateful for advice from the cooperative extension home economist. In this instance, the rationalizing of work processes might preserve the health of someone whose work load would otherwise be overwhelming.

Finally, it is obvious that in one of its incarnations, that of non-sex-specific sanitary and nutritional science, home economics belonged to an important development of the early twentieth century—the growth in knowledge about and improvement in the practice of public health, whereby the life expectancy of Americans made dramatic gains. If the average woman's life expectancy went from 45 in 1900 to 78 in 1985, then the sanitation experts must receive a large measure of credit. Ellen Richards may not have created many opportunities for women scientists despite her best efforts, but her research and the research of some of the other pioneers unquestionably prolonged lives.

Having said all this, we can now turn to the opposite side of the coin. The most fundamental criticism to be made of home economics is that it was a giant step backward with respect to sexual symmetry. The fascination with the scientific method was so strong that it could unite women as dissimilar in their ideal of home as Ellen Richards and Charlotte Perkins Gilman in the quest for purely technological solutions to the housewife's problems, thus moving away from the larger issue of the equitable distribution of domestic labor. Most of the pioneers believed that a woman's place is in the home, that home duties belong uniquely to women, and that their own research would make the status quo more palatable to women. Lillian Gilbreth went so far as to state, "This book makes no appeal for 'kitchen husbands' or 'kitchen sons.' . . ."[36] It was as if the ferment of the 1870s, with Antoinette Brown Blackwell as the most imaginative thinker pondering the possibilities for shared domestic responsibilities, had never taken place. Even those who believed it appropriate for a woman to take a public role or to be gainfully employed outside the home thought that home economics research, plus the removal of ever more functions from the home, could solve her problems without having to reorganize gender relations. In essence, men were let off the hook. Given the increasing trivialization of the home as an institution, it was unlikely that men would seek to challenge this situation.

The very closeness between Progressives and home economists that gave the new discipline its social dimension in the early years also meant that home economists would share in some of the less desirable characteristics of the Progressives, such as their Anglo-Saxonism. Whatever else the Progressive movement may have been—and for the foreseeable future, historians will be trying to define the movement with precision—it was in part a reaction to the millions of immigrants from southern and eastern Europe in the late nineteenth century—men and women who clustered in cities and seemed to be less assimilable than earlier waves of immigrants. Middle-class Amercans reacted to them with a complicated mixture of alarm, disdain, and a certain compassion.[37] What was rarely present was any kind of cultural relativism. Typical of this outlook was the Yankee home economists' assumption, as manifested in the New England Kitchen, that they could suggest a diet for immigrants that would be "better" than the immigrants' own cuisine. When ethnocentrism was wedded to the pervasive biological reductionism of the late nineteenth century, the result was the widespread interest in eugenics, the science of improving the qualities of the human race by the careful selection of parents. That Ellen Richards's favorite name for her new discipline when taught as part of the college curriculum was "euthenics" shows that she, along with millions of her fellow Americans, regarded it and eugenics as perfectly legitimate topics of research,[38] the former pointing the way to better living and the latter to an improved race.

Sincere desire to improve social conditions often coexisted with contempt for ordinary people—workers, housewives, immigrants—in the minds of Progressive reformers, including home economists. This explains the appeal of the expert and the desire to apply "scientific" knowledge to areas of life that had hitherto been matters of common sense. Thus, in addition to Anglo-Saxonism, elitism was a very characteristic attitude of Progressives, an attitude that the home economists fully shared.

The frequent attacks on tradition, individual taste, and common sense as bases for domestic practice are clear evidence of the over-arching elitism. When applied to cookery, this approach had especially unfortunate consequences. Without doubt, one of the most negative elements of the impact of home economics on women and all Americans, for that matter, has been an alienation from trust in one's own tastebuds. Throughout most of the twentieth century Americans have been warned that such trust is a bad idea because "unscientific." As we shall learn in the next chapter, the person so instructed becomes much easier to sell to—as advertisers learned to their profit. In a memorable if polemical phrase, John and Karen Hess refer to "the rape of the palate" whereby Americans "have grown so accustomed to mass-produced, artificially flavored foods that anything else tastes peculiar."[39] In this process, home economists played a big role because they set out to destroy good taste as a criterion of the American diet.

Lest it be thought that experts were merely trying to save women time and work, we can consider the subject of coffee. Several generations ago women routinely roasted and ground the coffee beans immediately before brewing coffee. It then became possible to purchase roasted coffee beans at a store, a savings of time for the housewife with no great loss of flavor in the taste of coffee as long as she was able to procure reasonably fresh beans. Enter the food-processing companies, and Americans were taught to buy canned, vacuum-packed, pre-ground coffee. This was more modern and hence more desirable. As increasing numbers of Americans have traveled to Europe in the postwar years, however, they have encountered a beverage very different from the usual American variety. It is now possible to buy whole beans in most American cities of any size, and many Americans have discovered that they can make coffee, akin to the European model, that costs no more money and very little more effort than the canned variety. One can speculate that only people who had been coaxed away from trusting their own tastebuds in the first place could have been persuaded to drink so flavorless a brew as the typical American coffee made from canned, ground beans.

Another negative consequence of the shrill attacks on the female craft tradition has to do with the declining status of the aging woman in the twentieth-century United States. Growing old is never easy, but some societies honor the wisdom of their elders more than do others. As we have seen, Harriet Beecher Stowe had celebrated the collective expertise of "aunties of high repute" in her New England novels. In fact, older women were the repositories of community wisdom respecting domesticity in the nineteenth century. If there was one theme that was universal in the writings of the pioneer home economists, however, it was disdain for such expertise. Blue-collar male workers have had to contend with similar attitudes owing to industrial engineering, but at least some men have had access to the type of job in which age is likelier to be seen as an asset—judge, for example. Until recently, such access was impossible for women. As a consequence, the decades "between menopause and death," to use Erma Bombeck's phrase, seem to have become much more problematic for older housewives than they had been in the nineteenth century.

Because they were trying to construct a model of a fully rationalized, scientific discipline out of materials that did not always lend themselves to the endeavor—domestically oriented emotions and values, and a craft tradition—the home economists not infrequently found themselves engaged in what can only be called a reductio ad absurdum approach to domesticity. Two pieces of evidence can be adduced to support this generalization although many others doubtless exist. In 1927, *The Farmer's Wife* decided to try to identify five "master home-makers" in each state where they could secure cooperation. People were supposed to nominate candidates, who would then be sent a forty-five-page work-sheet to fill out. The nominee was supposed to sketch the floor plan of her kitchen, reveal whether any member of her family suffered regularly from constipation, discuss the sleeping habits of her children, and list her ten favorite labor-saving devices, among other items. In a similar vein, a workbook from a home economics class in 1932, evidently a college-level course in home economics education, gives drills for opening and closing a sewing bag and using a thimble. This is the sewing bag drill:

1. Open the bag.
2. Take out work.
3. Arrange work on the desk.
4. Hold up the work.[40]

Finally, in assessing the impact of home economics on women, it seems evident that tying the discipline so closely to land grant colleges and the Department of Agriculture has made it appear to be part of an outmoded, rural past as the twentieth century has advanced and the American population has become increasingly urban/suburban in composition. This, in turn, may have helped to give domesticity itself an old-fashioned image for young women outside rural areas, who would nonetheless find their own later lives enmeshed in domesticity.

Having drawn up a balance sheet, then, we see that home economics was perhaps the major mode by which the culture of professionalism could accommodate the aspirations of women in the early twentieth century. But because the underlying assumptions of the culture of professionalism were antagonistic to what the home had stood for at the height of its esteem in the mid-nineteenth century, it was impossible for home economists to fulfill one of their most important goals, that of raising the status of the home.

By way of summation, we can examine two representative figures, each of whom was writing about the home in the early twentieth century: Mary Virginia Hawes Terhune, harking back to the nineteenth-century roots of home economics, and Christine Frederick, foreshadowing the twentieth-century future. Terhune (1830–1922), who wrote under the pen name of "Marion Harland," belonged to the phenomenon of literary domesticity of the 1850s and yet published well into the twentieth century because she lived to so vigorous an old age. In many ways her career and her writings exemplify the transitions about which we have been speaking. Indeed, in her forties she herself made the transition from novelist to author of cookbooks and giver of advice so that she was one of the women who helped to create the discipline of home economics, although not in an academic setting.

According to her own later account, the young Mary Virginia

Hawes had a childhood calculated to give her respect for the capacities of housewives. Born in Virginia to a Yankee father who had moved south and a mother whose family had been part of the South for generations, Terhune wrote in vivid detail about the domestic aspects of the Old South in her autobiography. She remembered, for example, that her mother had been one of the earliest subscribers to *Godey's*: "Every number was read aloud in the family circle gathered on cool evenings about my mother's work-stand."[41] She remembered her careful supervision of every aspect of household maintenance: "The notable housewife knew to a fraction how much of the raw products went to the composition of each dish she ordered. So much flour was required for a loaf of rolls, and so much for a dozen beaten biscuits. . . ."[42] Like Stowe's reminiscences of New England kitchens, Terhune's autobiography occasionally partakes of the quality of a genre painting:

> We had fried chicken and waffles, hot rolls, ham, beaten biscuits, honey, three kinds of preserves, and by special petition of all the children, a mighty bowl of snow and cream, abundantly sweetened, for supper. This dispatched, and at full length, the journey having made us hungry, and the sight of us having quickened the appetites of the rest, we sat about the fire in the great 'chamber' on the first floor that was the throbbing heart of the home, and talked until ten o'clock.[43]

Not surprisingly, given these experiences, when she began to write, first as a girl and then as a young woman, she produced work that fit comfortably into the mold of the domestic novel. Her best-known work of fiction, *Alone*, appeared in 1854 and eventually sold some 100,000 copies. Although the heroine, Ida Ross, is thoroughly conventional in her views about woman and her sphere, she is also thoroughly competent: an orphan, she reinstitutes a benign domestic order at the family plantation when she reaches maturity.

As we have seen, the domestic novel played itself out sometime in the 1870s, and at this juncture, Terhune, by now married to a Presbyterian clergyman, switched to new types of writing; the domestic advice treatise and the cookbook. If one examines her cookbooks one can see elements of both old and new. As early as 1878, for example, she was giving recipes that employed canned tomatoes and canned corn. Although she waxed lyrical about the beaten biscuits of her girlhood, her recipes called for chemical leavening, both soda and baking powder. On the other hand, the pound cake recipe she gave in 1896 was the real thing, with eggs as the only leavening. Moreover, that same cookbook has a recipe for a French chicken casserole, incorporating wine, salmon, and cucumber salad, that does not sound like something to gladden the heart of a rationalizing home economist.[44]

By the late nineteenth century, Marion Harland was the country's favorite domestic authority. Her columns appeared in a number of newspapers, and she received five hundred to a thousand letters per week asking for advice. Her autobiography was serialized in the *Ladies Home Journal* in 1920. Her literary output consisted of twenty-five novels, three volumes of short stories, twenty-five books of domestic advice, and twelve miscellaneous books of travel, biography, and history.[45]

The reason for going into detail about Terhune's life and emphasizing its rootedness in the nineteenth-century craft tradition is that she lived long enough to sell her services to advertisers in the twentieth century, thus becoming a one-woman bridge between the cult of domesticity and the culture of consumption. An advertising circular in the Warshaw Collection of Business Americana in the Smithsonian Institution gives a ringing endorsement by "Marion Harland" for the product in question.

If Terhune was a transitional figure who lived long enough to endorse products, then Christine Frederick (1883–1970) was a woman born at the right time to play a major role in the creation of the advertising industry.[46] Receiving a baccalaureate in science from Northwestern University in 1906, she married, gave birth to four children, and then began to study efficient procedures in the home by setting up a model kitchen, the Applecroft Home Experiment Station, at her own house in Greenlawn, Long Island. Soon the fame of her experiments spread, and in 1912 she became household editor for the *Ladies Home Journal*. Wedded to the utility of the scientific management model for home economics, she used her position at the *Journal* to proselytize for this approach. In addition to having all the right tools, housewives should learn to do everything exactly on schedule, she thought. "And it is this great question of the best way of dispatching housework and having it run on a schedule, just as a train does, that I want to show in my next article. I worked it out, I do it, and it works like a clock." Another cardinal principle had to do with standardization: "Standardize some household task so that you can do it every day in an identical manner *without much mental attention* [emphasis added]. Does this not make it seem less difficult?" She recommended that a housewife stick to just one task at a time, until *all* the sweeping, for example, is complete. She should work out a standard practice for each task, write it down, and then stick to it. While "cooking too often depends on the caprice of the family," laundry can be readily standardized.[47]

It should surprise no one to learn that evolutionary theory underlay her program: "The only reason that man is not still a savage is his capacity to analyze, study, and plan. Women have, however, relied far too much on custom and their emotions, with the result that they have not lifted their sphere of labour out of the hard physical drudgery era, as man has lifted his office and shop, by scientific management and invention."[48] As with so many others, her analysis required the intervention of outside experts like herself to improve the housewife's lot. She was confident that the results would be worthwhile: "by dignifying home economics as a *science,* and placing it on a level with other cultural studies, your daughter will learn to recognize and accept the dignity of housework and homemaking as she would never have learned it in your own home kitchen." This, in turn, would provide "a fine antidote against the unnatural cravings for 'careers.' "[49]

Like Lillian Gilbreth, Christine Frederick had a major influence on kitchen design. Insofar as that influence led to intelligent placement of drainboards, the construction of counters at the optimum height, and similar innovations, it was beneficial to women. But unlike the nineteenth-century progenitors, Catharine Beecher and Harriet Beecher Stowe, who argued for centrally located and cheerful kitchens, Frederick thought that small, unifunctional kitchens were greatly to be preferred. A big, old-fashioned kitchen is just not efficient, she thought.[50] In this instance, it is clear that efficiency had become a goal to be served for its own sake, irrespective of the emotional life of the housewife and her family, rather than a means to serve any larger purpose.

As with Terhune's cookbooks of the late nineteenth century, Frederick's *The New Housekeeping*, written in 1913, contains elements of old and new. More than once she mentions the power for good that a housewife has at her disposal in her capacity as family purchasing agent: "It is woman's privilege and duty as the possessor of the powerful weapon of purchaser that it be used to prevent social injustice."[51] Yet working at cross purposes to this socially responsible view of consumption was her opinion of the importance of brand names and packaging. "Women are still fickle in their buying," she thought. They would do better if they were to stick to brand names with which they were familiar.[52] In this passage she foreshadowed the opinions she would express in her *Selling Mrs. Consumer* of 1929, where, instead of advising women how to buy intelligently and responsibly, she advised advertisers how best to make their sales. This book is a key document of the culture of consumption and will be examined in more detail in the next chapter.

In the years between 1913 and 1929, Frederick moved from being a pioneering home economist to being a pioneering advertising woman. As her Applecroft Home Experiment Station became well known, manufacturers began to send her their products to test. If the product in question met with her approval, she would write promotional literature on its behalf, evidently never worrying about what this did to her credibility as an unbiased expert. Because in its infancy the advertising industry discriminated against women, she founded the League of Advertising Women in New York in 1912 and gave increasing time and attention to this pursuit.[53] As with Terhune, Frederick's metamorphosis is indicative of the ease with which corporate America would be able to "buy" home economists as spokeswomen, thereby undermining the independence of the discipline.

This happened not because home economists were weak women,

predisposed to sell out, but because the field had been misconceived in the first place. Under the influence of the intellectual trends of the late nineteenth and early twentieth century, such as the infatuation with science and efficiency, the pioneer home economists ignored most of .what had produced the esteem for domesticity in the early nineteenth century and the concomitant esteem for the housewife, and strove to make the home as much like a male workplace as possible. They thought that if this succeeded, it would not matter so much if one sex was assigned the public world of work and the other sex was consigned to the home. The idea that home can be a source of redemptive values for other institutions was completely disregarded.

Moreover, the field was misconceived because it is impossible to "help" a housewife while systematically disparaging her life experiences and judgment. Themselves women who were having to contend with invidious stereotypes of female nature and female abilities in the academy and the workplace, many of the pioneer home economists internalized the stereotypes and judged housewives accordingly. All the professions of beneficent intent with respect to the housewife—no doubt sincere—could not get around this difficulty.

Finally, when efficiency, expertise, and fidelity to the scientific method become the highest values, the ability to resist a good offer from an advertiser is greatly undermined. If the home is important because it is outside the cash nexus, because it celebrates values in opposition to marketplace values—the reason for its importance to people like Harriet Beecher Stowe and Theodore Parker—then there might be a reason to say no to General Foods or General Mills. In parting company with this tradition, the home economists in essence made ready to perform the role of Betty Crocker and the rest of her sisterhood.[54]

SEVEN

Domesticity and the Culture
of Consumption

I**N 1918 AND 1920 TWO NOVELS** appeared that are representative
of the changes in the American home—and consequently in the role
of the housewife—that came to fruition in the 1920s. Willa Cather's
My Antonia celebrated the sturdy farm wife whose multifarious
abilities could keep her family afloat. In her heroic portrayal of
Antonia Shimerda, Cather looked back to the nineteenth century.
On the other hand, in creating Carol Kennicott, the restless heroine
of *Main Street,* Sinclair Lewis gave the first significant depiction
in an American novel of what Betty Friedan would call "the problem
that has no name," that is, the pervasive emptiness of the middle-class
housewife's life. That the two novels appeared nearly back to back
is not surprising because a number of long-term trends suddenly
became visible and identifiable in the years following the First World
War. Indeed, the prewar home seems to resemble closely the Victorian domicile of some remote ancestor, while the servantless home
of the 1920s, filled with electrical appliances and brand-name products, is nearly as familiar as the home next door. And yet the distance
between those two homes was traversed with remarkable speed, so
that by 1930 the "home of consumption" was firmly entrenched in
American culture.

In effect, Willa Cather celebrated the female craft tradition just as it was becoming obsolete, the coup de grace being rendered by the commodification of the home after the war. Like Stowe before her, Cather created a gallery of competent housewives in *My Antonia* and then used domesticity as a counterweight to the violence that lurks both in human nature and in the environment. Unlike Stowe, however, she did not employ domesticity as part of an analysis of the larger realms of politics or religion. The ideology of domesticity had become too attenuated by 1918 to sustain that weight.

My Antonia is narrated by Jim Burden, a man who has known the title character since childhood. As children, Antonia and Jim arrive simultaneously in the rural Nebraska of the late nineteenth century, Jim to live with his grandparents and Antonia in company with her Bohemian family. Because her mother is mean-spirited and unskilled in housewifery, Antonia must learn about the domestic arts from a series of other women. (In this theme Cather echoes not only Stowe, but also Susan Warner in *The Wide, Wide World*.) As a sensitive observer, Jim takes note of Antonia's apprenticeship, the earliest portion of which is conducted by his own, highly skilled grandmother. He recalls that as a young girl "Antonia loved to help grandmother in the kitchen and to learn about cooking and house-keeping."

Cather makes it clear that pioneering on the Great Plains was not for the faint-hearted. People killed themselves out of homesickness; families underwent cruel privation during the long winters. What redeems the situation is the order created by skill—that of the farmer in taming the natural world and more especially that of his wife in maintaining the home. Recalling his first winter, Jim says:

> The basement kitchen seemed heavenly safe and warm in those days—like a tight little boat in a winter sea. The men were out in the fields all day, husking corn, and when they came in at noon, with long caps pulled down over their ears and their feet in red-lined overshoes, I used to think they were like Arctic explorers. In the afternoons, when grandmother sat up-stairs darning or making husking gloves, I read "The Swiss Family Robinson" aloud to her, and I felt that the Swiss family

had no advantages over us in the way of an adventurous life. I was convinced that man's strongest antagonist is the cold. I admired the cheerful zest with which grandmother went about keeping us warm and comfortable and well-fed. She often reminded me, when she was preparing for the return of the hungry men, that this country was not like Virginia; and that here a cook had, as she said, "very little to do with." On Sundays she gave us as much chicken as we could eat, and on other days we had ham or bacon or sausage meat. She baked either pies or cake for us every day, unless for a change, she made my favourite pudding, striped with currants and boiled in a bag.

Next to getting and keeping warm, dinner and supper were the most interesting things we had to think about. Our lives centered around warmth and food and the return of the men at nightfall.[1]

Here we encounter many more characteristics of the domestic novel during its first flowering: the kitchen as a bulwark against the world, the iteration of types of food to suggest comfort, the vivid and sympathetic description of interiors. Like Stowe recollecting her Connecticut grandmother's home of the early nineteenth century and using these interiors in *Old Town Folks* and others of the New England novels, Cather based the domestic scenes in *My Antonia* on her own childhood. She, like Jim Burden, had moved from Virginia to Nebraska in her tenth year (1883), and she, too, had witnessed the struggle of immigrant families to make homes in a new land. She understood the tension between the desire to cling to the old ways and the desire to assimilate, with food as an important resource in resisting the loss of cultural identity. Hence it was natural for her to focus on domesticity and, in particular, on the preparation of food.

As an instance in point, the adult Jim Burden returns to Nebraska after an absence of twenty years and goes to see Antonia, the mother of a large brood of offspring. The children are eager to introduce the visitor to the wonders of the fruit cave where their mother stores her preserved food:

Anna and Yelka showed me three small barrels; one full of dill pickles, one full of chopped pickles, and one full of pickled watermelon rinds.

"You wouldn't believe, Jim, what it takes to feed them all!" their mother exclaimed. "You ought to see the bread we bake on Wednesdays and Saturdays! It's no wonder their poor papa can't get rich, he has to buy so much sugar for us to preserve with. We have our own wheat ground for flour—but then there's that much less to sell."

Nina and Jan and a little girl named Lucie, kept shyly pointing out to me the shelves of glass jars. They said nothing, but, glancing at me, traced on the glass with their finger tips the outlines of the cherries and strawberries and crabapples within, trying by a blissful expression of countenance to give me some idea of their deliciousness. "Show him the spiced plums, mother. Americans don't have those," said one of the older boys. "Mother uses them to make *kolaches*," he added.[2]

Domesticity plays an altogether different role in *Main Street*. Twelve years younger than Cather, Sinclair Lewis had experienced a less heroic stage of the development of the Upper Midwest than had she. As a mature writer, he remembered the narrowness of small-town life in his native Sauk Centre, Minnesota, rather than the warmth and coziness of the homes, and the narrowness was what he emphasized in creating his fictional Gopher Prairie. Moreover, for his heroine there is no apprenticeship in housewifery because her work is seen as virtually meaningless and the older women as vicious gossips rather than as keepers of a tradition.

Main Street begins, as does *My Antonia*, with a character moving into a small rural town. Giving up her career as a librarian, Carol Milford marries Dr. Will Kennicott and moves from St. Paul to Gopher Prairie. Filled with a desire to improve and uplift small-town life in the abstract, she is dismayed by her first sight of the actual village of 3,000 people. Moreover, their home is far from welcoming. Lewis describes the interior as dingy, airless, and lugubrious. Even the furniture—family relics assembled by Will's mother—seems hostile:

"How could people ever live with things like this?" she shud-
dered. She saw the furniture as a circle of elderly judges, con-
demning her to death by smothering. The tottering brocade
chair squealed, "Choke her—choke her—smother her." The old
linen smelled of the tomb. She was alone in this house, this
strange still house, among the shadows of dead thoughts and
haunting repressions. "I hate it!" she panted. "Why did I
ever—."[3]

Before very much time has elapsed, Carol has to confront the fact
that the dullness and provincialism of Gopher Prairie combined with
her circumscribed role as a doctor's wife make her life so boring as
to be nearly unendurable. She has fixed up their home to her satisfaction and thereby exhausted the gratifications of housework.

Routine care was all she could devote to the house. Only by
such fussing as the Widow Bogart's could she make it fill her
time.
     She could not have outside employment. To the village doc-
tor's wife it was taboo.
     She was a woman with a working brain and no work.[4]

Trapped in a sterile domesticity, under the constant, prying surveil-
lance of older women, Carol stages a brief rebellion by going off to
Washington, D.C., to work but comes back to Dr. Will and Gopher
Prairie after two years. Her only hope is that her daughter's generation will have more success in changing the world than she has had—
she knows herself to be defeated.

In many ways *Main Street* seems to be a working-out in fiction
of Charlotte Perkins Gilman's ideas about home and the role of
women. In the first place, Carol's reaction to her mother-in-law's
furniture echoes the reaction of the narrator to the yellow wallpaper
in the story of the same name: a domestic interior symbolizes the
vacuousness of the housewife's life. Further, Lewis evidently shares
Gilman's low opinion of the usual expertise brought to bear on
housewifery. At one point Carol wonders "how many millions of
women had lied to themselves during the death-rimmed years
through which they pretended to enjoy the puerile methods persist-

ing in housework." Like Gilman, Lewis combines a proto-feminist critique of woman's oppression with considerable contempt for women themselves.[5]

There is, however, one sympathetic female character in *Main Street* besides Carol, and she is married to the most sympathetic male character. The Kennicotts have a Swedish maid, Bea Sorenson, who is cheerful, hard-working, and unpretentious. She leaves them to marry Miles Bjornstam, a handyman known as the Red Swede both because of his coloring and because of his unorthodox opinions. As devoted as his wife to the maintenance of a cheerful home, Miles buys Bea a phonograph: "While she was busy with the activities her work-hungry muscles found—washing, ironing, mending, baking, dusting, preserving, plucking a chicken, painting the sink; tasks which, because she was Miles's full partner, were exciting and creative—Bea listened to the phonograph records with rapture. . . ."[6] In this passage, Lewis seems to indicate that domesticity would not be so obnoxious were it coupled with sexual symmetry. On this point he departed from Gilman—for whom domesticity had no redeeming features whatsoever.

Looking back from the perspective of the 1980s, it is clear that Carol Kennicott has been close to being the representative middle-class American woman of the twentieth century, while Antonia Shimerda is the archetype of a tradition that has had an ever-decreasing salience for most Americans.[7] That 1920 was the year in which for the first time people living in towns and cities predominated in the census over people living in the country had much to do with this phenomenon. In fact, the heroic farm wife was on her way to virtual extinction as a cultural ideal by 1920 as her real-life counterparts diminished so substantially in number. And the industrialized home, foreshadowed in the late nineteenth century, would become a well-established reality during the ensuing decade.

Sinclair Lewis was far from the only American of his day to realize that the society was undergoing a sea change and that this change would have a profound impact on women. One of the masterpieces of American cultural analysis, *Middletown*, by Robert and Helen Lynd, was predicated on a similar awareness. The Lynds went to

Muncie, Indiana, in the mid-twenties, determined to uncover how the community was different from what it had been in 1890. They and a team of assistants spent a year and a half in Muncie, observing, interviewing, and surveying its inhabitants. The general outlines of what they found can be summarized as follows. The Muncie of 1925 had been penetrated by a variety of consumer goods, the automobile being the most important, and this had dramatically altered the way people spent their leisure time and the way they allocated their resources. Particularly noteworthy were the changes in homes and in household routines. Less than 5 percent of Muncie's homes had been wired for electricity in 1890, whereas in June 1925, 99 percent were wired. A small fraction of the homes had had running water in 1890, yet by 1925 approximately three-quarters possessed running water. The number of families with servants had declined by about 50 percent. The Lynds accounted for this phenomenon as follows: "Smaller houses, easier to 'keep up' labor-saving devices, canned goods, baker's bread, less heavy meals, and ready made clothing are among the places where the lack of servants is being compensated for and time saved today."[8]

That the patterns uncovered by the Lynds in Muncie were national as well as local has been confirmed by subsequent students of housework and domestic technology. Ruth Schwartz Cowan uses the word "revolutionize" in conjunction with the changes of the 1920s:

> Almost every aspect of household labor was revolutionized in the 20's; in good part this was due to electrification. In 1907 (the first year for which data are available) only 8% of dwellings in the U.S. had electric service; by the time we entered the war this had risen to 24.3% and by 1925 more than half the homes in America (53.2%) had been wired. If we consider the data for urban and rural non-farm dwellings the figures are even more striking: almost half of those homes had been electrified by 1920 (47.4%) and more than two-thirds by 1925 (69.4%). . . .
>
> A study of 100 Ford employees living in Detroit in 1929 revealed that 98 families had an electric iron, 80 had electric

sewing machines, 49 had electric washing machines, and 21 had electric vacuum cleaners. The benefits of technology were clearly not limited to the upper middle classes.[9]

Because the home was subject to so much technological innovation, many households could and did dispense with servants—again demonstrating that "Middletown" was typical of national patterns. The decade of the 1920s saw fundamental change in the nature of domestic service. First, except in the South where there was a supply of black women consigned to being domestics, the number of households with servants declined dramatically. Second, where servants persisted, they were much more likely to be day-workers rather than living-in, which had been the case in earlier periods.[10]

Yet another change of the 1920s was the introduction of frozen food. Clarence Birdseye, the pioneer of the frozen-food industry, received a patent in 1925 for the new technique, and by 1934 some 39 million pounds of frozen food were being processed annually.[11] When coupled with the burgeoning growth of the canning industry, this all added up to immense changes in cookery and in the American diet. Needless to say, there was also an impact on the way that the average housewife allocated her time.

"Birdseye" joined other brand names in processed foods and household products that were well established by the 1920s such as Nabisco (1898), Del Monte (1916), Crisco, Fels-Naptha, and Hoover. The emergence of a national market in the late nineteenth century and developments in packaging in the early twentieth century created an altogether different style of marketing and facilitated the work of the advertising industry in heightening consumer demand. Some brand names such as Jell-O, Kleenex, and Frigidaire became so well known as to enter the vocabulary. A related development was the introduction of the self-service grocery by the Piggly Wiggly chain in 1916, a change that would result in the decline of the "Mom and Pop" grocery store.

It is well known that the advertising industry came of age in the 1920s. Not only did the volume of advertising rise during the period but also copywriters pioneered new styles of layouts, used photography more extensively, and developed non-rational styles of appeal to the consumer. "I want advertising copy to arouse me," the associate editor of *Advertising and Selling* had written in 1919, "to create in me a desire to possess the thing that's advertised, even though I don't need it."[12] During the next ten years, the industry became increasingly sophisticated about achieving this goal.

Finally, another indication that new household patterns had taken shape and a new attitude toward consumer goods had come into being in the 1920s concerns installment buying. More and more people were able to buy more and more appliances (as well as automobiles) because of the frequency with which they could employ this means of paying for a purchase. According to the Lynds:

> Today Middletown lives by a credit economy that is available in some form to nearly every family in the community. The rise and spread of the dollar-down-and-so-much-per plan extends credit for virtually everything—homes, $200 overstuffed living-room suites, electric washing machines, automobiles, fur coats, diamond rings—to persons of whom frequently little is known as to their intention or ability to pay.[13]

Another contemporary scholar, the economist E. R. A. Seligman, wrote a book about installment buying in 1927, predicated on the insight that this method of obtaining credit was creating an economic revolution. He estimated that in 1926 installment sales accounted for $4.5 billion of a total national retail sales of $38 billion (which included food and clothing as well as consumer durables).[14]

All of these changes—brand names, installment buying, the heyday of American advertising—crystallized to produce what has been called the culture of consumption.[15] As Warren Susman argued in a recent essay, the culture of republicanism of the nineteenth century was based on limits, restraint, and sacrifice, with "character" as the essential mode of self-presentation. This culture gave way to one based on abundance, fulfillment, gratification, and consumption, with "personality" replacing character in importance.[16] The constellation of hedonistic attitudes that emerged in the 1920s, "the Jazz Age," symbolized the birth of a new era, an era that could not fail to have enormous consequences for the status of domesticity.

Let us look at the four significant functions that the home had gained by 1830 and assess their status one hundred years later in the light of these developments. As we have seen, the political function of the home had been eroded by changes in the late nineteenth century, chiefly the emergence of an evolutionary perspective that saw the home as irrelevant to human progress. The capacity for the home to serve as an arena for the display of female prowess had been greatly undermined by a combination of technological innovation and the arrogation to themselves of domestic expertise by the home economics profession. The religious function was unlikely to be especially salient in an increasingly secular society. The Lynds, for example, inferred the existence of "doubts and uneasiness" about Christian belief in Muncie in 1925 and noted that Sunday was well on its way to becoming a day for recreation rather than for the solemn observation of the Sabbath.

What was left, then, of the original foundation of the ideology of domesticity was the heightened emotional role home had gained by 1830. If anything, that role had become even more important by the early twentieth century. Yet the importance was tied to a new self-consciousness—not to say anxiety—about how well the women in charge of the home could meet their families' emotional needs. Moreover, home-centered values had so much competition from other sources of cultural value by the 1920s that housewives in effect had as much responsibility for the emotional well-being of the society as ever, along with a diminished capacity to meet that responsibility.

In an astute analysis of the development of youth culture in the twenties, Paula Fass argues that the trends in the Anglo-American family of the late eighteenth century—democratization, companionate norms, child-centeredness—had become even more full-blown by the early twentieth century. Freedom and affection were seen as the basis for child nurture, and a regiment of psychologists and other social scientists set out to explain to women how this ideal could best be achieved. Recognizing that the home was no longer a center of production, experts argued that it was uniquely suited to foster emotional health in an industrial society:

> Family sociologists thus greeted the affectionate family enthusiastically because it provided a rich medium for personal satisfactions. But while they wrote endlessly about individual needs, they worried constantly about social order. The experts were, in fact, proposing that the emotional family would do more than satisfy the individual. They believed that it would ensure the health of the society. The key was the concept of psychological adjustment. . . .[17]

The housewife thus became the party in charge of psychological adjustment and this in a Freudian age given to the frequent employment of such terms as "psychosis" and "neurosis." Given these trends, the women's magazines were quick to print advice by experts so that women could be kept up-to-date in their approach to child-rearing and home-making. For example, the *Woman's Home Companion* of January 1922 contained an article entitled "Are You a 100% Mother?" The author explained how women could rate themselves in a number of areas.

At least one contemporary observer remarked on the difficulties presented to women by the new psychology. In an article in the June 1927 issue of the *Ladies Home Journal,* Virginia Terhune Van de Water (Marion Harland's daughter) argued that mothers were no longer immune from criticism in the wake of the Freudian revolution: " 'Mother, Home, and Heaven!' used to form the pious three. Now the Home is more of an exception than a rule; Mother is cast down from her pinnacle; and a good many people are trying to take away Heaven." She noted that the new prescriptions for women contained contradictory elements. Mother was supposed to let go as her children grew up, to refrain from invoking any maternal authority over them, and yet to "Be There" should they need her.

At the same time, the experts were far from unanimous in their agreement about the best way to raise children. Against the chorus of praise for love and democracy as the basis for child nurture, John B. Watson, the noted behaviorist, raised his voice with contrary advice. Distrusting affection and adjustment as the basis of the social order, Watson placed his reliance on training and habit. No less than those who emphasized affection, Watson urged the mother to take seriously the consequences of her mistakes: "But once a child's character has been spoiled by bad handling, which can be done in a few days, who can say that the damage is ever repaired?"[18] Committed to the ideal of "scientific" child care as well as to his extreme environmentalism, he doubted that the home was the right environment to socialize children but realized that it was likely to continue as the locus of child-rearing for the foreseeable future. "It is a serious question in my mind whether there should be individual homes for children—or even whether children should know their parents. There are undoubtedly much more scientific ways of bringing up children, which will probably mean finer and happier children."[19] The mother who wanted to do a good job of child-rearing—to approximate laboratory conditions for child care—should stifle her emotions, sternly resist "spoiling" the child, and adhere to rigid schedules, in Watson's view. While his ideas never captured the majority, at least in their most doctrinaire form, they were widely disseminated in American society, and hence had an impact impossible to dismiss.[20]

The picture that emerges of the 1920s is thus one of ever-increasing self-consciousness about the home's expressive function, whether defined in positive or negative terms. Simultaneously, however, the home was losing ground to such attractions as the automobile and the movies in its ability to command allegiance, especially the allegiance of young people. In Muncie as early as 1925, the Lynds found that the automobile had fundamentally altered courtship patterns: even high-schoolers could and did remove themselves from the supervision of their parents or other adults while on a date. The Lynds found, further, that in the peak movie-going month of December 1923, four and a half times the total population of Muncie went to the movies. The content of the films they saw was in decided contrast to values fostered by the ideology of domesticity: "*Alimony*—brilliant men, beautiful jazz babies, champagne baths, midnight revels, petting parties in the purple dawn, all ending in one terrific smashing climax that makes you gasp."[21]

That traditional domestic values were losing ground is particularly well illustrated by an article in the *Ladies Home Journal* by F. Scott Fitzgerald. The fact that the prophet of the Jazz Age was welcome in the pages of so staid a publication is remarkable in itself. Even more remarkable is the tenor of the article, entitled "Imagination and a Few Mothers." Fitzgerald begins by proclaiming, "The average home is a horribly dull place. This is a platitude; it's so far taken for granted that it's the basis of our national humor." The husband wants his club, and the wife wants to go to the movies. This is because the home fails in imagination. Indeed, there has been an "age-old fight against domestic dullness." Despite this dilemma, however, Fitzgerald holds out the hope that an imaginative mother, one who resolutely purges herself of dullness, can compete with other attractions. He himself knows a Mrs. Paxton whose home was "a success because she had a good time in it herself." What is more she has never hesitated to tell her children when they are boring.[22] The home is thus being evaluated solely on its ability to keep its occupants entertained and without regard to its moral or social capacities. It would be hard to imagine a greater departure than this from the discussions of the virtuous household conducted during the antebellum period.

In effect, Fitzgerald was telling housewives to join in the spirit of Jazz Age hedonism and in the priorities it fostered. Another source of competition for domesticity in the twenties was the widely revered world of business, and housewives were being urged to emulate this, too, rather than cling to an alternate and, implicitly, outmoded set of values. As we have seen, there were many givers of domestic advice in the early twentieth century who thought that scientific management and efficiency were appropriate goals for the housewife. By the teens and twenties, articles urging this approach were regularly appearing in women's magazines. "Are business methods possible in the home?" queried an article of the same name in the *Journal* of May 1919. The answer was yes: young wives who went from the office to the home would be better equipped than their sisters who lacked business experience.

What all this meant was that the home—still defined as a haven

by most social scientists and most other Americans—lacked the critical, independent edge it had possessed in the antebellum years. Virginia Terhune Van de Water had noted that the mothers of the
1920s were supposed to Be There for other people on whom the
mothers could make no claims of their own. Similarly, the emotionally intense home of the 1920s, whose ability to produce psychological
adjustment in its inhabitants was an article of faith for most Americans, no longer represented values that could make serious demands
on those inhabitants. Where Sarah Josepha Hale, writing in *Godey's*,
had addressed middle-class housewives with unassailable certainty
about the moral superiority of home to any other institution, the
editors of the *Ladies Home Journal* seventy years later revealed no
such certainty. The housewife might need to be frivolous on occasion so as not to bore her family and businesslike at other times so
as to make the optimum use of her time and resources. None of this
was calculated to give the women in charge of the home any leverage in asserting their claims vis-à-vis husbands or children. About all
housewives could attempt was to be loving, and hope for the best.
Everyone told them that unhappiness stemmed from a mother's mistakes. But no one explained the practical steps whereby a mother
could insure that her family would heed her direction—as influenced
by the many experts.

At worst, domesticity might be seen as not merely irrelevant but
as a positive impediment to other, more meaningful goals. The most
forceful statement of this position appears in *Arrowsmith*, another
of Sinclair Lewis's novels of the 1920s and one that was instrumental
in his being awarded the Nobel Prize for Literature in 1930.[23]
Martin Arrowsmith is a young medical scientist who has to combat
a variety of enemies, including his second wife, before he is finally
able to do his research unimpeded. Lewis gives him a mentor, Dr.
Max Gottlieb, who exemplifies all the values of neutral, unemo-
tional, supposedly value-free science. Martin's most helpful ally is
his first wife Leora, who comes as close to being ego-free as a character can be. She makes no demands on "Sandy," as she calls her
husband, and has no life or interests of her own. She is not even
especially competent at being a housewife. She is happy to sit home,

wait for her husband, whose hours are extraordinarily irregular, and listen to him whenever he needs her. Her only fault lies in contracting a tropical disease, dying, and leaving her husband alone—or rather leaving him to a much more assertive second wife.

Joyce is everything that Leora was not. She expects Martin to attend dinner parties, she wants him to take an interest in their child, and she insists that he shape his life to suit her needs as well as his own. At one point, he groans, "Oh Lord, there's The Arranger—wants me to come to tea with some high-minded hen." Finally, he realizes that he will have to forsake his wife and child if he is to serve science to the fullest extent possible. He moves to the Vermont woods, where he and another researcher share facilities and devote themselves to their work. Terry, the other scientist, proposes to Martin that they bring in a few more researchers, lest in their isolation the two of them should quarrel: "[T]he laboratory scheme should be extended to include eight (but never more!) maverick and undomestic researchers like themselves. . . ." Under this regimen, Martin begins to hit his scientific stride: "[H]e became stronger and surer and no doubt less human."[24] Lewis makes it clear that becoming less human is not too high a price to pay for the achievement that lies within Martin's grasp. In effect, Lewis makes a virtue of what people later in the century have called "workaholism" and in so doing heaps disapproval on the wife who tries to assert the claims of home.

Whether the competition for domesticity stemmed from the male-oriented values centered in business and science or from the youth-oriented hedonism associated with the Jazz Age, the home had been sufficiently devalued so as to lose some of its ability to be an emotional haven. Yet at the same time it was losing so many of its nine-teenth-century functions, it was gaining a new one appropriate to the new culture of consumption that, as we have seen, came of age in the 1920s: it was the place where sufficient consumer demand must be generated to keep the economy afloat. And the supreme social duty of the housewife—mostly unstated, but no less real—became that of spending freely.

As awareness of gender-related issues has grown, a few economists have begun to analyze the twentieth-century housewife's role in the economy. Says one student of the subject: "Because housework does not create surplus value [in the technical sense] there has been no incentive for capitalism to encourage a reorganization of the work in order to increase productivity—that is, minimize labor time." In fact, capital's interests may be best served by the waste and inefficiency of the housewife's time and of material goods both.[25] Says another economist, John Kenneth Galbraith, "The conversion of women into a crypto-servant class was an economic accomplishment of the first importance."[26] This is because industrial capitalism requires a high level of consumer spending—optimally of a rather indiscriminate nature—and this task has been ascribed to women. Their "work" does not show up in calculations of the gross national product; hence until recently it has been largely ignored.

It is in this context that Christine Frederick's *Selling Mrs. Consumer* belongs. Rather than being aimed at women, as had been the case with her earlier books, *Mrs. Consumer* was aimed at the advertising industry and attempted to set forth the best means for inducing housewives to spend as much as possible. Frederick begins by describing Mrs. Average Consumer in no very flattering terms: with little education and a limited vocabulary, she is more illogical than a man. Moreover, "the present generation of women are not bound much by religious controls. . . ."[27] Implicitly, of course, all of this makes Mrs. Consumer the more manipulable.

Because it would be advantageous for the manufacturers with goods to sell were each household to consume as much as possible, Frederick coined the term "creative waste" to describe the goal toward which the advertising industry should urge women. What is creative waste? It is "looking to a large end, beyond the draining of the last bit of utility,"[28] the larger end presumably being the maintenance of prosperity. Why should women bother to make breadpudding out of leftover crusts, for example? An accelerating rate of obsolescence for products was all to the good, Frederick thought. All that was to be desired was that Mrs. Consumer "would waste more rather than less!"

She had similar ideas with respect to household appliances: "There should be vastly more household equipment sold." Toward this end, manufacturers had to take on the job of educating women: "The manufacturer must educate, train, and transfer a worker from a hand and craft technique, over into a tool technique."[29] Here we find an overt assault on what was left of the craft tradition. An earlier generation of advice-givers from Charlotte Perkins Gilman to the pioneer home economists had downgraded the value of women's own expertise in the name of science. Now, those who attacked female expertise more likely did so with a very concrete goal in mind—that of selling a product.

Another book from the 1920s that was aimed at the advertising industry was *Advertising to Women* by Carl Naether. The author stated that women were believed to buy 80 to 90 percent of the commodities in general use. Therefore, advertising copy should be written squarely with women in mind and employ "woman's own language." For example, in describing apparel, Naether suggested the use of the phrase "such sweet shades."[30] The point is that those who were writing advice for copywriters displayed little respect for the intelligence of the women who would be responding to the advertisements.

While Frederick and Naether were advising copywriters about how best to sell products to women, there was a whole discipline that stood ready to make itself available to corporate America for a similar purpose, and that was the home economics profession. In the pages of the women's magazines, both in articles and in advertisements, there was mounted a concerted effort, made credible to women by the endorsement of experts, to break down the resistance to new products.[31] Moreover, hundreds and eventually thousands of home economists found employment directly with large business firms such as General Mills and General Electric, where their expertise was used toward the goal of heightening the levels of consumption of particular products.[32]

A sample of articles from the *Ladies Home Journal* will demonstrate the tenor of the advice that was being given to women as the culture of consumption took firm hold. In February 1922 an article titled "What Science Has Done for the Housewife" urged women to use the new food substitutes wherever possible. Science had done "wonderful things" for women, Mary D. Warren contended, yet there were still housewives who clung to tradition and to the dead past, "who pass by the scientific food substitutes excellent as they are, for high-priced and scarce products." Why not use powdered milk, canned milk, and oleo margarine? Warren queried. At more or less the same time, an advertisement for Crisco read, "Why Make Such Expensive Cakes?" The housewife could substitute Crisco for butter and add a little salt. "It [Crisco] is always pure, fresh, colorless, taste-less, and odorless."[33]

The new electrical appliances also received endorsement: "My Favorite Coworker—Electricity" contained Clara Zillesen's enthusi-astic praise of these products in the February 1927 issue. She enu-merated as many types of small and large appliances as she could envision, including, in addition to the range, the dishwasher, and the washing wachine, such items as the electric fan, electric sewing machine, electric heater, electric clock, electric milk-bottle warmer, electric heating pad, and electric hair curler. "There's something so cuddly and comforting about an electric heating pad which helps any ache or ill where the hot-water bottle is so impersonal. . . ."

An ambitious series of articles by Gove Hambidge late in the decade proclaimed a new era in foods and housework. The food industry had received the benefit of "creative genius," Hambidge thought. "Poets and dreamers" had evolved new products and new ways of packaging so that in 1928, 90 percent of the grocery business was in packaged goods: "I talked with a man in the display room of a modern wholesale grocery—a grocery fanatic, always dreaming new packages, new ways of doing this, that and the other. For thirty years his senses have been passionately alert for every reaction of the consumer to the products of his firm." It was this kind of dedi-cation that had produced such striking results. " 'Do you think we could depend on taste alone in making our tomato soup?' " one man said. Only chemists could produce a truly uniform flavor for each can. " 'Can any home cook tie that one? And how many households would take the trouble to make a vegetable soup, as this company does, using over a dozen different vegetables?' " With respect to baked goods, too, Hambidge extolled the wonders of science: "The modern bakery selling and advertising its products all over the country is a tiled, window-lined sunlit sanitarium. Ingredients for bread go in at one end, and wrapped, sealed loaves, perfectly baked, come out at the other without a finger having touched them. Small wonder the woman who bakes bread in her own kitchen is almost as extinct as the ichthyosaurus." As for housework, ". . . we are so obsessed with the scientific viewpoint that we are applying it to every aspect of life," and the result was such a proliferation of objects that the home was truly being mechanized, Hambidge thought. There had been those who had expressed doubts as to whether this goal might be achievable. The pessimists were overlooking the fact that vacuuming a rug is "fun."[34]

Finally, in 1929 Lita Bane, past president of the American Home Economics Association, became an associate editor of the *Journal.* In a January 1930 article titled "Homemaking and the Scientific Spirit," she urged women not to cling with irrational fervor to "the good old days" and "the good old ways." The *Journal* wanted to become a clearing-house for the dissemination of new information. In a subsequent article Bane attributed women's dislike for housework to their resistance to new ideas. "Drudgery is compulsory work that we do not know how to do well!" Yet cooking alone was receiving added interest from scientific discoveries, standardized recipes, and new packaging, to say nothing of other areas of housework.[35]

The nineteenth century had seen the development of a cultural ideal of "notable" housewifery whose main properties were skill and frugality. The 1920s version of the good housewife as set forth by the women's magazines had a much more passive quality. Frugality was passé, and skill involved listening to the right experts. Again to emphasize the rapidity of the cultural transformation, the *Journal* had run an article as late as August 1920, "Your Economy Questionnaire," with literally dozens of suggestions for being frugal such as saving and clarifying fat, saving paraffin from year to year, using buttermilk as far as possible in cooking, doing the mending every week, and saving and selling old rags. The woman who had done all this would not have been able to pass muster with Scott Fitzgerald's Mrs. Paxton, who never bored her family, let alone with all the experts later in the decade who urged women not to cling to the dead past. She would, however, have been exercising her judgment by conserving rather than wasting all her materials, a housewifely feat that operated at cross-purposes to maintaining maximum levels of consumption.

What, then, was the significance for women of these rapid changes? In the first place, one can discern a schizoid quality in the advice to women about their proper sphere as reflected in the pages of the *Ladies Home Journal* in the early twenties. An article in the May 1919 issue by Emily Blair stated the issue succinctly: "What Are Women Going To Do?" The author argued that American women had learned during the war that they had a margin of spare time that they could employ for war work. With the war over, how would that time be spent? Should women go back to bridge, do useless things, fold their hands? Blair thought that the answer lay in club work, especially work with activist clubs like the National Consumers League. The woman not gainfully employed would then be offering her leisure as her family's contribution to the public good. This, of course, was an updated version of domestic feminism, but it would founder as new priorities involving less socially oriented uses for leisure time asserted their claims in the ensuing decade.

Women should be publicly active, but only up to a point, and the *Journal* tried to set limits in a "credo for the new woman" in August 1920 (simultaneous with the ratification of the Nineteenth Amendment giving women the vote):

> I believe in woman's rights; but I believe in woman's sacrifices also.
>
> I believe in woman's freedom; but I believe it should be within the restrictions of the Ten Commandments.
>
> I believe in woman's suffrage; but I believe many other things are vastly more important.
>
> I believe in woman's brains; but I believe still more in her emotions.

There is an uneasy sense being conveyed in this article that the old verities are inadequate for the new age—no doubt the later decision to publish Fitzgerald's piece stemmed from this sense—coupled with reluctance to part entirely with traditional notions of woman's sphere.[36]

While advice-givers debated as to the best use for woman's time and the appropriate content of woman's sphere, women themselves were reallocating their time in response to the new consumer goods, with a further net loss both of craft and of human contact. As has already been suggested in Chapter 4, the decade of the twenties was the period when the housewife's job began to metamorphose into a post-industrial one. Although production of basic commodities like textiles and soap had left the home early in the nineteenth century (except in frontier areas), women continued to be producers of clothing, skilled cookery and baking, and needlework for another hundred years. But the culture of consumption militated against their being producers of anything of substance. There were at least two reasons for this. In the first place, brand-name processed foods were widely available. In the second place, the tone of advice in the women's magazines suggested that it would be almost atavistic to make one's own soup, say, when canned soup was so much more scientifically correct than the homemade variety. At the same time, the diffusion of the automobile, the declining number of servants, and the new types of merchandising put middle-class housewives squarely into the service mode, whether chauffeuring children, running errands, or shopping in a self-service market. Increasingly, after the twenties, they would move from isolation in their homes via isolation in their cars to the relatively impersonal supermarket, with its hygienically packaged goods.[37]

Most significant for women, perhaps, was the fact that the home of consumption conferred no special claims to cultural influence on housewives. Because home was no longer a moral beacon, the woman in charge of the home had little rationale for speaking out publicly in its name. Those who did so were likely to be dismissed as silly or sentimental. At least one scholar, Paula Baker, dealing with the female political culture and seeking to explain women's failure to form a separate voting bloc after 1920, singles out the devaluation of domesticity as an important part of the story. By the 1920s, "Women [had] thus abandoned the home as a basis for a separate political culture. . . . Their rejection of the woman's sphere as an organizing principle discouraged women from acting as a separate political bloc."[38] It is, of course, the argument of this study that women did not so much abandon the home as a basis for their culture as have it so badly undermined as to be worthless for justifying female political claims. Nonetheless, it is striking that one who was studying female activism and not necessarily focusing on the home came to this conclusion.

Yet another consequence of the culture of consumption concerned the status of older women. The attack on traditional female expertise and the authority of older women already mounted by home economists proved to be congruent with the purposes of the advertising industry in promoting the sale of new products. For example, an advertisement for Cannon sheets proclaimed: "I taught Aunt Sue a lesson—She'd been living in the past!" The copy continued: "Bob and I both are crazy about Aunt Sue. We try to do things right when she visits. But when she saw the luxurious sheets on her bed, she thought that we were living beyond our means. That's because she didn't know about Cannon's sensibly priced percale . . ." The point is that the culture of consumption enhanced the essential irrelevancy of older women to the rest of society. The message conveyed by the advertising industry was that older women should be brushed off, politely and kindly of course, should they have the temerity to give advice.[39]

IF ONE COULD accurately pinpoint the exact time when the phrase "Just a housewife," made its first appearance, it seems likely that the period under discussion might have been that time. Certainly the likelihood that domesticity could be a fully adequate prop for female self-esteem had greatly diminished by 1930. The consumer culture along with the hedonism it spawned sounded the death knell both for housewifery as a skilled craft and for mother as a moral arbiter. And yet the overwhelming majority of American women were still housewives for the better part of their lives.

We might well ask why, if the commodification of the home had so deleterious an impact on women, they consented to it. Are consumers sheep, to be manipulated by any corporation that has enough money to spend on an advertising campaign? Although there is no easy answer to this question, it seems worth pointing out that women resisted the process for quite some time. For instance, most housewives refrained from using bakers' bread until after 1900, preferring to make their own bread despite the work involved.[40] When processed food and brand-name products began to carry the day, they did so not only in response to the promptings of copywriters but undergirded also by the advice of home economists and ultimately by the enormous authority of modern science.[41]

By whatever means—and scholars have only begun to analyze adequately the genesis and diffusion of the culture of consumption—the commodification of the home took place. One indication that women were far from being beneficiaries of this development was the appearance in 1920 of a book entitled *The Nervous Housewife* by Dr. Abraham Myerson (whose work also appeared in magazines). Although Dr. Myerson had a certain propensity for blaming the victim, he also possessed sympathetic insight into the nature of the housewife's problems. Perhaps most striking was his contention, based on his clinical experience, that housewifely nervousness was virtually universal: "Most housewives are nervous, both in their own eyes and in those of their husbands, yet rightly they are not regarded as sick. They are uncomfortable, even unhappy, and the way out seems impossible to find."[42]

Myerson thought that at least part of the difficulty lay in the nature of housework in an industrial society. Although it is menial work like ditch-digging, housework nonetheless carries an enormous emotional baggage, and hence is glorified in unrealistic ways: "In its aims and purposes housekeeping is the highest of professions; in its methods and techniques it ranks among the lowest of occupations."[43] At least no one tries to convince ditch diggers or garbage collectors that their work is anything but disagreeable, and they are better off for this honesty.

Myerson identified the isolation of the individual housewife as well as the boring nature of the work as particularly acute problems: "Work that is in the main lonely; and work that on the whole leaves the mind free, leads almost inevitably to day dreaming and intro-spection. These are essentials, in the housework—monotony, day-dreaming, and introspection."[44] Household efficiency experts such as Christine Frederick had, of course, been urging women to work toward the precise goal of standardizing and routinizing their tasks. What no one had foreseen was the fact that routinized housework would continue to fill women's time while it starved their brains. This was because running errands and acting as general factotum more than filled the time women saved by standardizing work prac-tices or by the use of labor-saving devices.

Ten years later Myerson published an article in the *Journal* en-titled "Remedies for the Housewife's Fatigue." In addition to the factors eroding the possibility of contentment in the role of house-wife that he had already identified, he brought up a new one—the devaluation of motherhood. He spoke of the good old days when "Freud had not yet corroded the delight of the infant's attachment to the mother nor the mother's joy in the child, and [John B.] Watson had not yet destroyed the self-esteem of the mother by making her worse than worthless in her own eyes."[45] That a clinician singled out the de-skilling and devaluation of the housewife's job as creating so much female misery suggests that the impact of the changes on women was substantial. Only research in the letters and diaries of women themselves can document the exact nature of that impact.

Finally, one measure of the trivialization of domesticity that had occurred by 1930 was an article that appeared that year in the soon-to-be-defunct *Woman's Journal.* Entitled "I Rebel at Rebellion," it must have made the feminist founders of that periodical uneasy in their graves. The author claimed to be tired of the new freedom. All she wanted was to stay home. Happy to be supported by her husband, she had no regrets about not supporting herself. The article had more in the same vein.[46] Rather than bearing any relationship to the socially conscious, nineteenth-century ideology of domesticity, the article anticipated the privatized "Feminine Mystique" that became full-blown in the 1950s. As we shall learn, the American home at mid-century, cut loose from social, religious, or political moorings, was sacred only to "Family Togetherness." And the housewife who was the chief votary of this cult was supposed to eradicate any vestige of personal ambition or independent thought in order to keep her family happy.

EIGHT

Naming the Problem

*I*N 1963 BETTY FRIEDAN published *The Feminine Mystique.* In it she wrote feelingly about the "problem that has no name," as she called the malaise she thought to be afflicting the middle-class housewife. The book evoked an outpouring of letters from other women, stirred the publication of responses, and engendered enough controversy to ensure that Betty Friedan would become one of the best-known women in the United States. In this chapter we will explore the context for that publishing event. Why did *The Feminine Mystique* appear when it did, and why was the response so powerful?

In order to situate fully *The Feminine Mystique,* we must return to the interwar years. The depression decade of the 1930s produced few changes with respect to domesticity after the tumultuous developments of the preceding ten years. Moreover, the women's magazines conveyed little of the earlier élan about modern science. Since the disastrous economic downturn had tarnished the prestige of American business, there were fewer articles demonstrating how the housewife could emulate the world of business. That most Americans had far less in the way of disposable income than had been the case earlier had a dampening effect, too, on the growth of the culture of consumption.

One generalization that can be made about the advice to house-wives in the pages of the *Ladies Home Journal* in the years just before the attack on Pearl Harbor is that women were being told to tend to their knitting—literally. Where Harriet Beecher Stowe and Julia Ward Howe had been virtual embodiments of the Union cause during the Civil War, and Jane Addams had symbolized for many the American ability to meet the challenge of the new urban-industrial order in the early twentieth century—in all cases demon-strating the salience of domesticity for the society—there was no parallel female figure as the nation underwent the dual stress of economic hardship and anxiety about fascism.[1] Repeatedly, the *Journal* published editorials, articles, or columns in which women were congratulated on their lack of involvement with large issues and were enjoined to continue this state of affairs.

A particularly noteworthy example of the genre was the editorial by Bruce and Beatrice Gould in the September 1938 issue. The female reader's husband had probably been coming home for years and making speeches about world problems, speeches that she could not understand, so the Goulds suggested: "Be glad you're dumb about all these earth-shaking questions. They don't affect you nearly so much as a lot of other things much nearer home. . . . The great problems of the world are all Greek to you—but the problems of your home and family and community are right down your alley. Be glad you're dumb while your husband is saving the world—be brave and you can save the home." The editorial then went on to caution women against wasting too much time on books, lectures, or discus-sions. Even Sarah Josepha Hale, who had resolutely opposed woman suffrage and had refrained from discussing slavery in *Godey's*, had assumed more political and intellectual awareness than did the Goulds—and the Goulds were part of the post-suffrage era.

Dorothy Thompson, one of the leading journalists of the interwar years, gave advice of a similar nature: "It happens that I have led most of my life in the thick of problems of the outside world. It has been an interesting life, and I should not like to have changed it. But I should hate to see most women so exteriorize their lives as I have done!" She worried about what would become of the domestic sphere should this happen. Therefore, she thought that women might well stay home and knit. When they attended their clubs, those gatherings should not engage in "superficial" discussions of vast world problems, she contended. In this way the solid achievements of women's clubs both in educating their members and in agitating for change were dismissed.[2]

If housewives were being told to abjure any interest in changing the world, they were also being told much more explicitly than ever before to render personal service to their husbands and to be dependent, especially if they happened to have jobs outside the home. One expert, after advising working wives to be sure that their husbands had received an adequate quota of small personal services, addressed husbands as follows: "Make your wife as dependent on you as you can in all matters relating to the management of your home and life. There must be a greater percentage of dependence on the part of a wife than a husband; if this isn't financial, it will have to be in other matters."[3]

Given the tenor of these articles, it is not surprising to discover that Nobel Prize laureate Pearl Buck was shocked by the low status of American women when she arrived in the United States after having spent most of her life in China. In a remarkable book published in 1941, *Of Men and Women,* she described her reaction to this situation and anticipated many of the points that Friedan would make some twenty years later. That Buck's book appeared at a time of international crisis is part of the explanation for the fact that it failed to generate much discussion. More to the point, the changes of the 1940s and 1950s would make "the problem that has no name" much more acute, hence more likely to attract public attention. In any event, Buck's dissection of the housewife's role was far in advance of the contemporary conventional wisdom.

She began by asserting that "woman's influence is almost totally lacking in the centers of American national life." A woman's feminine qualities were "despised," a phenomenon of which the woman herself was quite well aware, so much so that she was the conduit of these attitudes to the next generation. "What is one to think of women who deliberately teach their sons to despise women?" That the dis-esteem entertained by American women for their own gender struck so forcibly a woman who had spent the better part of her life in a traditional society not known for prizing women is startling evidence of the toll taken by the devaluation of domesticity.

Buck's description of a housewife's day in a prosperous household is chilling: "She listens to as much as they will tell her, she reads as much as she is inclined, she potters about on the fringes of the world which really goes on without her and comforts herself by having a good hot dinner ready at night anyway. It is not enough. The feeling one has after coming to know American women is that they are starving at the sources."[4] Identifying this as the "Carol Kennicott problem," Buck was astute about what had caused it. As difficult as the impact of economic and technological change may have been for housewives, most fundamental was the loss of moral stature. "More serious to woman even than the removal of the need for her physical labor is the fact that she is no longer the spiritual and moral influence she was once to man and child in the home."[5] Because a woman's loneliness could be so sharp and her talents so underutilized, Buck urged that husbands begin to take a fair share of domestic responsibility so that their wives could live "a rounded life."

If Buck thought that American housewives were in a crisis state, from which only the cooperation of husbands could rescue them, there were many men who thought, to the contrary, that husbands were the ones who were put-upon. Indeed, in the post–World War I years a major theme of the American novel and short story was the predatory housewife. Although one could cite innumerable examples of this genre, we can examine another of Sinclair Lewis's novels, *Dodsworth* (1947), in order to make the acquaintance of a prototypical "Great American Bitch."[6]

Sam Dodsworth is a successful businessman, with more culture and sensitivity than most, but he has felt inadequate for most of his married life because his wife Fran is an expert at inducing such feelings:

> She had a high art of deflating him, of enfeebling him, with one quick, innocent sounding phrase. By the most careless comment on his bulky new overcoat she could make him feel

like a lout in it; by crisply suggesting that he "try for once to talk about something besides motors and stocks" while they rode to a formidable dinner to an elocutionary senator, she could make him feel so unintelligent that he would be silent all evening. The easy self-confidence which weeks of industrial triumphs had built up in him she could flatten in five seconds. She was, in fact, a genius at planting in him an assurance of his inferiority.[7]

Sexually cold, emotionally immature, and spoiled, Fran insists that the two of them take an extended vacation in Europe, a trip that brings out the worst in her personality. She unloads her husband for a European count, is herself cast off in turn, but fails to win Sam back. The book ends with Sam's decision to make a new life with a more understanding woman—American, too, but much less spoiled than Fran. At one point, Lewis, speaking of "American wives whom living in England had not weakened in their view of women's right to forbid men's rights," suggests that Fran's negative qualities may be more or less pandemic among American women.[8]

In plays, too, the predatory housewife appears. In 1925, George Kelly introduced Harriet Craig in his *Craig's Wife*, a Pulitzer Prize-winning play that was subsequently made into a movie starring Rosalind Russell in 1936, and remade with Joan Crawford in 1950. Harriet Craig is unambiguously manipulative. As she first enters, she is fretting about the screen door being open. We soon learn that she worships her house, is obsessed with order, and regards her husband principally as the means whereby she can achieve a stable home. At one point, she cautions her niece that a woman must not allow romance to put her in the position of "primitive feminine dependence and subjection." Harriet would never be that sentimental herself. By the end of the play Walter Craig has come to understand Harriet's hunger for control. Like Sam Dodsworth, he leaves his wife—after accusing her of a campaign to reduce him to "one of those wife-ridden sheep."[9]

In a pioneering article identifying the literary theme of the bitch/housewife, Dolores Barracano Schmidt points out that, surprisingly, the figure who so threatened the male personae of authors such as

F. Scott Fitzgerald, Ernest Hemingway, and Sinclair Lewis was not a career woman or an austere intellectual but rather a conventional housewife. The housewife's mistake was to be too bossy or to be a free-spending "parasite," or both. This literary pattern provides further evidence of the devaluation of domesticity because the wife who asserted her claims or defended her values could no longer legitimize her position through the home. Female assertiveness thus came to be defined as bitchery. Moreover, the shift in the nature of the housewife's role from production to consumption made it seem less like real work. There began to be a pervasive male fear that women were getting off too easy, reflected in literature in the interwar years and more generally in the society after World War II.[10] Finally, the bitch/housewife came to literary prominence in the decade when women had not only achieved suffrage, but also the old domestic feminist goal of prohibition, a goal whose capacity to provoke male anger and a heightened sexual politics we have already discovered. It is worth pointing out that characters such as Sam Dodsworth and Walter Craig are especially angry when their wives monitor their smoking or drinking behavior.

Whether or not the average middle-class housewife had enough work to occupy her time in 1940, she was certainly likely to find that she had work in 1943. By that time, of course, millions of housewives had gone into the labor force. Those who did not still found nearly every aspect of their work routine to be adversely affected by the war: housing was scarce, rationing created long lines at the grocery store, and millions of soldiers' wives had to be both mother and father to their children. That the war had a profound impact on American women because it transformed the character of the female labor force is so well known as to be a cliché. That it also had a profound impact on domesticity is only beginning to be understood.[11]

We can start by examining the way the war affected the American diet. Lasting more than twice as long as the American involvement in World War I and thus calling on far more resources, World War II saw the introduction of a thorough-going rationing of food that necessitated new recipes and enhanced the acceptability of food substitutes. Before the war, women had been using canned goods and packaged products such as crackers and factory-made bread. During the war, as a result of the shortage of butter, margarine made its way onto the American table, and so did convenience foods and meat stretchers. An advertisement for General Mills suggested extending butter with gelatin, an instance of the adjustments that people had to make in their ideas about what tastes good.[12] By April 1945, the *Ladies Home Journal* contained advertisements for such products as Junket quick fudge mix and Chef Boy-ar-dee spaghetti dinner with sauce, pasta, and cheese all in one box. No doubt the sheer volume of sales to the military market had given food processors new ideas about packaging convenience items.[13] Furthermore, it was difficult to bake and put up preserves at home during the war because of sugar rationing. Then, too, millions of women war workers had less time than ever before for preparing meals. In consequence, the war's legacy to the American palate was cake mix—and other types of processed foods that were closer to being ready-to-eat than anything before. And the level of skill that housewives needed to bring to cookery declined further.

While women struggled, often unsuccessfully, to provide meals for their families that approximated prewar meals, they also had to contend with other problems, petty and large. Household appliances, parts, and repairmen were all in short supply, for example. It was hard to find such items as paring knives or egg-beaters. The percentage of families owning refrigerators and washing machines actually fell during the war because consumer durables were hardly the most urgent priority of American industry.[14] Perhaps most painful was the fact that the wife who was not gainfully employed—who was, in fact, filling the role she had been trained all her life to fill—might be subject to subtle or not-so-subtle hints that she was falling short in her patriotic duty. One instance of this was the fact that a columnist for the *Detroit Free Press* actually suggested that a housewife should surrender her seat on a bus to a woman war worker.[15]

The war created geographic mobility on a vast scale because people moved to get higher-paying war work. This exacerbated a housing shortage that persisted even into the postwar years. In the late forties about two and a half million families were still "doubling up" in housing.[16] The large-scale shifts in population also created strains on school systems. As a consequence, many schools had to institute half-day sessions. And this in turn meant that thousands of mothers had their children underfoot for much of the day, often in cramped quarters.

A novel by Harriette Arnow, *The Dollmaker,* gives a vivid depiction of what wartime shortages and dislocations mean to a family that has moved from Kentucky to Detroit. This subject also gives Arnow the opportunity to deal with the broader topic of the loss of a craft tradition in the transition to a modern industrial society. The heroine of the novel, Gertie Nevels, is a country woman whose passion is not so much housewifery as it is the "male" work of farming and the "male" hobby of whittling. Nonetheless, Gertie savors the comfort of her mother's kitchen:

> She paused an instant looking around the great room. She glanced into the wide-mouthed fireplace where her great-grandmother had baked the bread and cooked all the Kendrick food, and smiled a little on an unusually large Dutch oven, one her father had always prized. . . . She crossed the kitchen to the great cookstove with its high curving legs, and rolled back the warming-oven door.
>
> . . . It was for an instant as it had been before she married, when this was home and if she grew hungry at any time of the day or night she had only to come to the warming oven or go to the cherry cupboard, where a selection of jams and jellies and canned and baked goods, especially gingerbread, were kept. Endlessly replenishing the kitchen, like the widow's barrel, were the smokehouse, the springhouse, and roothouse.[17]

Gertie takes pride in her own cooking, too, because when she serves food to her family, she realizes that "everything, even the meal in the bread, was a product of her farming."

Gertie's husband, Clovis, takes a job in Detroit, as did so many rural men and women during the war, lured by the high salaries. When Gertie arrives in Michigan with the five children, she is horrified by the housing Clovis has arranged for them. Their apartment is tiny and shed-like, with a kitchen like a "large closet." To make matters worse, it is near a steel mill. The children's school, on half-sessions, is inadequately provisioned and operating without a cafeteria. The wartime produce is so bad and Gertie is trying so hard to save money that she finds it nearly impossible to provide appealing meals for her family. At one point, one of the children refuses to finish her breakfast, and Gertie wonders what to do: "She looked at the half-eaten egg, flat-yolked, gray, rubbery white, the biscuit burned on the bottom, too pale on top, smeared with margarine instead of butter. She wasn't any good at coloring the stuff, but butter cost so. None of them ate the way they had back home."[18] On another occasion, Clovis complains, "Gert, that grub wasn't fitten fer a dawg."

Arnow contrasts the solid, craft-oriented way of life back in Kentucky with the meretricious consumer culture they encounter in Detroit. When Clovis surprises Gertie with a huge "Icy Heart" refrigerator, for example, one of the neighbors is able to recite the "Icy Heart" radio commercial from memory: "Every woman dreams of a ten-cubic-foot Icy Heart in her kitchen—Icy Heart power—Icy Heart. We must hurry up and win the war so we can all go out and buy Icy Hearts."[19] Only her whittling enables Gertie to hang on to some of her traditional culture. But as the novel ends, even that is taken away from her. Clovis, fully attuned to the machine age, has fixed up a jig-saw so that she can turn out her wooden dolls more quickly. " 'Law, Law, Gert,' Clovis said, too pleased that the contraption had worked to be real quarrelsome. 'You just want something you can make in a hurry an sell cheap; they could be money in sich. Sell 'em, say, around Christmas; that hand carven takes too long ever to make much.' "[20] Because they badly need the money, she has no choice but to assent.

If the housewife at home had to contend with innumerable new difficulties, the married war worker, "Rosie the Riveter," had special problems of her own as she tried to discharge all of her domestic responsibilities. Most pressing was the lack of adequate child care for the hundreds of thousands of mothers who had entered or re-entered the labor force. National magazines published articles containing horror stories about the expedients that were being adopted by desperate mothers. For example, an article in the *Woman's Home Companion* quoted a social worker who had testified to a Senate committee: "I have seen children locked in cars in parking lots in my valley [the San Fernando Valley] and I have seen children chained to trailers in San Diego."[21] Despite the entry of six million women into the labor force, many of whom were the mothers of young children, the federal government's efforts to meet the need for child care were pathetically inadequate.[22] Given this and given the suddenness of the demand, the private sector's ability to supply that demand was inadequate as well. Grandmothers were pressed into service, children lived with relatives other than their parents in some instances, and most mothers doubtless found more humane solutions to their problems than locking their children in a car. Nonetheless, the toll on mothers and children both—in anxiety and neglect respectively—was substantial.

Another grave difficulty for the woman war worker was the length of her workday. The case histories of such women in national magazines tell of grueling work schedules involving swing shifts and seven-day work weeks combined with all of the domestic difficulties imposed by rationing and shortages. The United Auto Workers sent out a questionnaire to its women members, asking what would make their lives easier. The respondents asked for help with child care, better shopping hours, shorter work days, better transportation, and better planned production.[23] What women war workers actually received was very little in the way of publicly supported services. In Britain there were several types of special services for gainfully employed housewives, such as one free afternoon a week for shopping, central kitchens that served over three million meals a week at cost, and welfare officers at war plants.[24] In America, a gainfully employed housewife was on her own.

Despite the pious proclamations that our boys were fighting to protect the American home, the American home was not deemed worthy of any genuine investment of societal resources. Both the scarcity of supplies for domestic purposes and the paucity of services for Rosie the Riveter conveyed this message. Given this, the woman who was "just a housewife" could hardly have escaped wondering whether her contribution to her society was appreciated.[25]

In some instances, the message of disdain for the American housewife during the war years was explicit rather than implicit. Most notorious was the attack on "Mom" by Philip Wylie in his bestselling diatribe, *A Generation of Vipers*. Wylie directed his main artillery against the "third sex" of post-menopausal women. In the good old days, "mom folded up and died of hard work somewhere in the middle of her life." Now, because she has a man to maintain her, she survives "to stamp and jibber . . . a noisy neuter by natural default or a scientific gelding."[26] No matter what she turns to, she brings disaster in her wake. Her presence at the ballot box has been responsible for a "new all-time low in political scurviness." Her clubs afford her merely the opportunity to nose into other people's business. And Wylie thought there were so *many* "moms." "Never before has a great nation of brave and dreaming men absent-mindedly created a huge class of idle, middle-aged women."[27]

Beyond the substance of his attack—most of which has to do with Mom's idleness and her consequent attempts to bind her sons to her so as to fill her time—the language he employs indicates rage rather than mere criticism. He speaks of the "beady brains behind their beady eyes" and the "stones in the center of their fat hearts." Mom is "a middle-aged puffin." That anger so excessive fueled a book going into numerous printings suggests that *A Generation of Vipers* had tapped a fund of inchoate male rage in the larger society.

Mom became a popular scapegoat. "Are American Moms a Menace?" queried an article in the *Journal* in November 1945. The author, Amram Scheinfeld, pointed out that "among abject failures we find a high proportion of mother's sons"—like Adolf Hitler. Shortly before the war ended, *Life* ran an editorial on "American Women." "Draft Them? Too Bad We Can't Draft Their Grandmothers" proclaimed the subtitle. Obviously influenced by Wylie, the editorial alleged extensive female idleness. "American women, as a class, even more than men, have a lot to learn about the responsibilities of all-around citizenship and their role in the modern world."[28] Two years later, *Life* ran a long feature on the "American

Woman's Dilemma." No woman's dilemma was more acute than that of the woman over forty, according to the article: "The Bureau of Labor Statistics lists 20 million women, nearly half of all adult female Americans, as essentially idle. They do not have children under 18, they are not members of the labor force, they do not work on farms, nor are they aged or infirm. With not nearly enough to do, many of them are bored stiff." While the tone of the writing conveys a certain sympathy for this plight, the illustrations accompanying the article perpetuate Wyliesque stereotypes. There are pictures of bored-looking women playing bridge and depictions of the "props for idle hours" like *Photoplay*, pills, chocolate, or a dog. All of this documents a "desert of wasted time."[29] There could be no more cruel reminder of the essential functionlessness of the older woman in the culture of consumption than the reduction of the last several decades of a woman's life to "a desert of wasted time."

However idle an older woman might have been deemed to be, no one was encouraging women to pursue careers on the same terms as men. Quite the contrary. The women's magazines celebrated the woman who was willing to sacrifice her own ambition for the more important goal of her husband's career. In April 1945, for example, the regular "How America Lives" feature of the *Journal* (a feature that ran for more than twenty years and hence provides an excellent source for the historian) focused on the Eck family. Mrs. Eck had had a promising career on the concert stage, but the tension of trying to fill multiple roles had induced a nervous breakdown. As a consequence, she gave up her career so as to devote herself to her children and to furthering her husband's career as a supermarket manager. Reflecting on her choice, she said, "The career I am educating them [her daughters] for is marriage, pure and simple. . . . It's the only lasting happiness a woman can have. . . . The sooner a woman makes a real home for a man, the sooner he will become successful and can give her a better house, servants, lovely clothes and so on. . . . Few men ever amount to much when their wives work."

Indeed, it is a scholarly commonplace that the rapid changes ushered in by the war contributed to considerable anxiety about the role of women in the postwar years. "Moms" were blamed for the high rate of emotional instability among inductees into the army, and working mothers received the blame for juvenile delinquency. The very health and survival of American society required women to maintain their traditional roles in the eyes of many commentators.[30] The most sophisticated presentation of this general argument appeared in *Modern Woman: The Lost Sex* by Ferdinand Lundberg and Marynia Farnham. Acknowledging that the changes of the past century had removed many functions from the home and had left housewives in increasing isolation, Lundberg and Farnham nonetheless insisted that the feminist response to these changes had been inherently neurotic, based on "deep illness." In fact, they argued, women have become so maladjusted that they have been responsible for widespread unhappiness: "Throughout, it will be seen, women are the principal transmitting media of the disordered emotions that today are so widely spread throughout the world and are reflected in the statistics of social disorder."[31] Only if women were to reestablish their essential dependence on men and stay home could they and their families achieve contentment.

Yet as housewifery became increasingly de-skilled, staying home became increasingly unsatisfying. An article in the April 1947 issue of the *Journal* discussed the phenomenon of radio soap opera in this context. In the eyes of the author, Aloise Buckley Heath, herself a housewife, the housewife's day was something to be endured rather than enjoyed because of the "many daily activities of a woman which require utter mindlessness." Soap operas helped fill the fourteen hours every day in which she had "work on her hands and nothing on her mind." That the specific content of the soap opera may have mattered less than its ready accessibility to a stay-at-home woman is suggested by another article a few years later. In this, the plight of a family newly arrived in a small city was discussed. With four small children and few acquaintances, the woman in question could go for days with hardly any adult conversation. Her method of filling the void in her life was to read her way through a thirty-volume encyclopedia. That way she could keep from being overwhelmed by loneliness.[32]

By the early 1950s the contours of what Betty Friedan would label "the feminine mystique" had emerged clearly. After the privations of depression and war, early marriage and large families had come into fashion. The grim events of the preceding twenty years had made it difficult to believe in the individual's capacity to have a positive influence on his or her society. Therefore, the home once more became a haven, but an apolitical one, unlike the home of the antebellum years. In an age of anxiety engendered by the Cold War and the nuclear threat, the chief quality desired of women was that they be soothing. An article in the series "Making Marriage Work" in the *Journal* advised a wife in this fashion: "Cater to his tastes—in food, in household arrangements, even in your appearance. Indulging his wishes, even if they are whims, is a sure way of convincing him that you really want to please him."[33] The woman who was reluctant to cater to the whims of another adult was unfeminine, according to the best wisdom of the day.

The 1950s' woman projected her femininity in her clothing, too. Not since the late nineteenth century had women's clothes so emphasized the wasp waist nor been so constraining. Women wore "Merry Widow" brassieres that cinched in their waists, crinoline petticoats under full skirts, tight girdles under straight skirts, and spike heels. If the good wife was supposed to think constantly and selflessly about how best to please her husband, the dictates of fashion reinforced the message that women existed to please men rather than as beings in their own right who warranted comfort.

The message that female ambition was not to be taken seriously was found not only in psychological treatises like *Modern Woman: The Lost Sex* but also in the new medium of television. The most famous housewife in the United States in the early fifties was Lucy Ricardo of "I Love Lucy." Week after week, Lucy connived at getting into her husband's nightclub act. Week after week, her loving, tolerant, yet firm husband foiled her attempts. Lucy's place was at home or else in the company of her best friend Ethel Mertz, and not in the public eye. When she attempted to perform, she was invariably ridiculous.[34]

The career woman was a well-identified threat to the social order, but so, too, was the housewife who had insufficiently purged herself of her unfeminine traits. In December 1956, *Life* ran an article entitled "Changing Roles in Modern Marriage." After explaining how feminism, although a thing of the past, had nonetheless produced the fatal error of the career woman syndrome, the author went on to caution that, even if the wife did not have a career, there might still be problems: "If there is such a thing as a 'suburban syndrome,' it might take this form: the wife, having worked before marriage, or at least having been educated and socially conditioned toward the idea that work (preferably some kind of intellectual work, in an office, among men) carries prestige," may well become depressed about being "just a housewife." Even if she avoids this, "her humiliation still seeks an outlet. This may take various forms: in destructive gossip about other women, in raising hell at the PTA, in becoming a dominating mother. . . . In her disgruntlement, she can work as much damage to the lives of her husband and children (and her own life) as if she were a career woman, and indeed sometimes more."[35] The "normal," feminine woman would be happy staying at home. One who was unhappy was, in fact, by definition not normal.

Yet the sources of self-esteem for the housewife were still dwindling. Arguably, the nadir of American cookery came in the fifties. This was the heyday of prepared foods and the cream-of-mushroom-soup school of cuisine whereby the cook could pour a can of this product over anything that was not a dessert and create a culinary treat according to the standards of the day. Although Friedan was to contend that women in the 1950s were being enjoined to chain themselves to their stoves, such was not the case. The women's magazines promoted "quick and easys," using convenience foods, canned goods, and the like. One issue of the *Journal*, for example, contained recipes calling for canned pears, canned sweet potatoes, frozen broccoli, pudding mix, canned salmon, and bakery apple pie to which the housewife was supposed to add a slice of cheese.[36] In 1960, Peg Bracken published the *I Hate To Cook Book*, whose animating spirit was summarized as follows: "Some women, it is said, like to cook. This book is not for them."[37] One might well ponder what there was to like about cooking as it was usually practiced circa 1960. One hundred years earlier, techniques and recipes had been zealously preserved treasures. In 1960 "creativity" consisted in combining a pudding mix with a cake mix and adding extra salad oil rather than merely following the instructions on the package of cake mix.

Perhaps the most consequential development for housewives in the 1950s, however, was the simultaneous growth of suburban housing tracts and of the highway system, changes that represented the maturation of the culture of consumption after World War II. Inexpensive homes and financing after the war plus "practically universal car ownership" combined to produce 37 million suburban residents by 1950, a figure that would nearly double by 1970. Suburbia has been subjected to a great deal of easy and clichéd criticism, and in fact there is not much positive to say about it as a locale for the stay-at-home housewife. Suburban housing patterns reinforced a woman's isolation from most of the world of adults. And the percentage of a woman's day spent chauffeuring other family members about increased exponentially. Even if she was not gainfully employed outside the home, she often needed to resort to convenience foods in order to maintain the driving schedule intact. Moreover, as a result of these changes, she began to seem like a servant to her children as well as to her husband.

By the mid-fifties the women's magazine began to reflect concern about the plight of the young housewife—although their analyses fell far short of what Friedan would achieve a few years later. The *Journal* sponsored a forum that brought together four young mothers, assorted experts, and the magazine's editors to discuss the subject. Too much was expected of the young mother, and she suffered from too much isolation—these were the major conclusions. The anthropologist Ashley Montagu suggested that women should organize to improve their situation. Beatrice Gould of the *Journal* thought that this was unlikely to happen because the housewife's self-esteem had been too badly eroded for her to be capable of advocacy on her own behalf.[38]

While the women's magazines were alternately promoting family "togetherness," a campaign launched by *McCall's* in 1954, and acknowledging the existence of widespread female misery, the magazines aimed at the male market took a rather different approach to male-female relations. As Barbara Ehrenreich demonstrates in *The Hearts of Men*, whether promoting indoor recreation à la *Playboy* or outdoor recreation à la *True*, these magazines resolutely rejected togetherness as an appropriate goal for the American male. What is more, rather than displaying any sympathy for a housebound wife, the editors were likely to run features displaying either undisguised contempt for her or else resentment of her "idleness."

> Tired of the Rat Race?
> Fed up with Job Routine?

> Well, then . . . how would you like to make $8000, $20,000—*as much as $50,000 and more*—working at home in your Spare Time? No selling! No commuting! No time clocks to punch

> BE YOUR OWN BOSS! ! !

> Yes, an Assured Lifetime Income can be yours *now*, in an easy, low-pressure, part-time job that will permit you to spend most of each and every day as *you please* . . .[39]

This was the way an article in *Playboy* satirized the housewife's job in 1963. Again, the point must be made that the contrast with the literature aimed at men in the antebellum years could not have been greater. At that time, male readers had been cautioned that moral striving would be required before they could be worthy of the angels to whom they were wed. The tenor of advice to men after World War II was that they had a right to be self-centered and self-indulgent. The wife who would not accept this was, by implication if not by explicit charge, a bitch.

Ehrenreich makes the further point that in the fifties the bread-winner role to many commentators began to seem so onerous as to be dangerous to men's health. In addition, then, to the other reasons for catering to her husband and ministering to his ego, a wife began to receive warnings in the pages of the women's magazines that failure to do her utmost to take care of her man might well result in his early death by heart attack.[40] *Playboy* told him to enjoy himself;

the *Journal* told her that she could not be too cautious about protecting his health.

By the 1950s domesticity was no longer capable of inspiring literary treatment by women other than as a source of pathology. And no woman writer had more negative things to say about domesticity than Anne Sexton—perhaps because no other major woman writer of the period had been so thoroughly immersed in the housewife role herself. Anne Gray Harvey eloped to marry Alfred Sexton in August 1948, when she was nineteen years old. Having been too rebellious a teenager to be a good student, she was launched into the world of adult responsibilities without much in the way of an education. She came, therefore, to her vocation of poet by a circuitous route—as a form of therapy after being hospitalized for suicidal depression:

> Until I was twenty-eight I had a kind of buried self who didn't know she could do anything but make white sauce and diaper babies. I didn't know I had any creative depths. I was a victim of the American Dream, the bourgeois, middle-class dream. All I wanted was a little piece of life, to be married, to have children. I thought the nightmares, the visions, the demons would go away if there was enough love to put them down. I was trying my damnedest to lead a conventional life for that was how I was brought up, and it was what my husband wanted of me. But one can't build little white picket fences to keep nightmares out. The surface cracked when I was about twenty-eight. I had a psychotic break and tried to kill myself.[41]

Discussing this passage, her biographer, Diane Middlebrook, comments, "Like many of the housewives Betty Friedan was interviewing for her book *The Feminine Mystique,* Sexton experienced the home as a sphere of confinement and stultification."

From the mid-fifties, when she first received encouragement for her poetry, to her death by suicide in 1974, the outward events of Sexton's life were remarkable. As Middlebrook puts it:

> In April 1960, Anne Sexton for the first time wrote "poet" rather than "housewife" in the "occupation" block of her in-

come tax return. Married since 1948, mother of two daughters, Sexton had been publishing poetry for three years. The change in her status as citizen was significant for Sexton and for American literature. No poet before her had written so frankly of the female realm of family life, nor of its pathologies. And few poets, women or men, achieved success so expeditiously: nine years from drafting her first poem to being awarded the Pulitzer Prize.[42]

Domesticity was for Sexton as constricting a prison as it had been for Charlotte Perkins Gilman. When the illness became acute, Sexton was incapable of maintaining household routines or of caring for her children—sometimes for years at a time. One of her letters reveals that occasionally she experienced a sense of repose and peace while at home:

> I feel today at home at home. You remember I said I didn't feel at home in life. Well that was almost always any life—not just the outside world—more the outside than my home here. But sometimes, all my life really, I've stayed home hiding from the world. Hiding is different from being "at home." Today, just now, I was working around the kitchen singing at the top of my lungs.[43]

The evidence of the poetry suggests, however, that these moods were rare. More often, home represented not so much solace as defeat and denial of one's full humanity. And her long-term identity as a housewife inspired revulsion:

HOUSEWIFE

Some women marry houses.
It's another kind of skin; it has a heart,
a mouth, a liver and bowel movements.
The walls are permanent and pink.
See how she sits on her knees all day
faithfully washing herself down.
Men enter by force, drawn back like Jonah
into their fleshy mothers.

A woman *is* her mother.
That's the main thing.[44]

Sexton published this poem in a collection entitled *All My Pretty Ones* that came out in 1962. From the late fifties, when her first poems started appearing in print, she wrote in an entirely unprecedented way about the particulars of the female condition such as menstruation, abortion, and mother-daughter relationships. Because she so captured the public imagination, one can only infer that she was articulating the feelings of other women. To be a housewife in the United States in 1960 might well open a woman up to negative emotions.

Perhaps the quintessential suburban housewife of the 1950s in a novel by a male writer was Betsy Rath, wife of Tom Rath, the title character in *The Man in the Gray Flannel Suit*. The Raths struggle with such typical issues of the day as suburban housing developments and better school systems. Betsy, although not gainfully employed and not in possession of many ideas of her own, does have an attractive spunky quality. Nonetheless, she is at best an adjunct to her husband as he goes through a series of moral crises, which he decides on his own. And the author, Sloan Wilson, reveals no real insight into what this situation might cost a woman of spirit. One passage in particular embodies the conventional wisdom that the American housewife of the period was "spoiled."

> "You're talking like a typical American Woman," Tom said disgustedly. "You want it both ways. 'Don't play it safe,' you say, 'and can we get a new car tomorrow?' "[45]

Tom then accuses Betsy of having had an easy life. On another occasion (when he is confessing an episode of wartime adultery) he urges, "Try to be adult about this."

In *Mrs. Bridge*, a novel that appeared just a few years after *The Man in the Gray Flannel Suit*, Evan Connell does demonstrate insight into the housewife's dilemma. The title character, married to a successful man and the mother of three children, lives with her family in Kansas City. A thoroughly conventional woman, devoted to her family's interests and eager to please, Mrs. Bridge gradually loses the ability to know her own mind enough to render opinions on subjects of any consequence. When the Bridges go out for a social evening, Mrs. Bridge is happiest if they are with another couple, both members of which are predictable. Then she can tell the husband what he wants to hear without needing to do much guesswork. A telling episode is the suicide of one of Mrs. Bridge's close friends, Grace Barron:

> She often wondered if anyone other than herself had been able to divine the motive; if so, it went unmentioned. But she herself had found it instinctively less than an instant after hearing the news: her first thought had been of an afternoon on the Plaza when she and Grace Barron had been looking for some way to occupy themselves, and Grace had said, a little sadly, "Have you ever felt like those people in the Grimm fairy tale—the ones who were all hollowed out in the back?"[46]

Unlike Wilson, Connell had figured out that starvation of the ego was bad for the development of an adult personality.

There were, then, a few glimmerings of insight into female malaise that went beyond blaming "neurotic" women for their illegitimate aspirations that appeared before Friedan published her indictment of the problem that has no name. For the most part, however, the media paid little attention to them. The election of John F. Kennedy in 1960 signaled the coming of a new, more vigorous generation into power and the start of a new dispensation in American society. No doubt this contributed to the reception accorded to Friedan's book when it appeared in 1963.

In the 1980s *The Feminine Mystique* must be dealt with in two ways: as a document and as an analysis. In the first instance, the book is an invaluable source; in the second instance, its value is undercut by the author's lack of historical perspective. Friedan was angry about the developments of the 1950s and exaggerated the novelty of the suburban housewife's plight relative to earlier decades. Also, writing before the rebirth of women's history, she lacked any insight into the nineteenth-century version of domesticity.

The genesis of the book came in Friedan's decision to survey some two hundred of her classmates in the Smith College Class of 1942 fifteen years after graduation. Sifting through their responses and pondering her own life, she came to believe that there was a radical disjunction between the popular image of the suburban housewife surrounded by the bounty of a consumption-oriented society and the private reality of women's lives. The strongest part of the book lies in her exposition of the housewife's malaise, "the strange, dissatisfied voice stirring within her."

> It is no longer possible to ignore that voice, to dismiss the desperation of so many American women. This is not what being a woman means, no matter what the experts say. For human suffering there is a reason; perhaps the reason has not been found because the right questions have not been asked, or pressed far enough. I do not accept the answer that there is no problem because American women have luxuries that women in other times and lands never dreamed of. . . .
>
> If I am right, the problem that has no name stirring in the minds of so many American women today is not a matter of loss of femininity or too much education or the demands of domesticity. It is far more important than anyone recognizes. It is the key to these other new and old problems which have been torturing women and their husbands and children, and puzzling their doctors and educators for years. It may well be the key to our future as a nation and a culture. We can no longer ignore that voice within women that says, "I want something more than my husband and my children, and my home."[47]

Having begun by sketching out the dimensions of the problem, Friedan went on to identify multiple sources of difficulty for women, including Freudian psychology, functionalist social science that enshrined the status quo as the norm, educators who failed to respect female intellectual abilities, and the manipulations of advertisers eager to sell products to housewives. Too angry to be altogether fair, she assumed that the housewife role was merely something from which women needed to be liberated. She gave no consideration to the issue of how many interesting careers the society might have at its disposal, and whether there would be enough to go around.

Would the woman who could only find a menial job outside the home be that much better off than the housewife? This, too, was an issue that Friedan ignored. Finally, were there any components of the housewife role that might be worth preserving? If there were, Friedan did not mention them. Rather, she argued that women needed "some higher purpose than housework and thing-buying." Moreover, she claimed that *"women have outgrown the housewife role"* [emphasis in the original]. Clearly, she herself had internalized the societal contempt for housewifery that lay just beneath the pious surface. Like Charlotte Perkins Gilman, she seriously undervalued the female contribution to society.

Although the analysis might have been flawed, *The Feminine Mystique* deserves to take its place as one of the most influential books written by an American in the twentieth century. Friedan had named the problem, and the public discourse about the housewife was never again the same. Before she published her book, women were most often blamed personally for their unhappiness. Afterwards, there began to be an appreciation that social arrangements could receive some of the blame for female unhappiness.

As soon as the book appeared, Friedan found herself at the center of a media blitz. The women's magazines, initially hostile to her approach, could no longer ignore her. *Life, McCall's, Harper's, TV Guide,* and the *Ladies Home Journal* all ran articles by or about her. Interviewed on television, alternately praised and vilified, she consistently challenged the conventional wisdom about women. As a result, she began to receive letters from women all over the country, many filled with outrage and many others with relief. These letters, with the writers' names inked out for privacy, are now housed at the Schlesinger Library at Radcliffe. A perusal of a small sample of them confirms that Friedan had touched a responsive chord in the minds of many women:

> But who cares about a "helpless" lonely housewife's life being wasted away by the kitchen sink. About all the millions of potentialities whittling away in quiet desperation . . .
>
> Thank you so much for *The Feminine Mystique.* It was such a

relief to find my feelings and thoughts are not so outrageous after all. For the last three years I was convinced I was becoming ill. No one will ever know how many times I have fled into the bathroom to cry because I couldn't conquer that horrible, restless, all at ends feeling.

As I sat down to read it, I had the strangest sensation that you had studied me and then written a book concerning the whole "nameless problem."

I feel so moved to express my thanks to you that I have not even waited to finish reading your wonderful book, *The Feminine Mystique*. It seemed to me, as I read, that I was saying almost every page or quote, "Why that's me. That's the way I have felt." I found I was reading with absorption that left me physically trembling.[48]

The most carefully thought-out response to Friedan from the other side came from Phyllis McGinley in her book, *Sixpence in Her Shoe*, published in 1964. A poet and the mother of two daughters, McGinley insisted that her role as a housewife had given her great satisfaction. In essence, she restated the doctrine of separate male and female spheres in order to bolster the position of the housewife. In an ideal society, "the two nations, male and female, would each inhabit a sphere snugly suited to its ordained capabilities." Conceding that some women might be better off gainfully employed than at home, she nonetheless insisted that society requires carefully drawn boundaries between gender roles. Toward that end, women must be "self-immolators."[49]

McGinley's critics may well have wondered how much she had practiced self-immolation herself. Few people who publish multiple volumes of poetry, as she had, do so out of the desire to obliterate their own egos. Moreover, we may also wonder how much McGinley understood of the contemporary suburban housewife's situation. Herself one of the small minority of housewives with live-in domestic help, in touch with the literary world of New York, she could hardly have identified with the plight of the woman who tried to read her way through the entire encyclopedia for company. Yet McGinley did understand that the housewife role was being undervalued by most Americans.

The developments of the last twenty years—such as the rebirth of feminism and feminism's relationship to its housewife constituency—would furnish the subject for a book in their own right. A study conducted in 1970, whose subjects came to maturity when the "Feminine Mystique" was flourishing, can, however, provide a coda to our discussion of the devaluation of domesticity. In a doctoral dissertation in psychology undertaken at Michigan, Judith Birnbaum studied a group of eighty-one women of approximately the same age and educational background, all of whom had graduated from college between 1945 and 1955. One-third were housewives, one-third were married professionals, and one-third were single professionals. Birnbaum gave her subjects a forty-one-page, self-administered questionnaire that included a number of open-ended questions. Interestingly, not only did the housewives display lower self-esteem in general, but they also had lower self-esteem than did the married professionals in their assessment of their own child-care skills. The housewives were lonelier, were more negative about menopause, and experienced far more uncertainty about what they wanted from life than did the married professionals. Birnbaum concluded, "It is not surprising that involutional melancholia is so common among middle-aged, middle-class women, and unfortunately the homemaker seems already a vulnerable pushover to just such difficulties."[50]

One housewife's response, apologetic because of her tardiness in returning the questionnaire, epitomizes the erosion of self about which Friedan had written:

> Please excuse me for being so long completing the booklet. I am very poor at writing and as the years go by, my bad habit of "putting off" difficult tasks becomes worse. I hope this is not too late to be of some assistance. I feel rather guilty with some of my responses—but I guess it is because I never admitted them to anyone but myself.[51]

The writer, a forty-six-year-old mother of four, had been, as had been all of Birnbaum's subjects, a gifted student. No matter. Years of being "just a housewife" had left their imprint. By the 1960s, the woman who was supposed to provide emotional support for her family and in essence underwrite the psychological well-being of her society was all too likely to be herself in a state of demoralization.

Thus the complex of social, political, and cultural factors that had created the ideology of domesticity and an enhanced possibility for self-respect on the part of the housewife had dissolved by the mid-twentieth century. As we have seen, the rise of an urban-industrial society in the late nineteenth century and the rapid conquest of educated opinion by evolutionary theory combined to make the home seem ineffectual. The female craft tradition succumbed to de-skilling and devaluation by experts who, ironically enough, were dedicated to "helping" women. Moreover, where a nineteenth-century notable housewife had been assumed to play an active role in promoting the good society, the culture of consumption that took shape in the 1920s required her to play the passive role of spending freely. After World War II the level of skill involved in cooking—no doubt that area of housework with the most potential for inspiring job satisfaction—declined to an all-time low. And in the 1950s millions of women found themselves living in suburbs and therefore spending many hours each week performing the service role of chauffeur, instead of engaged in productive work.

The "problem" took generations to develop, but after Friedan named it, the explosive pace of change within a relatively short time demonstrates how many women were affected by it. As Pearl Buck had written in 1941, they were "starving at the sources."

Afterword

$\mathcal{I}$N THE MORE THAN TWENTY YEARS since the publication of *The Feminine Mystique* there have been vast changes in the lives of American women, most of them for the better. The majority of women, including those who are married, are now gainfully employed outside the home. Although most women workers are still underpaid relative to men and are still disproportionately employed in the "pink collar ghetto," the fact remains that women today have opportunities that were undreamed-of twenty years ago. A powerful feminist movement came into being in the late sixties and early seventies and mobilized women to effect change. Public policy began to be responsive to the needs of women in an unprecedented fashion. Women now make up a substantial portion of the classes at law and medical schools. Higher education is beginning to have a more equitable representation of women faculty, and curricular changes have afforded woman-centered topics more time in the classroom. A "gender gap" has materialized in the voting behavior of men and women, thus creating a new interest on the part of politicians in their female constituents. Women are beginning to be taken seriously as candidates for major office, and a woman sits on the Supreme Court. In other words, women have more access to social, economic, and political power than ever before.

As is well known, the civil rights and student movements of the 1960s played critical roles in catalyzing the rebirth of feminism. Young women who came together to fight for social justice or to protest the war in Southeast Asia discovered that they shared "the bonds of womanhood" (as had their sisters of the nineteenth century in the abolitionist movement). Tragically, many of these young white women felt alienated from the woman's culture represented by their own mothers, whose lives were subject to the demoralizing influences we have been discussing. It was, therefore, especially important for young white women in the sixties to go south, as so many did, and to encounter black women whose roles in their communities were altogether different than those of middle-class white women in the North.

Perhaps the only positive way in which domesticity played a role in the formulation of modern feminism was in this encounter between southern black women and the young northerners to whom they were inspirational figures. The southern black women belonged to households in which the consumer goods of twentieth-century America were relatively less available than they were in middle-class strata of society. The black women's domestic skills were thus more immediately apparent to their families and to outsiders. In fact, many northerners wrote letters home in which they extolled the cooking of the southerners. (Moreover, black women have always been gainfully employed outside the home at a greater rate than in the white community, another way in which they could be seen as making a material contribution to the welfare of their families.) For many reasons, then, the black women seemed admirable to northern students.[1]

With this exception, modern feminism might be said to have been born out of the repudiation of women's traditional roles and not out of the desire both to glorify and to expand those roles as in the nineteenth century. In no other country in the world was there such a contradiction between woman's nominal freedom to do anything and the actual contempt for female capabilities, especially those manifested in the housewife, as in the United States in 1963. Moreover, few, if any, Americans retained knowledge of a nineteenth-century female craft tradition that had empowered women to effect change. For these reasons, feminists were unable to use either their own history or woman's culture to fashion a movement. The loss of this history as well as the widespread contempt for housewives in the culture made it difficult for feminists to build bridges to their potential housewife constituency.

There are signs that this situation may be changing, however. In the resurgence of interest in food I see more than merely a manifestation of the affluent at play. After so many decades of sensory deprivation where their palates are concerned, Americans of varied circumstances are rediscovering one of life's more important pleasures, a good meal. Younger women and men are increasingly willing to prepare food from scratch. Perhaps it is not too much to hope that a craft tradition in cookery is being reborn.

Furthermore, many feminists are beginning to talk about their domestic priorities. Recognizing the divergent approaches to domesticity based on regional, racial, and class differences, I think that we have enough in common to develop a program that would enable us to ask the state for better policy, employers for more flexible work arrangements—especially where the interests of young children are concerned—and our loved ones for more equitable sharing of domestic responsibility. This, in turn, might enable the building of bridges to more traditional women.

Can home, the site where many of the emotions that make us most fully human are fostered, survive and prosper in the late twentieth century? Can it survive and prosper without entailing the exploitation of women? Can technology be tamed to serve human needs? These are open questions. What is not an open question is the fact that all of us need home, whatever our particular household arrangements might be. Inevitably, in a complex, bureaucratic society, workplace decisions must be made on meritocratic grounds. The marketplace revolves around the cash nexus. If our social geography is to have any locale where love counts for more than merit or profit, then home will have to be that place. To say this does not mean that the private sphere has more intrinsic worth than the public sphere.

Rather, there are certain important values that are generated in each realm. A disproportionate emphasis on one realm at the expense of the other impoverishes the whole of life.

We cannot go back—nor would we want to—to the nineteenth-century home. But we can learn from history, and we can be sustained by the heritage of women and men like Harriet Beecher Stowe, Antoinette Brown Blackwell, and Samuel May. It seems to me that the essence of what they have to teach us is as follows: the good society and the good home are inextricably intertwined.

Notes

Introduction

1. The Schlesinger Library of Women's History at Radcliffe College, Cambridge, Mass., has the Friedan papers, which include the letters received by Friedan in response to the publication of *The Feminine Mystique*.

ONE *The Emergence of a New Ideology*

1. Ruth Schwartz Cowan, *More Work for Mother: The Ironies of Household Technology from the Open Hearth to the Microwave* (New York: Basic Books, 1983), chapter 2 *passim*.

2. Mary Beth Norton, *Liberty's Daughters: The Revolutionary Experience of American Women, 1750–1800* (Boston: Little, Brown, 1980), 38.

3. *Ibid.*

4. See Edmund Morgan, *The Puritan Family: Religion and Domestic Relations in Seventeenth-Century New England* (New York: Harper & Row, 1966), and Jay Fliegelman, *Prodigals and Pilgrims: The American Revolution against Patriarchal Authority, 1750–1800* (Cambridge: Cambridge Univ. Press, 1982).

5. Cowan, *More Work for Mother*; Laurel Thatcher Ulrich, *Good*

Wives: Image and Reality in the Lives of Women in Northern New England, 1650–1750 (New York: Alfred A. Knopf, 1982).

6. Carole Shammas, "The Domestic Environment in Early Modern England and America," *Journal of Social History* 14 (Fall 1980): 4–24; Lois Green Carr and Lorena S. Walsh, "Inventories and the Analysis of Wealth and Consumption Patterns in St. Mary's County, Maryland, 1658–1777," *Historical Methods* 13 (Spring 1980): 81–104.

7. Shammas, "The Domestic Environment," 14.

8. Cowan, *More Work for Mother*, 21–24.

9. Sally Smith Booth, *Hung, Strung, & Potted: A History of Eating in Colonial America* (New York: Clarkson N. Potter, 1971), 174. On the diet of New England see Sarah Frances McMahon, " 'A Comfortable Subsistence': A History of Diet in New England," Ph.D. dissertation, Brandeis Univ., 1982.

10. Norton, *Liberty's Daughters*, 155.

11. Linda K. Kerber, *Women of the Republic: Intellect and Ideology in Revolutionary America* (Chapel Hill: Univ. of North Carolina Press, 1980), 283f.

12. Amelia Simmons, *American Cookery*, a facsimile of the first edition, 1796, with an essay by Mary Tolford Wilson (New York: Oxford Univ. Press, 1958). A paperback reprint (Boston: Rowan Tree Press, 1982) has helpful annotations, too. It should be pointed out that Amelia Simmons borrowed freely from English sources. On the changing culinary standards of the eighteenth century see Sarah Frances McMahon, " 'A Comfortable Subsistence.' "

Though other approaches might be possible—using needlework, for example—I will use cookbooks to document the ebb and flow of a craft tradition among American housewives wherever appropriate because I feel competent to generalize in this area. I have learned a great deal from Joseph Carlin and the other Culinary Historians of Boston. Anthropologists, not the least of whom has been Claude Levi-Strauss, have been aware of the cultural significance of food and cookery for quite some time. It is high time for cultural historians to use this approach, too.

13. Fliegelman, *Prodigals and Pilgrims*, 2–13.

14. Carl Degler, *At Odds: Women and the Family from the Revolution to the Present* (New York: Oxford Univ. Press, 1980), 8.

15. Lawrence Stone, *The Family, Sex and Marriage in England, 1500–1800* (New York: Harper & Row, 1977).

16. Degler, *At Odds*, 8. See also Jan Lewis, *The Pursuit of Happiness:*

Family and Values in Jefferson's Virginia (Cambridge: Cambridge Univ. Press, 1983).

17. Bernard Wishy, *The Child and the Republic: The Dawn of Modern Child Nurture* (Philadelphia: Univ. of Pennsylvania Press, 1968); Nancy Cott, *The Bonds of Womanhood: "Woman's Sphere" in New England, 1780–1835* (New Haven: Yale Univ. Press, 1977).

18. Dudden, *Serving Women: Household Service in Nineteenth-Century America* (Middletown, Conn.: Wesleyan Univ. Press, 1983). I suspect that only the very wealthiest women held themselves entirely aloof from doing housework. See, for example, Catherine Clinton's descriptions of the heavy domestic responsibilities of plantation mistresses in her *The Plantation Mistress: Woman's World in the Old South* (New York: Pantheon, 1982). See further, Susan Strasser, *Never Done: A History of American Housework* (New York: Pantheon, 1982), 163. Strasser points out that in 1870 the United States census listed only one domestic servant for every 8.4 families in the population.

19. Dudden, *Serving Women*, 44.

20. John Mack Faragher, *Women and Men on the Overland Trail* (New Haven: Yale Univ. Press, 1979), 70f.

21. Kathleen Ann Smallzreid, *The Everlasting Pleasure: Influences on America's Kitchens, Cooks and Cookery from 1565 to the Year 2000* (New York: Appleton-Century-Crofts, 1956), 120.

22. Faragher, *Women and Men on the Overland Trail*, 70f.

23. Cowan, *More Work for Mother*, 54.

24. *Ibid.*, 53–62.

25. Simmons, *American Cookery*, 12.

26. I have been very much influenced by John L. Hess and Karen Hess's lively polemic, *The Taste of America* (New York: Grossman, 1977). After cooking out of a large number of old cookbooks, the Hesses state unequivocally that American cookery was at its high point during this period. See also Waverly Root and Richard de Rochemont, *Eating in America: A History* (New York: William Morrow, 1976), 145, whose judgment is that antebellum cookbooks reflect considerable skill and a willingness to experiment with flavors, "even exotic ones."

27. See Hess and Hess, *The Taste of America*, and also William Weaver's introduction to Elizabeth Ellicott Lea, *A Quaker Woman's Cookbook*, William Woys Weaver, ed. (Philadelphia: Univ. of Pennsylvania Press, 1982).

28. Eliza Leslie, *The Lady's Receipt Book* (Philadelphia: Carey and

Hart, 1847). I used the cookbook collection at the Schlesinger Library at Radcliffe College.

29. Mary Randolph, *The Virginia Housewife or Methodical Cook* (Baltimore: Plaskitt, Fite, 1838).

30. *The Housekeeper's Book* (Philadelphia: William Marshall, 1838).

31. Lea, *A Quaker Woman's Cookbook*, 111–25.

32. *Ibid.*, 61. I have also been influenced in this judgment by conversations with Joseph Carlin of the Culinary Historians of Boston. Not only is Mr. Carlin a nutritionist, but he has his own extensive collection of antebellum cookbooks, which he graciously allowed me to consult.

33. Mary P. Ryan, *Cradle of the Middle Class: The Family in Oneida County, New York, 1790–1865* (Cambridge: Cambridge Univ. Press, 1981), 198.

34. Harriet Beecher Stowe, *Oldtown Folks* (New York: Viking, 1982), 1209.

35. Elizabeth Wetherell [Susan Warner], *The Wide, Wide World* (New York: G. P. Putnam, 1853), 125.

36. *Ibid.*, 156f.

37. *Ibid.*, 170f.

38. See the discussion of this work in Nina Baym, *Woman's Fiction: A Guide to Novels by and about Women in America, 1820–1870* (Ithaca: Cornell Univ. Press, 1978), 143–50.

39. Susan Swan, *Plain and Fancy: American Women and Their Needlework, 1700–1850* (New York: Holt, Rinehart and Winston, 1977), 204.

40. On this subject see Lyle Koehler, *A Search for Power: The "Weaker Sex" in Seventeenth-Century New England* (Urbana: Univ. of Illinois Press, 1980).

41. William G. McLoughlin, *The American Evangelicals, 1800–1900*, an anthology (New York: Harper & Row, 1968), introduction *passim*. For the quote about Lyman Beecher see George M. Fredrickson, "A Founding Family," *New York Review of Books* 45 (Nov. 9, 1978), 38. For a different interpretation of the relationship between nineteenth century and domesticity, see Ann Douglas, *The Feminization of American Culture* (New York: Alfred A. Knopf, 1977).

42. Barbara M. Cross, *Horace Bushnell: Minister to a Changing America* (Chicago: Univ. of Chicago Press, 1958), 61–63. See also David P. Handlin, *The American Home: Architecture and Society,*

1815–1915 (Boston: Little, Brown, 1979), 6–11 for a discussion of the impact of Bushnell and "home religion" on American architecture.

43. Horace Bushnell, *Christian Nurture* (New York: Charles Scribner's Sons, 1890), 19f.

44. *Ibid.*, 406.

45. Steven Mintz, *A Prison of Expectations: The Family in Victorian Culture* (New York: New York Univ. Press, 1983), 146.

46. Henry Ward Beecher, *Norwood or Village Life in New England* (New York: Fords, Howard and Hulbert, 1887), 12.

47. *Ibid.*, 72.

48. As quoted in Lawrence A. Cremin, *American Education: The Colonial Experience, 1607–1783* (New York: Harper & Row, 1970), 486–89.

49. See Russell Blaine Nye, *The Cultural Life of the New Nation, 1776–1830* (New York: Harper & Row, 1960), 221–27.

50. Theodore Parker, "Phases of Domestic Life," *Lessons from the World of Matter*, vol. 5 of the *Works of Theodore Parker* (Boston: American Unitarian Association, 1908), 187–98.

51. Kerber, *Women of the Republic*, chapter 7 *passim*; Anne Firor Scott, "What, Then, Is the American: This New Woman?" *Journal of American History* 65 (Dec. 1978): 679–703.

52. Benjamin Rush, "Of the Mode of Education Proper in a Republic," *The Selected Writings of Benjamin Rush*, Dagobert D. Runes, ed. (New York: Philosophical Library, 1947), 95f.

53. Degler, *At Odds*, 308–9. This statistic applies to whites only.

54. Nathaniel Hawthorne referred to his female competition as "that damned mob of scribbling women" and most scholars have taken their cue from Hawthorne. See, for example, Henry Nash Smith, "The Scribbling Women and the Cosmic Success Story," *Critical Inquiry* 1 (1974): 47–70. In *The Feminization of American Culture*, Ann Douglas uses these novels as evidence of the effeteness of Victorian culture in the United States. On the other hand, Helen Waite Papashvily sees the strength of the novels but views this characteristic as unfortunate evidence of man-hating on the part of the novelists. See Papashvily, *All the Happy Endings: A Study of the Domestic Novel in America, the Women Who Wrote It, the Women Who Read It, in the Nineteenth Century* (New York: Harper & Row, 1956).

55. Baym, *Woman's Fiction*; Mary Kelley, *Private Woman, Public*

Stage: Literary Domesticity in Nineteenth-Century America (New York: Oxford Univ. Press, 1984); Jane Tompkins, *Sensational Designs: The Cultural Work of American Fiction, 1790–1860* (New York: Oxford Univ. Press, 1985).

56. Frances [Mrs. William] Parkes, *Domestic Duties or Instructions to Young Married Ladies* (New York: J. and J. Harper, 1829), 48f. I am not certain how widely read Mrs. Parkes's book might have been, but I did come across a mention of a later edition in *Godey's*.

57. *Ibid.*, 161.

58. Kirk Jeffrey, "Marriage, Career, and Feminine Ideology in Nineteenth-Century America: Reconstructing the Marital Experience of Lydia Maria Child, 1828–1874," *Feminist Studies* 2 (1975): 113–30.

59. The Collected Correspondence of Lydia Maria Child, 1817–1880, #758, Aug. 31, 1849, copyright by Patricia J. Holland and Milton Meltzer, Schlesinger Library, Radcliffe College.

60. *Ibid.*, #48, June 23, 1831.

61. *Ibid.*, Letter to Henrietta Sargent, #1614, Jan. 8, 1865.

62. Lydia Maria Child, *The American Frugal Housewife*, 12th ed. (Boston: Carter, Hendee, 1833), 81.

63. *Ibid.*, 71.

64. *Ibid.*, 5.

65. *Ibid.*, 96.

66. Catharine Sedgwick, *Home* (Boston and Cambridge: James Munroe, 1835), 28f. Mary Kelley points out that *Home* went through twelve editions in two years. *Private Woman, Public Stage*, 13.

67. Sedgwick, *Home*, 64.

68. Lydia Sigourney, *Letters to Young Ladies* (Hartford: P. Canfield, 1833), 27.

69. Lydia Sigourney, *Letters to Mothers*, 6th ed. (New York: Harper & Brothers, 1841), 192.

70. *Ibid.*, 12.

71. *Ibid.*, 59.

72. *Ibid.*, 195.

73. William A. Alcott, *The Young Husband or Duties of Man in the Marriage Relation* (Boston: George W. Light, 1839), 153f. See the discussion of Alcott in Arthur M. Schlesinger, *Learning How To Behave: A Historical Study of American Etiquette Books* (New York: Macmillan, 1946).

74. Timothy Shay Arthur, *Advice to Young Men on Their Duties and Conduct in Life* (Boston: Phillips, Sampson, 1850), 96f.

75. *Ibid.*, 99.

76. Henry Clarke Wright, *Marriage and Parentage: or, The Reproductive Element in Man, as a Means to His Elevation and Happiness* (Boston: Bela Marsh, 1866), 296. See also Wright, *The Empire of the Mother over the Character and Destiny of the Race* (Boston: Bela Marsh, 1863), and Lewis Perry, *Childhood, Marriage and Reform: Henry Clarke Wright, 1797–1870* (Chicago: Univ. of Chicago Press, 1980). For the discussion of a counter-tradition among men, one that celebrated male freedom from restraint, see Carroll Smith-Rosenberg, "Davy Crockett as Trickster: Pornography, Liminality, and Symbolic Inversion in Victorian America," in Smith-Rosenberg, *Disorderly Conduct: Visions of Gender in Victorian America* (New York: Oxford Univ. Press, 1985).

77. Daniel Scott Smith, "Family Limitation, Sexual Control, and Domestic Feminism in Victorian America," in *Clio's Consciousness Raised,* Mary Hartman and Lois W. Banner, eds. (New York: Harper & Row, 1974); Degler, *At Odds,* 189.

78. Nancy F. Cott, "Passionlessness: An Interpretation of Victorian Sexual Ideology, 1790–1850," *Signs* 4 (Winter 1978): 219–36. See Ryan, *Cradle of the Middle Class,* for a community study depicting the interplay between domestic ideals and the changing dynamics of family life.

79. Claudia L. Bushman, *"A Good Poor Man's Wife": Being a Chronicle of Harriet Hanson Robinson and Her Family in Nineteenth-Century New England* (Hanover, N.H.: Univ. Press of New England, 1981), 120f. See chapter 7, "Housekeeping," for a detailed description of Robinson's routine.

80. *Ibid.,* 121.

81. Mary Kelley, "At War with Herself: Harriet Beecher Stowe as Woman in Conflict within the Home," *American Studies* 19 (Fall 1978): 23–40; the quote from Stowe is taken from Forrest Wilson, *Crusader in Crinoline* (Philadelphia: J. B. Lippincott, 1941), 219f. For a description of the water cure see Kathryn Kish Sklar, *Catharine Beecher: A Study in American Domesticity* (New York: W. W. Norton, 1973), 205–9.

82. Annie Fields, *Life and Letters of Harriet Beecher Stowe* (Houghton, Mifflin, 1897), 98.

83. Eunice Beecher, *All Around the House; or How to Make Homes Happy* (New York: D. Appleton, 1879). For a discussion of Eunice Beecher's health see Clifford E. Clark, Jr., *Henry Ward Beecher: Spokesman for a Middle-Class America* (Urbana: Univ. of Illinois Press, 1978).

84. Catharine Beecher, *A Treatise on Domestic Economy* (Boston: Marsh, Capen, Lyon, and Webb, 1841), 18, 19.

85. Sklar, *Catharine Beecher,* 204.

86. See Dudden, *Serving Women,* on the difficulty of life for most domestics.

87. Suzanne Lebsock, *The Free Women of Petersburg: Status and Culture in a Southern Town, 1784–1860* (New York: W. W. Norton, 1984), 24, 40–46.

88. See Mary Patricia Ryan, "American Society and the Cult of Domesticity, 1830–1860," Ph.D. dissertation, Univ. of California at Santa Barbara, 1971, for information on the social origins of the authors of the advice manuals.

89. Sigourney, *Letters to Young Ladies,* 27 (emphasis added).

90. See Julie Roy Jeffrey, *Frontier Women* (New York: Hill & Wang, 1979), and Faragher, *Women and Men on the Overland Trail,* for a discussion of this theme.

91. Clinton, *The Plantation Mistress,* 137.

TWO The Golden Age of Domesticity

1. On women's culture in the nineteenth century, see Ellen DuBois, Mari-Jo Buhle, Temma Kaplan, Gerda Lerner, and Carroll Smith-Rosenberg, "Politics and Culture in Women's History: A Symposium," *Feminist Studies* 6 (Spring 1980): 26–64. This symposium features a sharp disagreement between those who fear that overstressing women's culture may result in the neglect of politics (DuBois is the spokesperson for this point of view) and those who emphasize the positive impact of women's culture on women's lives in the nineteenth century (Smith-Rosenberg is the spokesperson for this point of view). For a discussion of the interplay between women's culture and politics that suggests that the former may have promoted women's involvement in the latter, see Paula Baker, "The Domestication of Politics: Women and American Political Society, 1780–1920," *American Historical Review* 89 (June 1984): 620–47.

2. Kirk Jeffrey, "Family History: The Middle-Class American Family

in the Urban Context, 1830–1870," unpublished Ph.D. dissertation, Stanford Univ., 1972, p. 99.

3. Ralph Waldo Emerson, "Domestic Life," *Emerson's Complete Works*, VII (Boston: Houghton Mifflin, 1893), 113.

4. *Ibid.*, 113.

5. Anne C. Rose, *Transcendentalism as a Social Movement, 1830–1850* (New Haven: Yale Univ. Press, 1981), 100.

6. Emerson, "Domestic Life," 108f.

7. Elizabeth Oakes Smith Papers, New York Public Library, Box 1.

8. Ellen Tucker Emerson, *The Life of Lidian Emerson*, Delores Bird Carpenter, ed. (Boston: Twayne, 1980), 96f.

9. Nathaniel Hawthorne, *The House of the Seven Gables* (New York: Bantam, 1981).

10. *Ibid.*, 53.

11. *Ibid.*, 200.

12. As quoted in Clifford E. Clark, Jr., "Domestic Architecture as an Index to Social History: The Romantic Revival and the Cult of Domesticity in America, 1840–1870," *Journal of Interdisciplinary History* 7 (Summer 1976): 33–56, p. 56.

13. On the moral significance of architecture in England and the United States under the influence of John Ruskin, see David Handlin, *The American Home: Architecture and Society, 1815–1915* (Boston: Little, Brown, 1979), 41.

14. Andrew Jackson Downing, *The Architecture of Country Houses*, with introduction by J. Stewart Johnson (New York: Dover, 1969), 79. The sales figures are in the introduction to this edition.

15. Gwendolyn Wright, *Building the Dream: A Social History of Housing in America* (New York: Pantheon, 1981), 84.

16. Mary Kelley, *Private Woman, Public Stage: Literary Domesticity in Nineteenth-Century America* (New York: Oxford Univ. Press, 1984), 27.

17. Henry Clay to Sarah Josepha Hale, March 6, 1848, Hale Papers, Huntington Library, San Marino, Calif.

18. Oliver Wendell Holmes to Sarah Josepha Hale, Nov. 20, 1872, Hale Papers, Huntington Library, San Marino, Calif.

19. See *Hearth and Home*, Oct. 30, 1869, for the article on cooperative housekeeping. See the issue of Aug. 7, 1869, for Stowe's reply to Horace Bushnell.

20. See the splendid biography of Beecher by Kathryn Kish Sklar,

Catharine Beecher: A Study in American Domesticity (New York: W. W. Norton, 1976).

21. See also Susan Hill Lindley, "Woman's Profession in the Life and Thought of Catharine Beecher: A Study of Religion and Reform," unpublished Ph.D. dissertation, Duke Univ., 1974.

22. Anne Firor Scott, "The Ever-Widening Circle: The Diffusion of Feminist Values from the Troy Female Seminary, 1822–72," *History of Education Quarterly* 19 (Spring 1979): 3–25. On the radicalism of suffrage see Carl Degler, *At Odds: Women and the Family from the Revolution to the Present* (New York: Oxford Univ. Press, 1980), and Ellen Carol DuBois, *Feminism and Suffrage: The Emergence of an Independent Women's Movement in America, 1848–1869* (Ithaca: Cornell Univ. Press, 1978).

23. Sklar, *Catharine Beecher*, 161.

24. Catharine E. Beecher, *A Treatise on Domestic Economy for the Use of Young Ladies at Home and at School* (Boston: Marsh, Capen, Lyon, and Webb, 1841), 9.

25. Catharine E. Beecher, *The True Remedy for the Wrongs of Woman with a History of an Enterprise Having That for Its Object* (Boston: Phillips, Sampson, 1851), 51.

26. *Ibid.*, 59.

27. Beecher, *A Treatise on Domestic Economy*, 314.

28. Catharine E. Beecher and Harriet Beecher Stowe, *The American Woman's Home* (New York: J. B. Ford, 1870), 19.

29. Harriet Beecher Stowe to Sarah Josepha Hale, undated but ca. 1850, Hale Papers, Huntington Library, San Marino, Calif.

30. Mrs. Edward Beecher to Stowe as quoted in Forrest Wilson, *Crusader in Crinoline* (Philadelphia: J. B. Lippincott, 1941), 252.

31. As quoted in Harriet Beecher Stowe, *Uncle Tom's Cabin*, Kenneth S. Lynn, ed., The John Harvard Library, Howard Mumford Jones, editor-in-chief (Cambridge, Mass.: Belknap Press, 1962), xxvi.

32. Harriet Beecher Stowe to Lord . . . , Jan. 20, 1853, Huntington Library, San Marino, Calif.

33. Jane Tompkins, "Sentimental Power: *Uncle Tom's Cabin* and the Politics of Literary History," *Glyph* 8 (1981): 79–102, p. 81.

34. Harriet Beecher Stowe, *The Minister's Wooing* (New York: Viking, 1982), 527, 561, 560.

35. Mary Virginia Terhune, *Marion Harland's Autobiography: The Story of a Long Life* (New York: Harper & Brothers, 1910), 339.

36. Harriet Beecher Stowe, *Uncle Tom's Cabin* (New York: New American Library, 1966), 156.

37. *Ibid.*

38. Alice C. Crozier, *The Novels of Harriet Beecher Stowe* (New York: Oxford Univ. Press, 1969), 167–77.

39. Stowe, *Uncle Tom's Cabin*, 224f.

40. On the home of Simon Legree as an "anti-home" see the pioneering discussion in William Robert Taylor, *Cavalier and Yankee: The Old South and American National Character* (New York: G. Braziller, 1961).

41. These articles are reprinted in Harriet Beecher Stowe, *Household Papers and Stories*, vol. 8 of *The Writings of Harriet Beecher Stowe* (Cambridge: Houghton Mifflin, 1896).

42. Annie Fields, "Days with Mrs. Stowe," *Atlantic Monthly* (Aug. 1896), as reprinted in Elizabeth Ammons, ed., *Critical Essays on Harriet Beecher Stowe* (Boston: G. K. Hall, 1980), 292.

43. On Stowe's conservative turn in her later life see Dorothy Berkson, "Millennial Politics and the Feminine Fiction of Harriet Beecher Stowe," in Ammons, *Critical Essays on Harriet Beecher Stowe*.

44. Annie Fields, *Life and Letters of Harriet Beecher Stowe* (Boston: Houghton Mifflin, 1897), 210, 211.

45. Theodore Parker, "Home Considered in Relation to Its Moral Influence," *Sins and Safeguards of Society*, vol. 9 in *The Works of Theodore Parker* (Boston: American Unitarian Association, 1908), 214; "The Public Function of Women," in *Sins and Safeguards of Society*, *ibid.*, 204, 205.

46. Parker, "Home Considered in Relation to Its Moral Influence," 213.

47. Parker was, for example, one of the "Secret Six" who advanced help to John Brown prior to the raid on the arsenal at Harper's Ferry in 1859.

48. On Blackwell see Elizabeth Cazden, *Antoinette Brown Blackwell: A Biography* (Old Westbury, N.Y.: Feminist Press, 1983); Blanche Glassman Hersh, *The Slavery of Sex: Feminist-Abolitionists in America* (Urbana: Univ. of Illinois Press, 1978); William Leach, *True Love and Perfect Union: The Feminist Reform of Sex and Society* (New York: Basic Books, 1980).

49. Blackwell to Lucy Stone, 1850, Blackwell Family Papers, Library of Congress, Container 92.

50. Cazden, *Antoinette Brown Blackwell*, 162, 199.

51. Blackwell to Susan B. Anthony, Oct. 25, 1859, Blackwell Family Papers, Schlesinger Library, Radcliffe College, Reel 2, Folder 34.

52. Blackwell to Lucy Stone, April 1859, Blackwell Family Papers, Library of Congress, Container 92.

53. Blackwell to Lucy Stone, Dec. 9, 1879, Blackwell Family Papers, Library of Congress, Container 92.

54. Antoinette Brown Blackwell, "The Relation of Woman's Work in the Household to the Work Outside," *Papers and Letters Presented at the First Woman's Congress of the Association for the Advancement of Women . . . New York, October, 1873,* as quoted in Cazden, *Antoinette Brown Blackwell*, 163.

55. Antoinette Brown Blackwell, *The Sexes Throughout Nature* (New York: G. P. Putnam's Sons, 1875), 112.

56. Antoinette Brown Blackwell, "Work in Relation to the Home," *Woman's Journal*, May 2, 1874.

57. Antoinette Brown Blackwell, "Work in Relation to the Home, Part II," *Woman's Journal*, May 9, 1874.

58. Samuel J. May, "The Rights and Condition of Women; Considered in 'The Church of the Messiah,'" Nov. 8, 1846 (Syracuse: Stoddard and Babcock), collection of the Boston Public Library.

59. Letter from Samuel May to Woman's Rights Convention, Worcester, Mass., Oct. 1850, reprinted in Thomas Wentworth Higginson, Woman's Rights Tracts no. 8, collection of the Boston Atheneum.

60. *Memoir of Samuel Joseph May* (Boston: Roberts Brothers, 1873), 277.

61. Mary Beth Norton, "The Evolution of White Women's Experience in Early America," *American Historical Review* 89 (June 1984): 593–619, 615f. See also Donald G. Mathews, "The Second Great Awakening as an Organizing Process, 1780–1830: An Hypothesis," *American Quarterly* 21 (Spring 1969): 23–42; Nancy F. Cott, "Young Women in the Second Great Awakening in New England," *Feminist Studies* 3 (Fall 1975): 17–29.

62. As quoted in Anne Firor Scott, "Women's Voluntary Associations in the Forming of American Society," in Scott, *Making the Invisible Woman Visible* (Urbana: Univ. of Illinois Press, 1984), 280.

63. Norton, "The Evolution of White Women's Experience in Early America," 617. Norton points out that the American situation whereby women took this responsibility was unique. On the role of voluntary

associations in a frontier community see Don Harrison Doyle, *The Social Order of a Frontier Community: Jacksonville, Illinois, 1825–1870* (Urbana: Univ. of Illinois Press, 1978).

64. Suzanne Lebsock, *The Free Women of Petersburg: Status and Culture in a Southern Town, 1784–1860* (New York: W. W. Norton, 1984), 205.

65. Mary P. Ryan, "The Power of Women's Networks," *Feminist Studies* 6 (Spring 1979): 66–85, pp. 68f.

66. Paula Baker, "The Domestication of Politics," 625.

67. Virginia Sapiro, *The Political Integration of Women* (Urbana: Univ. of Illinois Press, 1983).

THREE *Domestic Feminism and the World Outside the Home*

1. See Ellen Carol DuBois, *Feminism and Suffrage: The Emergence of an Independent Women's Movement in America, 1848–1869* (Ithaca: Cornell Univ. Press, 1978).

2. For this definition of domestic feminism see Karen J. Blair, *The Clubwoman as Feminist: True Womanhood Redefined, 1868–1914* (New York: Holmes and Meier, 1980), 8.

3. See Mary Kelley, *Private Woman, Public Stage: Literary Domesticity in Nineteenth-Century America* (New York: Oxford Univ. Press, 1984).

4. Elizabeth Wetherell [Susan Warner], *The Wide, Wide World* (New York: G. P. Putnam, 1853), vol. II, p. 54.

5. *Ibid.*, 86.

6. Harriet Beecher Stowe, "Homekeeping Versus Housekeeping," *Household Papers and Stories*, vol. VIII in *The Writings of Harriet Beecher Stowe* (Cambridge: Houghton Mifflin, 1896), 27.

7. Mary P. Ryan, *Cradle of the Middle Class: The Family in Oneida County, New York, 1790–1865* (Cambridge: Cambridge Univ. Press, 1981), 232.

8. In fact, Nina Baym read fourteen of Southworth's novels from the 1850s and "found only one thoroughly good man, the father in *The Lost Heiress*. Most are of limited intelligence and overwhelming vanity." Baym, *Woman's Fiction: A Guide to Novels by and about Women in America, 1820–1870* (Ithaca: Cornell Univ. Press, 1978), 115.

9. E. D. E. N. Southworth, *The Deserted Wife* (New York: D. Appleton, 1850), 78.

10. *Ibid.*, 143.

11. Says Nina Baym, "Southworth's women want to make a place for themselves where men can be distanced and controlled." Baym, *Woman's Fiction*, 116.

12. Augusta J. Evans, *St. Elmo* (New York: Carleton, 1866), 467f. Southworth, on the other hand, supported suffrage. See the Aug. 13, 1868, issue of *The Revolution* for a letter memorializing Congress on behalf of suffrage for women in the nation's capitol. Southworth signed the letter.

13. See the discussion of Evans in Baym, *Woman's Fiction*, chapter 10 *passim*.

14. *Godey's* 47 (July 1853), 84f.

15. Sarah Josepha Hale, *Manners or Happy Homes and Good Society All the Year Round* (Boston: J. E. Tilton, 1868), 20f.

16. *Ibid.*, 74f.

17. Mary H. Grant, "Domestic Experience and Feminist Theory: The Case of Julia Ward Howe," *Woman's Being, Woman's Place*, Mary Kelley, ed. (Boston: G. K. Hall, 1979), 224.

18. Julia Ward Howe, *Reminiscences, 1819–1899* (Boston: Houghton Mifflin, 1900), 213–15.

19. As quoted in Deborah Pickman Clifford, *Mine Eyes Have Seen the Glory* (Boston: Little, Brown, 1979), 197. By no means am I trying to suggest that the Howes' marriage was typical of either those of reformers or of the larger society. I am merely trying to suggest the possibility of a sexual politics using domesticity as the chief terrain of battle. Indeed, Blanche Glassman Hersh argues convincingly that the Howes were atypical of reformers, most of whom had harmonious marriages. See Hersh, *The Slavery of Sex: Feminist Abolitionists in America* (Urbana: Univ. of Illinois Press, 1978).

20. Howe, *Reminiscences*, 216f.

21. See DuBois, *Feminism and Suffrage*, 189–200.

22. See Barbara Leslie Epstein, *The Politics of Domesticity: Women, Evangelism, and Temperance in Nineteenth-Century America* (Middletown, Conn.: Wesleyan Univ. Press, 1981), for insights into antagonistic male and female cultures in the late nineteenth century. In my view, however, Epstein fails to grasp the full value of domesticity for women.

23. The account of Twain's life is based on the following: Justin Kaplan, *Mr. Clemens and Mark Twain: A Biography* (New York: Simon and Schuster, 1966); Everett Emerson, *The Authentic Mark Twain: A*

Literary Biography of Samuel L. Clemens (Philadelphia: Univ. of Pennsylvania Press, 1984); Susan K. Harris, *Mark Twain's Escape from Time: A Study of Patterns and Images* (Columbia: Univ. of Missouri Press, 1982). This particular episode is related by Michael Patrick Hearn in his introduction to *Huckleberry Finn* (New York: Clarkson N. Potter, 1981).

24. Kaplan, *Mr. Clemens and Mark Twain*, 80.

25. As quoted in *ibid.*, 115.

26. Nook Farm in Hartford was also the home of Harriet Beecher Stowe.

27. Harris, *Mark Twain's Escape from Time*, 116.

28. Mark Twain, *The Adventures of Tom Sawyer* (Berkeley: Univ. of California Press, 1982), 11.

29. *Ibid.*, 48.

30. *Ibid.*, 199.

31. *Ibid.*, 161, 162.

32. *Ibid.*, 255.

33. As quoted in Hearn's introduction to *Huckleberry Finn*, 28.

34. Clarence Cook, *The House Beautiful: Essays on Beds and Tables, Stools and Candlesticks* (New York: Scribner, Armstrong, 1878).

35. Mark Twain, *Adventures of Huckleberry Finn*, 165, 171.

36. *Ibid.*, 176, 183.

37. As quoted in Emerson, *The Authentic Mark Twain*, 128.

38. Harris, *Mark Twain's Escape from Time*, 58f.

39. Hearn, introduction to Huckleberry Finn, 35.

40. Benjamin P. Shillaber, *Life and Sayings of Mrs. Partington* (New York: J. C. Derby, 1854). The relationship between Mrs. Partington and Ike was evidently one source of inspiration for the relationship between Aunt Polly and Tom Sawyer.

41. Thomas Bailey Aldrich, "The Story of a Bad Boy," in *Our Young Folks: An Illustrated Magazine for Boys and Girls* V (May 1869), 277.

42. Benjamin P. Shillaber, *Ike Partington; or, The Adventures of a Human Boy and His Friends* (Boston: Lee and Shepard, 1879), 10f.

43. George William Peck, *The Grocery Man and Peck's Bad Boy* (Chicago and New York: Belford, Clarke, 1883), 26.

44. Louisa May Alcott, *Little Men* (Cleveland and New York: World Publishing, 1950), 129.

45. I was unable to secure a copy of *Reveries of a Bachelor*. I did, however, peruse *Fudge Doings: Being Tony Fudge's Record of the Same,*

2 vols. (New York: Charles Scribner, 1855), where I encountered the following passage (p. 29) in which Tony Fudge explains his marital condition:

> I am married—only to the world; which I find to be an agreeable spouse something fat, and with streaks of ill-temper; but, upon the whole, as good-natured and yielding as a moderate man ought to expect.

46. The extent to which Social Darwinism entered into American thought and life is still subject to scholarly debate. The classic treatment is Richard Hofstadter, *Social Darwinism in American Thought*, rev. ed. (Boston: Beacon, 1955). A recent critic is Robert C. Bannister, *Social Darwinism: Science and Myth in Anglo-American Thought* (Philadelphia: Temple Univ. Press, 1979).

47. On the cult of the strenuous life see George Fredrickson, *The Inner Civil War: Northern Intellectuals and the Crisis of the Union* (New York: Harper & Row, 1965), chapter 11; on Theodore Roosevelt see Kathleen Dalton, "Why America Loved Teddy Roosevelt or, Charisma Is in the Eyes of the Beholders," *Psychohistory Review* 8 (Winter 1979): 16–26; on definitions of masculinity in the 1890s see Peter Gabriel Filene, *Him/Her/Self: Sex Roles in Modern America* (New York: Harcourt Brace Jovanovich, 1974), chapter 3. A pathbreaking article by John Higham published more than twenty years ago identified the heightened interest in virility in the 1890s, adducing the popularity of writers like Owen Wister and Jack London as evidence:

> In effect, these and other writers were answering James Lane Allen's plea of 1897 for a reassertion of the masculine principle of virility and instinctive action in a literature too much dominated by the feminine principle of refinement and delicacy.

Higham, "The Reorientation of American Culture in the 1890s," in *The Origins of Modern Consciousness*, John Weiss, ed. (Detroit: Wayne State Univ. Press, 1965), 30.

48. Letter from Miss M. C. W. Dawson to Frances Willard, Dec. 14, 1874, Temperance and Prohibition Papers, Harvard Univ. Library, Reel 11.

49. Ruth Bordin, *Woman and Temperance: The Quest for Power and Liberty, 1873–1900* (Philadelphia: Temple Univ. Press, 1981), 22.

50. Mark Twain, "The Temperance Crusade and Woman's Rights," *The Works of Mark Twain: Europe and Elsewhere* XXIX (New York: Gabriel Wells, 1923), 24–30.

51. Says Ruth Bordin, the most recent student of the WCTU, "The Woman's Christian Temperance Union was unquestionably the first mass movement of American women." Bordin, *Woman and Temperance*, 156.

52. Twain, "The Temperance Crusade and Women's Rights," 29.

53. As quoted in Mari-Jo Buhle, *Women and American Socialism, 1870–1920* (Urbana: Univ. of Illinois Press, 1981), 65.

54. Timothy Shay Arthur, *Woman to the Rescue: A Story of the New Crusade* (Philadelphia: J. M. Stoddart, 1874), 218f.

55. Theodore Parker, "The Public Function of Women," *Sins and Safeguards of Society*, vol. 9 of *The Works of Theodore Parker* (Boston: American Unitarian Association, 1908), 200.

56. The *Woman's Journal* was the official publication of the American Woman's Suffrage Association, founded by Lucy Stone, Henry Ward Beecher, and others. AWSA, unlike NWSA, accepted the Reconstruction amendment that gave black men the vote.

57. *Woman's Journal*, Jan. 8, 1881.

58. *Woman's Journal*, Nov. 25, 1911.

59. Marion Talbot and Sophonisba P. Breckinridge, *The Modern Household* (Boston: Whitcomb and Barrows, 1912), 86.

60. Jane Addams, "Why Women Should Vote," *Ladies Home Journal* (Jan. 1910), 21.

61. On this subject see Marjorie Julian Spruill, "Sex, Science, and the 'Woman Question': *The Woman's Journal* on Woman's Nature and Potential," unpublished M.A. thesis, Univ. of Virginia, 1980.

62. Blackwell Family Papers, Library of Congress, Container 85.

FOUR   *Toward an Industrialized Home*

1. See Mary Beth Norton, "The Evolution of White Women's Experience in Early America," *American Historical Review* 89 (June 1984): 593–619. Says Norton, "The image of the republican mother represented a successful fusing of contradictory collective and individualistic tendencies within republican ideology itself, tendencies that quickly proved irreconcilable with respect to men. On the one hand, republicanism looked to the past and preached the necessary sacrifice of the individual will to the good of the whole. On the other, it looked to the future and sang the praises of unencumbered individualism. . . . both aspects could be incorporated into the definition of a woman's role as mother"

(p. 617). On republicanism see John Thomas, *Alternative America: Henry George, Edward Bellamy, Henry Demarest Lloyd, and the Adversary Tradition* (Cambridge: Belknap Press of Harvard Univ. Press, 1983), chapter 1; on artisanal republicanism, see Sean Wilentz, *Chants Democratic* (New York: Oxford Univ. Press, 1984); on late-nineteenth-century malaise see T. J. Jackson Lears, *No Place of Grace: Antimodernism and the Transformation of American Culture 1880–1920* (New York: Pantheon, 1981).

2. Edward Bellamy, *Looking Backward, 2000–1887* (New York: Modern Library, 1951), 104f.

3. On housework reform, see Dolores Hayden, *The Grand Domestic Revolution: A History of Feminist Designs for American Homes, Neighborhoods, and Cities* (Cambridge, Mass.: MIT Press, 1981).

4. Faye E. Dudden, *Serving Women: Household Service in Nineteenth-Century America* (Middletown, Conn.: Wesleyan Univ. Press, 1983).

5. *Ibid.*, chapter 4.

6. Lucy Maynard Salmon, *Domestic Service*, 2nd ed. (New York: Macmillan, 1901), 57, 54. It seems likely that the older pattern survived in rural areas until well into the twentieth century. For example, my father Glen Ingles recalls "standing up" for a hired girl at her wedding in the rural South Dakota of the teens.

7. Anna Smith to HBS, Summer 1839, Beecher Stowe Collection, Radcliffe Women's Archives, Schlesinger Library, Folder 236.

8. Catharine Sedgwick, *Home* (Boston and Cambridge: James Munroe, 1835), 72. Dudden discusses this character, too. See Dudden, *Serving Women*, 23.

9. Daniel E. Sutherland, *Americans and Their Servants: Domestic Service in the United States from 1800 to 1920* (Baton Rouge: Louisiana State Univ. Press, 1981), 33.

10. David M. Katzman, *Seven Days a Week: Women and Domestic Service in Industrializing America* (New York: Oxford Univ. Press, 1978), 33.

11. Harriet Beecher Stowe, "The Lady Who Does Her Own Work," *Household Papers and Stories*, vol. VIII in *The Writings of Harriet Beecher Stowe* (Cambridge: Houghton Mifflin, 1896), 94.

12. Mrs. Horace Mann, "Co-operative Housekeeping," *Hearth and Home* (Oct. 30, 1869).

13. Zena Peirce to Frances Willard, Aug. 1877, Elizabeth Boynton

Harbert Collection, Huntington Library, Box 8, Folder 123. See Dolores Hayden's discussion of Peirce in *The Grand Domestic Revolution*, chapter 4.

14. Hayden, *The Grand Domestic Revolution*, 117; Parker Pillsbury, "Cooperative Housekeeping," *The Revolution* (July 29, 1869); M. F. Peirce, "Co-operation," *Papers of the 4th Congress of Women, October 1876* (Washington, D.C.: Todd Brothers, 1877); *Godey's* (Oct. 1869). Hayden provides a list of the cooperative ventures in her appendix.

15. Harriet Beecher Stowe, "A Model Village," *The Revolution* (April 2, 1868).

16. Harriet Beecher Stowe, "Servants," *Household Papers and Stories*, 152f.

17. "Veni Vidi," *Hearth and Home* (July 18, 1874).

18. Abby Morton Diaz, *A Domestic Problem: Work and Culture in the Household* (Boston: J. R. Osgood, 1875), 11f.

19. Edward Bellamy, "A Vital Domestic Problem," *Good Housekeeping* (Dec. 21, 1889).

20. Hayden, *The Grand Domestic Revolution*, 3.

21. Catharine E. Beecher and Harriet Beecher Stowe, *The American Woman's Home* (New York: J. B. Ford, 1870), 74; *Report of the Committee on Awards of the World's Columbian Commission: Special Reports upon Special Subjects or Groups*, vol. I (Washington: Government Printing Office, 1901), 849.

22. The two standard works on the technology of housework are Ruth Schwartz Cowan, *More Work for Mother: The Ironies of Household Technology from the Open Hearth to the Microwave* (New York: Basic Books, 1983), and Susan Strasser, *Never Done: A History of American Housework* (New York: Pantheon, 1982). Both have much to offer although Cowan has to strain occasionally to make all the evidence fit her thesis that the industrialization of the home has had only—or largely—the effect of creating more work for the housewife.

23. Sandra L. Myres, ed., *Ho for California: Women's Overland Diaries from the Huntington Library* (San Marino: Huntington Library, 1980), 18, 100.

24. Lydia Maria Child to Louisa Loring, Dec. 12, 1840, #219 in the Collected Correspondence of Lydia Maria Child, 1817–1880, copyright by Patricia J. Holland and Milton Meltzer, Schlesinger Library, Radcliffe College.

25. *Godey's* (July 1860).

26. *World's Columbian Commission Report*, vol. II, p. 1405.

27. Annie Fields, *Life and Letters of Harriet Beecher Stowe* (Boston: Houghton Mifflin, 1897), 35f.

28. *World's Columbian Commission Report*, vol. II, p. 1371.

29. Warshaw Collection of Business Americana, Smithsonian Institution. The circular is a fascinating document with respect to racial, ethnic, and class stereotypes. The Irish and black maids are depicted in highly similar stances with similarly coarse features while the middle-class women who are supposed to be their employers are depicted with delicate features and refined manners.

30. Strasser, *Never Done*, 73. See also Siegfried Giedion, *Mechanization Takes Command: A Contribution to Anonymous History* (New York: Oxford Univ. Press, 1955), 544.

31. *Woman's Journal* (Nov. 14, 1891).

32. Mary Beals Vail, "Approved Methods for Home Laundering," (Cincinnati: Proctor and Gamble, 1906), Warshaw Collection of Business Americana, Smithsonian Institution.

33. Alfred D. Chandler, "The Beginnings of 'Big Business' in American History," *Business History Review* 33 (Spring 1959), reprinted in *Pivotal Interpretations of American History*, vol. II, Carl N. Degler, ed. (New York: Harper and Row, 1966).

34. "Adventures of Del Monte," *Fortune* 18 (Nov. 1938), 77.

35. John L. Hess and Karen Hess, *The Taste of America* (New York: Grossman, 1977), 96; see also William Weaver's introduction to Elizabeth Ellicott Lea, *A Quaker Woman's Cookbook*, edited with an introduction by William Woys Weaver (Philadelphia: Univ. of Pennsylvania Press, 1982), Waverly Root and Richard de Rochemont, *Eating in America: A History* (New York: William Morrow and Company, 1976), 145, and Laura Shapiro, *Perfection Salad: Women and Cooking at the Turn of the Century* (New York: Farrar, Straus and Giroux, 1986).

36. Introduction to Mary Randolph, *The Virginia Housewife*, a facsimile of the 1st ed., 1824, with historical notes and commentaries by Karen Hess (Columbia: Univ. of South Carolina Press, 1984).

37. *Hearth and Home* (March 27, 1869).

38. Nina Baym, *Woman's Fiction: A Guide to Novels by and about Women in America, 1820–1870* (Ithaca: Cornell Univ. Press, 1978), 296.

39. Stephen Crane, *Maggie: A Girl of the Streets*, Thomas A. Gullason, ed. (New York: W. W. Norton, 1979), 9.

40. *Ibid.*, 11.

41. On the centrality of *Norwood,* see William McLoughlin, *The Meaning of Henry Ward Beecher: An Essay on the Shifting Values of Mid-Victorian America, 1840–1870* (New York: Alfred A. Knopf, 1970), 56, 82–90.

42. Charles M. Sheldon, *In His Steps* (Chicago: John C. Winston, 1937), 249.

43. *Ibid.*, 127.

44. *Ibid.*, 204.

45. Washington Gladden, *Applied Christianity: Moral Aspects of Social Questions* (Boston: Houghton Mifflin, 1886), 187–97.

46. Walter Rauschenbusch, *Christianity and the Social Crisis* (New York: Macmillan, 1910), 279.

47. Julia McNair Wright, *The Complete Home* (Philadelphia: J. C. McCurdy, 1879), 176–80.

48. The classic study is Joann Vanek, "Keeping Busy: Time Spent in Housework, United States, 1920–1970," unpublished Ph.D. dissertation, Univ. of Michigan, 1973. See also Cowan, *More Work for Mother.*

49. Cowan, *More Work for Mother,* 85.

50. John Thomas refers to the Leete household as "affectless" and points to the lack of emotional communion there: "The household is harmonious because passion has been banished." Thomas, *Alternative America,* 255. On the relation between the need for emotional intimacy and capitalism, see Eli Zaretsky, *Capitalism and Family Life* (New York: Harper and Row, 1976), and Zaretsky, "The Place of the Family in the Origins of the Welfare State," in *Rethinking the Family: Some Feminist Questions,* Barrie Thorne, ed., with Marilyn Yalom (New York: Longman, 1982). To acknowledge the human need for intimacy is not to accede to a Parsonian approach that would make women largely responsible for maintaining the life of the emotions.

51. Hayden, *The Grand Domestic Revolution,* 299.

FIVE *Darwinism and Domesticity*

1. Richard Hofstadter, *Social Darwinism in American Thought,* 2d ed., rev. (Boston: Beacon, 1955).

2. On Darwinism in the United States, see Robert C. Bannister, *Social Darwinism: Science and Myth in Anglo-American Social Thought* (Philadelphia: Temple Univ. Press, 1979), and Cynthia Eagle Russet, *Darwin*

in America: The Intellectual Response 1865–1912 (San Francisco: W. H. Freeman, 1976). On Darwin and women, see Ruth Bleier, *Science and Gender: A Critique of Biology and Its Theories of Women* (New York: Pergamon, 1984), Ruth Hubbard, "Have Only Men Evolved?," in *Women Look at Biology Looking at Women: A Collection of Feminist Critiques*, Ruth Hubbard, Mary Sue Henifin, and Barbara Fried, eds. (Cambridge, Mass.: Schenkman, 1979), and Rosalind Rosenberg, *Beyond Separate Spheres: Intellectual Roots of Modern Feminism* (New Haven: Yale Univ. Press, 1982).

3. Stephen Jay Gould, *The Panda's Thumb: More Reflections in Natural History* (New York: W. W. Norton, 1980), 51.

4. As quoted in Peter Brent, *Charles Darwin: "A Man of Enlarged Curiosity"* (London: Heinemann, 1981), 247.

5. *Ibid.*

6. Donald Fleming, "Charles Darwin, the Anaesthetic Man," *Darwin*, Philip Appleman, ed. (New York: W. W. Norton, 1970). Fleming quotes not only from Darwin's journal but also from Charles Dickens's novel, *Hard Times*. In this novel Dickens depicts the emotional wreckage created by the efforts of Thomas Gradgrind to eliminate poetry and other such foolishness from the experience of his children. Says Fleming, "In his resolve to be one of the great Truth-Bearers, Darwin strove to perfect himself as a fact-and-dust man, more abundant in learning and insight, more generous in spirit, and more divided than Thomas Gradgrind, but endeavoring to stand for the same thing and indeed opening out cosmic vistas for application of the Gradgrind philosophy." Fleming, "Charles Darwin," 586.

7. Charles Darwin, *The Descent of Man; and Selection in Relation to Sex* (New York: A. L. Burt, 1874), 643.

8. *Ibid.*, 643, 644.

9. *Ibid.*, 645.

10. Herbert Spencer, *The Study of Sociology* (New York: D. Appleton, 1875), 373, 374. See the discussion of this topic in Rosenberg, *Beyond Separate Spheres*, chapter 1 *passim*.

11. *Ibid.*, 375.

12. George Fredrickson, *The Black Image in the White Mind* (New York: Harper & Row, 1971), 235. See also Stephen Jay Gould, *The Mismeasure of Man* (New York: W. W. Norton, 1981) for a discussion of the pseudoscientific attempts to "measure" the brains of women and less favored races in the late nineteenth century.

13. Stephen Jay Gould, "Evolution as Fact and Theory," *Science and Creationism*, Ashley Montagu, ed. (New York: Oxford Univ. Press, 1984).

14. Hubbard, "Have Only Men Evolved?," 31. One could argue that sexual selection gave females the dignified role of choosing mates, but neither Darwin nor Spencer seems to have made much of this.

15. Edward J. Pfeifer, "United States," *The Comparative Reception of Darwinism*, Thomas F. Glick, ed. (Austin: Univ. of Texas Press, 1974), 194–96.

16. *Ibid.*, 198, 199.

17. Charles E. Rosenberg, *No Other Gods: On Science and American Social Thought* (Baltimore: Johns Hopkins Univ. Press, 1976), 3.

18. Rosenberg argues that Darwinism has convinced educated minds with such ease that the opposition to it has been class and regional in origin. *Ibid.*

19. Russet, *Darwin in America*, 67.

20. As quoted in Carroll Smith-Rosenberg and Charles Rosenberg, "The Female Animal: Medical and Biological Views of Women," *No Other Gods*, 55. See also Lester Frank Ward, "Our Better Halves," *The Forum* 6 (Nov. 1888): 266–75. Ward was reacting to a rash of articles that had employed biology to keep women in their place.

21. Edward H. Clarke, *Sex in Education; or, A Fair Chance for the Girls* (Boston: James R. Osgood, 1873), 39. See also the discussion of Dr. Clarke in Rosalind Rosenberg, *Beyond Separate Spheres*, chapter 1.

22. Julia Ward Howe, *Sex and Education: A Reply to Dr. E. H. Clarke's "Sex in Education"* (Boston: Roberts Brothers, 1874), 19.

23. Antoinette Brown Blackwell, "Sex and Evolution," *The Feminist Papers: From Adams to de Beauvoir*, Alice S. Rossi, ed. (New York: Columbia Univ. Press, 1973), 357.

24. *Ibid.*, 367.

25. Antoinette Brown Blackwell, *The Sexes Throughout Nature* (New York: G. P. Putnam's Sons, 1875), 135.

26. On Blackwell, see Rosalind Rosenberg, "In Search of Woman's Nature," *Feminist Studies* 3 (Fall 1975): 141–54. See also Elizabeth Cazden, *Antoinette Brown Blackwell: A Biography* (Old Westbury, N.Y.: Feminist Press, 1983), and William Leach, *True Love and Perfect Union: The Feminist Reform of Sex and Society* (New York: Basic Books, 1980).

27. Bleier, *Science and Gender*, 22.

28. Gould, *The Panda's Thumb*, 83.

29. Hubbard, "Have Only Men Evolved?," 26.

30. Hofstadter, *Social Darwinism in American Thought*, 81.

31. Lester Frank Ward, *Dynamic Sociology*, vol. I (New York: D. Appleton, 1898), 648.

32. Ward, *Dynamic Sociology*, vol. II, p. 437f.

33. See Paula Baker, "The Domestication of Politics: Women and American Political Society, 1780–1920," *American Historical Review* 89 (June 1984): 620–37 for an article arguing that women's voluntary associations were so pervasive and important that they were responsible for the existence of a female political culture in the nineteenth century.

34. Ward, *Dynamic Sociology*, vol. II, p. 616.

35. Gilman, *The Living of Charlotte Perkins Gilman* (New York: Harper & Row, 1975), 31.

36. *Ibid.*, 89.

37. *Ibid.*, 187.

38. Gilman, "The Yellow Wallpaper," *The Charlotte Perkins Gilman Reader*, Ann Lane, ed. (New York: Pantheon, 1980).

39. Carl Degler, "Charlotte Perkins Gilman," *Notable American Women, 1607–1950*, 3 vols., Edward James, Janet James, and Paul S. Boyer, eds. (Cambridge: Belknap Press of Harvard Univ. Press, 1971), II, pp. 39–42.

40. Mary Wollstonecraft, *A Vindication of the Rights of Woman* (London: J. Johnson, 1792), 402.

41. Blanche Glassman Hersh, *The Slavery of Sex: Feminist-Abolitionists in America* (Urbana: Univ. of Illinois Press, 1978), 235.

42. *Ibid.*, 93.

43. *Woman's Journal*, March 12, 1898.

44. As quoted in Elizabeth Griffith, "Elizabeth Cady Stanton on Marriage and Divorce: Feminist Theory and Domestic Experience," *Woman's Being, Woman's Place*, Mary Kelley, ed. (Boston: G. K. Hall, 1979), 240, 241.

45. *The Revolution*, April 1, 1869.

46. *The Revolution*, April 21, 1870.

47. "Homes of Single Women," speech in 1877, Susan B. Anthony Papers, Library of Congress, Reel 7.

48. Anthony to Merritt Anthony, July 8, 1891, Anthony Papers, Library of Congress, Reel 1.

49. Letter from Miriam O. Cole, *Woman's Journal*, Oct. 15, 1870.

50. Leach, *True Love and Perfect Union*, 198. As we saw in the preceding chapter, this discussion had ended by the last two decades of the nineteenth century, perhaps because technology seemed to be promising an easier solution to the housework problem than reorganizing gender relations would be, and perhaps also because of the declining interest taken in the home by intellectuals.

51. Gilman, *Women and Economics: The Economic Factor between Men and Women as a Factor in Social Evolution*, Carl N. Degler, ed. (New York: Harper & Row, 1966), 5.

52. Gilman, *The Home: Its Work and Influence* (New York: Mc-Clure, Phillips, 1903), 83.

53. Gilman, *Women and Economics*, 69, 70, 74.

54. *Ibid.*, 180.

55. Gilman, *The Home*, 32; Gilman, *The Man-Made World or Our Androcentric Culture*, 3 ed. (New York: Charlton, 1914), 64.

56. Gilman, *The Home*, 135f.

57. For a discussion of the negative implications for women in the formulation of the culture of professionalism see Joan Jacobs Brumberg and Nancy Tomes, "Women in the Professions: A Research Agenda for American Historians," *Reviews in American History* 10 (June 1982): 275–96, and Margaret Rossiter, *Women Scientists in America: Struggles and Strategies to 1940* (Baltimore: Johns Hopkins Univ. Press, 1982), chapter 4, "A Manly Profession," *passim*.

58. Catt, "An Eight-Hour Day for the Housewife—Why Not?" *Pictorial Review* (Nov. 1928).

59. For brilliant insights into this dilemma—that is, the chasm between reason and emotion in the wake of Darwin—see Fleming, "Charles Darwin, the Anaesthetic Man."

SIX *The Housewife and the Home Economist*

1. As quoted in Caroline L. Hunt, *The Life of Ellen H. Richards* (Washington, D.C.: American Home Economics Association, 1980), 37. The account of Ellen Richards's life is also based on the entry on her by Janet Wilson James in *Notable American Women, 1607–1950*, 3 vols., Edward James, Janet Wilson James, and Paul S. Boyer, eds. (Cambridge: Belknap Press of Harvard Univ. Press, 1971), III, pp.

143–46, and Margaret W. Rossiter, *Women Scientists in America: Struggles and Strategies to 1940* (Baltimore: John Hopkins Univ. Press, 1982).

2. Lita Bane, *The Story of Isabel Bevier* (Peoria, Ill.: Chas. A. Bennett, 1955).

3. Rosalind Rosenberg, *Beyond Separate Spheres: Intellectual Roots of Modern Feminism* (New Haven: Yale Univ. Press, 1982), 49.

4. Rossiter, *Women Scientists in America,* 69, 70.

5. *Godey's* (Jan. 1867); Isabel Bevier and Susannah Usher, *The Home Economics Movement, Part I* (Boston: Whitcomb and Barrows, 1912), chapter 1; Emma Seifert Weigley, "It Might Have Been Euthenics: The Lake Placid Conferences and the Home Economics Movement," *American Quarterly* 26 (March 1974): 79–96.

6. Hunt, *Ellen Richards,* 115.

7. *Ibid.,* 108.

8. Burton J. Bledstein, *The Culture of Professionalism: The Middle Class and the Development of Higher Education in America* (New York: W. W. Norton, 1976). See also Rossiter, *Women Scientists in America,* chapter 4, "A Manly Profession," and Joan Jacobs Brumberg and Nancy Tomes, "Women in the Professions: A Research Agenda for American Historians," *Reviews in American History* 10 (June 1982): 275–96.

9. Henrietta Goodrich, "Standards of Living: Food," *Lake Placid Conference on Home Economics, Proceedings of the Fourth Annual Conference* (Lake Placid, N.Y., 1902), 43.

10. Mrs. Mary L. Wade, "Refined Life on Small Incomes or The Woman Who Does Her Own Work," *Lake Placid Conference on Home Economics, Proceedings of the First, Second, and Third Annual Conference* (Lake Placid, N.Y., 1901), 97.

11. Mrs. Lewis Kennedy Morse, "Report of Committee on Standards for Routine Work in the Home," *Lake Placid Conference on Home Economics, Proceedings of the Sixth Annual Conference* (Lake Placid, N.Y., 1904), 60.

12. Ellen Richards, "Domestic Industries—In or Out—Why Not," *Proceedings of the Sixth Annual Conference,* 27–30; "Ten Years of the Lake Placid Conference on Home Economics: Its History and Aims," *Lake Placid Conference on Home Economics, Proceedings of the Tenth Annual Conference* (Lake Placid, N.Y., 1908), 19f.

13. This point is made in Marjorie East, *Home Economics: Past,*

Present, and Future (Boston: Allyn and Bacon, 1980), 8–19. Indeed, East lists at least four frameworks for home economics, all of which showed up at the Lake Placid conferences: a) management of the household; b) the application of science towards improving the environment—human ecology; c) learning by doing à la John Dewey applied to cooking and sewing; d) the education of women for womanhood.

14. The syllabus can be found in the Elizabeth Boynton Harbert Collection, Huntington Library, Box 11, Folder 154. See Mary A. Hill, *Charlotte Perkins Gilman: The Making of a Radical Feminist, 1860–1896* (Philadelphia: Temple Univ. Press, 1980), 242 for information about Campbell's career.

15. Marion Talbot and Sophonisba P. Breckinridge, *The Modern Household* (Boston: Whitcomb and Barrows, 1912), 42f.

16. *Ibid.*, 47.

17. Samuel Haber, *Efficiency and Uplift: Scientific Management in the Progressive Era, 1890–1920* (Chicago: Univ. of Chicago Press, 1964), ix.

18. Harry Braverman, *Labor and Monopoly Capital: The Degradation of Work in the Twentieth Century* (New York: Monthly Review Press, 1974), chapter 4 *passim*.

19. *Ibid.*, 102–6.

20. Helen Campbell, *Household Economics* (New York: G. P. Putnam's Sons, 1897), 182, 16f., 141.

21. *Ibid.*, 120, 196, 145f.

22. Isabel Bevier, *The House: Its Plan, Decoration and Care*, vol. I in *The Library of Home Economics* (Chicago: American School of Home Economics, 1907), 163.

23. Martha Bensley Bruere and Robert W. Bruere, *Increasing Home Efficiency* (New York: Macmillan, 1914), 177.

24. *Ibid.*, 291.

25. Lillian M. Gilbreth, *The Home-Maker and Her Job* (New York: D. Appleton, 1929), chapter 5.

26. Frank B. Gilbreth, *Time Out for Happiness* (New York: Thomas Y. Crowell, 1970), 1.

27. Paul V. Betters, "The Bureau of Home Economics: Its History, Activities and Organization," Service Monographs of the United States Government, No. 62 (Washington, D.C.: Brookings Institution, 1930), 4–6.

28. *Ibid.*, 10.

29. *Ibid.*, 38.

30. "Women Confer on Plans for New Bureau of Home Economics," typescript, Records of the Bureau of Human Nutrition and Home Economics, National Archives, R.G. 176, Box 601.

31. Betters, "The Bureau of Home Economics," 1.

32. The report on the planning conference is in an untitled typescript, Records of the Bureau of Human Nutrition and Home Economics, R.G. 176, Box 601; E. W. Allen, "Standards for Research in Home Economics under the Purnell Act," mimeo, R.G. 176, Box 601.

33. Harbert Collection, Box 11, Folder 154.

34. La Follette Family Papers, Library of Congress, Series B, Containers 9, 10, 11, 12, and 13. For the correspondence between Louise Stanley and Caroline Hunt, see Records of the Bureau of Human Nutrition and Economics, R.G. 176, Box 601.

35. "Nellie Kedzie Jones's Advice to Farm Women: Letters from Wisconsin, 1912–1916," Jeanne Hunnicutt Delgado, ed., *Wisconsin Magazine of History* (Autumn 1973): 3–27, p. 17.

36. Gilbreth, *The Home-Maker and Her Job*, 47.

37. One of the best documents for understanding how all these attitudes could coalesce in one person is Jacob Riis, *How the Other Half Lives* (Cambridge: Belknap Press of Harvard Univ. Press, 1970), originally published in 1890. Riis writes out of outrage over the newcomers' sufferings but every page demonstrates his distaste for many of their cultural practices.

38. More than one commentator has pointed out that it took Hitler, Aryan supremacy, and Nazi experimentation to discredit eugenics.

39. Mary Bralove, *Wall Street Journal*, as quoted in John L. Hess and Karen Hess, *The Taste of America* (New York: Grossman, 1977), 5.

40. The work-sheet survives in the papers of the Bureau of Human Nutrition and Home Economics, National Archives, R.G. 176, Box 601. The work book is catalogued as the Bertha Davis Sampler, Schlesinger Library, Radcliffe College.

41. Mary Virginia Terhune, *Marion Harland's Autobiography: The Story of a Long Life* (New York: Harper and Brothers, 1910), 84.

42. *Ibid.*, 111.

43. *Ibid.*, 164.

44. Mary Virginia Terhune, *The Dinner Year Book* (Charles Scribner's Sons, 1878); Terhune and Christine Terhune Herrick, *The National Cook Book* (New York: Charles Scribner's Sons, 1896).

45. See the discussion of Terhune in Mary Kelley, *Private Woman, Public Stage: Literary Domesticity in Nineteenth Cenutry America* (New York: Oxford Univ. Press, 1984), and the entry by Merritt Cross in *Notable American Women, 1670–1950,* III, pp. 439–41.

46. In later life she lived in Laguna Beach and worked as an interior decorator where—as a child—I knew her.

47. Christine Frederick, "The New Housekeeping," *Ladies Home Journal* (Sept. 1912); Frederick, *Household Engineering: Scientific Management in the Home* (Chicago: American School of Home Economics, 1920), 96, chapter 4, p. 211.

48. Christine Frederick, *The New Housekeeping: Efficiency Studies in Home Management* (Garden City, N.Y.: Doubleday Page, 1913), 189f.

49. *Ibid.,* 233.

50. *Ibid.,* 46.

51. *Ibid.,* 227.

52. *Ibid.,* 224.

53. Caroline Shillaber, "Christine McGaffey Frederick," *Notable American Women,* Barbara Sicherman and Carol Hurd Green, eds. (Cambridge: Belknap Press of Harvard Univ. Press, 1980), 249, 250.

54. In her recent book on women and cookery at the turn of the century, Laura Shapiro presents arguments very congruent with my own analysis:

> The task faced by home economists was to change the focus of domesticity from the past to the future, demolishing the rule of sentiment and establishing in its place the values manifest in American business and industry. American business, in fact, was eager to embrace home economics, and the food industry became a prominent ally in the assault on mother's cooking.

Shapiro, *Perfection Salad: Women and Cooking at the Turn of the Century* (New York: Farrar, Straus and Giroux, 1986), 190.

SEVEN *Domesticity and the Culture of Consumption*

1. Willa Cather, *My Antonia* (Boston: Houghton Mifflin, 1918), 65, 66.

2. *Ibid.,* 337, 338.

3. Sinclair Lewis, *Main Street* (New York: Harcourt, Brace, 1920),

31. It should be noted that Willa Cather, too, dealt with the limitations of small-town life in some of her other works.

4. Ibid., 85.

5. According to Lewis's biographer, Lewis had been very impressed by one of Gilman's articles. See Mark Schorer, *Sinclair Lewis: An American Life* (New York: McGraw-Hill, 1961), 112.

6. Lewis, *Main Street*, 319.

7. A brief survey of the critical discussions of Lewis's work before the rebirth of feminism discloses a void insofar as sympathetic understanding of Carol Kennicott's plight is concerned. She is discussed in terms of the vacuousness of American idealism rather than in terms of the housewife's dilemma.

8. Robert S. Lynd and Helen Merrell Lynd, *Middletown* (New York: Harcourt, Brace and World, 1956), 98, 171. See Richard Wightman Fox, "Epitaph for Middletown: Robert S. Lynd and the Analysis of Consumer Culture," in Richard Wightman Fox and T. J. Jackson Lears, *The Culture of Consumption: Critical Essays in American History, 1880–1980* (New York: Pantheon, 1983), for an account of the genesis of the study.

9. Ruth Schwartz Cowan, "Two Washes in the Morning and a Bridge Party at Night: The American Housewife Between the Wars," *Women Studies* 3 (1976): 147–72, p. 159.

10. David M. Katzman, *Seven Days a Week: Women and Domestic Service in Industrializing America* (New York: Oxford Univ. Press, 1978), 95, 130.

11. Siegfried Giedion, *Mechanization Takes Command: A Contribution to Anonymous History* (New York: Oxford Univ. Press, 1955), 604.

12. As quoted in Otis Pease, *The Responsibilities of American Advertising: Private Control and Public Influence, 1920–1940* (New Haven: Yale Univ. Press, 1958), 35.

13. Lynd and Lynd, *Middletown*, 46.

14. Edwin R. A. Seligman, *The Economics of Installment Selling: A Study in Consumers' Credit with Special Reference to the Automobile* (New York: Harper and Brothers, 1927), 118.

15. For a collection of brilliant essays dealing with this subject, see Fox and Lears, *The Culture of Consumption*.

16. Warren I. Susman, "Scarcity vs. Abundance: A Dialectic of Two Cultures," *The Nation* (Feb. 16, 1985).

17. Paula S. Fass, *The Damned and the Beautiful: American Youth in the 1920s* (New York: Oxford Univ. Press, 1977), 98.

18. John B. Watson, *Psychological Care of Infant and Child* (London: George Allen and Unwin, 1928), 9.

19. *Ibid.*, 11.

20. There is an excellent, balanced discussion of Watson in Fass, *The Damned and the Beautiful*, 100–107. She insists that he never represented the "major tendency" of child-care thought in this country. One reason that I am convinced that Watson did have a significant influence, however, is the testimony of my mother, Alberta Ingles. Although she has never mentioned Watson by name, she has described a child-care orthodoxy that existed around the time of my birth (1938) that placed so much emphasis on rigid schedules and sternness that she felt guilty every time that she picked me up.

21. Lynd and Lynd, *Middletown*, 266.

22. *Ladies Home Journal* (June 1923).

23. The contrast between Lewis's view of the legitimacy of a woman's demands on her husband in *Main Street* and in *Arrowsmith* is quite dramatic. Evidently his own first marriage had gone sour in the intervening years.

24. Sinclair Lewis, *Arrowsmith* (New York: New American Library, 1964), 419, 427, 428.

25. Marilyn Power Goldberg, "Housework as a Productive Activity: Changes in the Content and Organization of Household Production," unpublished Ph.D. dissertation, Univ. of California, Berkeley, 1977, p. 20f.

26. John Kenneth Galbraith, *Economics and the Public Purpose* (Boston: Houghton Mifflin, 1973), 33.

27. Christine Frederick, *Selling Mrs. Consumer* (New York: Business Bourse, 1929), 23.

28. *Ibid.*, 81.

29. *Ibid.*, 177–80.

30. Carl A. Naether, *Advertising to Women* (New York: Prentice-Hall, 1928), 27.

31. I should make it clear that I am not trying to argue that there was any conspiratorial intent. The home economists no doubt believed that they were acting in the best interests of women themselves as well as in the interests of manufacturers.

32. Although I do not have the figures for the 1920s, I do have them

for the modern period. In a book published in 1980, Marjorie East gives the total of 225,000 home economists in the country; about 75,000 are involved in education (teachers, extension home economists), 5,000 of them "develop or promote or interpret products," and the rest work for public agencies and the like. See East, *Home Economics: Past, Present, and Future* (Boston: Allyn and Bacon, 1980), 4.

33. *Ladies Home Journal* (Jan. 1920). In her witty book about women and cooking at the turn of the century, Laura Shapiro singles out Crisco as the quintessential product symbolizing the attempt to alienate consumers from their taste buds.

> With the Crisco white sauce, scientific cookery arrived at a food substance from which virtually everything had been stripped except a certain number of nutrients and the color white. Only a cuisine molded by technology could prosper on such developments, and it prospered very well. . . . Between World War I and the 1960s, generations of women were persuaded to leave the past behind when they entered the kitchen, and to ignore what their senses told them while they were there.

Shapiro, *Perfection Salad: Women and Cooking at the Turn of the Century* (New York: Farrar, Straus and Giroux, 1986), 215f.

34. The articles were in the Nov. 1928, May 1929, June 1929, and Dec. 1929 issues of the *Journal*.

35. "Science Serves the Homemaker" (April 1933).

36. See also Eleanor Gilbert, "Why I Hate My Independence," *Ladies Home Journal* (March 1920); Eugene Davenport, "You Can Change the World," *Ladies Home Journal* (Jan. 1922); Corra Harris, "The Happy Woman," *Ladies Home Journal* (Nov. 1923).

37. Susan Strasser, *Never Done: A History of American Housework* (New York: Pantheon, 1982), chapter 13 *passim*.

38. Paula Baker, "The Domestication of Politics: Women and American Political Society, 1780–1920," *American Historical Review* 89 (June 1984): 620–47, pp. 644, 645.

39. The advertisement was in the *Ladies Home Journal* of Feb. 1938, p. 51. See the discussion of this theme in Stuart Ewen, "The Captains of Consciousness: The Emergence of Mass Advertising and Mass Consumption in the 1920s," Ph.D. dissertation, State Univ. of New York at Albany, 1974, pp. 181–85.

40. Waverly Root and Richard de Rochemont, *Eating in America: A History* (New York: William Morrow, 1976), 225. These authors state

that in 1900, 95 percent of all flour sold was for home use and by 1970 the figure was only 15 percent. Laura Shapiro points out that women proved frustratingly (to the home economists) resistant to scientific advice at first. Shapiro, *Perfection Salad*, 172, 173.

41. For a brilliant discussion of the theoretical issues involved in explaining the ascendancy of modern advertising, see T. J. Jackson Lears, "The Concept of Cultural Hegemony: Problems and Possibilities," *American Historical Review* 90 (June 1985): 567–93. According to Lears, "As [Antonio] Gramsci understood, the hegemonic culture depends not on the brainwashing of 'the masses' but on the tendency of public discourse to make some forms of experience readily available to consciousness while ignoring or suppressing others" (p. 577). As I see it, the public discourse of the early twentieth century made nothing available to women that would have given them the leverage to resist the persuasion of advertisements—especially when the advertisements were echoed by the advice of experts.

42. Abraham Myerson, *The Nervous Housewife* (Boston: Little, Brown, 1920), 231.

43. *Ibid.*, 77.

44. *Ibid.*, 78.

45. Abraham Myerson, "Remedies for the Housewife's Fatigue," *Ladies Home Journal* (March 1930).

46. Marian Castle, "I Rebel at Rebellion," *Woman's Journal* (July 1930).

EIGHT   Naming the Problem

1. One could make a case for Eleanor Roosevelt. It seems to me, however, that her greatest acceptance and greatest achievement came in her widowhood after the war.

2. "It's a Woman's World," *Ladies Home Journal* (July 1940); see also Rose Wilder Lane, "Woman's Place Is in the Home," *Ladies Home Journal* (Oct. 1936), and Mary Roberts Rinehart, "I Speak for Wives," *Ladies Home Journal* (Feb. 1937).

3. Olga Knopf, M.D., "Marriage and a Job," *Ladies Home Journal* (March 1941).

4. Pearl S. Buck, *Of Men and Women* (New York: John Day, 1941), 44.

5. *Ibid.*

6. Dolores Barracano Schmidt, "The Great American Bitch," *College English* 32 (May 1971): 900–905.

7. Sinclair Lewis, *Dodsworth* (New York: Random House, Modern Library, 1947), 23f.

8. *Ibid.*, 94.

9. George Kelly, "Craig's Wife," (New York: Samuel French, 1926).

10. Schmidt, "The Great American Bitch"; see also Barbara Ehrenreich, *The Hearts of Men: American Dreams and the Flight from Commitment* (Garden City, N.Y.: Anchor Press/Doubleday, 1983).

11. See, for example, Karen Anderson, *Wartime Women: Sex Roles, Family Relations, and the Status of Women During World War II* (Westpost, Conn.: Greenwood Press, 1981); D'Ann Campbell, *Women at War with America* (Cambridge: Harvard Univ. Press, 1984).

12. *Woman's Home Companion* (Oct. 1943), 101.

13. General Foods' sales to the federal government went from $1,477,000 in 1941 to $37,840,000 in 1944. See Richard J. Hooker, *Food and Drink in America: A History* (Indianapolis: Bobbs-Merrill, 1981), 333.

14. Campbell, *Women at War with America*, 172–74.

15. Anderson, *Wartime Women*, 90, 91.

16. Susan M. Hartmann, *The Home Front and Beyond: American Woman in the 1940s* (Boston: Twayne, 1982), 166.

17. Harriette Arnow, *The Dollmaker* (New York: Macmillan, 1954), 59f.

18. *Ibid.*, 188.

19. *Ibid.*, 253.

20. *Ibid.*, 448.

21. Alfred Toombs, "War Babies," *Woman's Home Companion* (April 1944). See also "Eight-Hour Orphans," *Saturday Evening Post* (Oct. 10, 1942).

22. William H. Chafe, *The American Woman: Her Changing Social, Economic, and Political Roles, 1920–1970* (New York: Oxford Univ. Press, 1972), 159–72. For a case study of one state, see George N. Otey, "New Deal for Oklahoma's Children: Federal Day Care Centers, 1933–1946," *Chronicles of Oklahoma* 60 (Fall 1984): 296–311.

23. Elizabeth Hawes, "Woman War Worker: A Case History," *New York Times* (Dec. 26, 1943); "How America Lives," *Ladies Home Journal* (Oct. 1942).

24. Chafe, *The American Woman*, 160–62.

25. Karen Anderson concludes that the war was responsible for a "relative decline in the status of homemaking." Anderson, *Wartime Women*, 90, 91.

26. Philip Wylie, *Generation of Vipers* (New York: Rinehart and Company, 1955), 199.

27. *Ibid.*, 200.

28. *Life* (Jan. 29, 1945).

29. *Life* (June 16, 1947).

30. See the discussion in Chafe, *The American Woman*, chapters 8 and 9.

31. Ferdinand Lundberg and Marynia Farnham, *Modern Woman: The Lost Sex* (New York: Harper and Brothers, 1947).

32. Eileen Sharpe, "Strangers in Town," *Ladies Home Journal* (Aug. 1956).

33. Clifford R. Adams, *Ladies Home Journal* (Sept. 1950).

34. The mention of Lucy Ricardo is a tantalizing reminder of how rich the materials on depictions of housewives in the media must be. That, however, would be another study.

35. Robert Coughlin, *Life* (Dec. 24, 1956).

36. Louella G. Shover, "Quick and Easys for Two," *Ladies Home Journal* (Jan. 1948).

37. Peg Bracken, *The I Hate To Cook Book* (New York: Harcourt, Brace and World, 1960).

38. "The Plight of the Young Mother," *Ladies Home Journal* (Feb. 1956).

39. "Love, Death and the Hubby Image," *Playboy*, 1963, as quoted in Ehrenreich, *The Hearts of Men*, 48.

40. *Ibid.*, chapter 6, "Reasons of the Heart," *passim*.

41. As quoted in Diane Middlebrook, "Becoming Anne Sexton," *Denver Quarterly* 18 (Winter 1984): 23–34, p. 23f.

42. Diane Middlebrook, "Housewife into Poet: The Apprenticeship of Anne Sexton," *New England Quarterly* (June 1984): 483–503, p. 483.

43. Anne Sexton to Anthony Hecht, May 24, 1961, in *Anne Sexton: A Self Portrait in Letters*, Linda Gray Sexton and Lois Ames, eds. (Boston: Houghton Mifflin, 1977), 123.

44. "Housewife," in *Anne Sexton: The Complete Poems* (Boston: Houghton Mifflin, 1981), 77.

45. Sloan Wilson, *The Man in the Gray Flannel Suit* (New York: Simon and Schuster, 1955), 206.

46. Evan S. Connell, Jr., *Mrs. Bridge* (New York: Viking, 1959), 238. I am indebted to Michael Morey for calling this book to my attention.

47. Betty Friedan, *The Feminine Mystique* (New York: Dell, 1963), 21, 27.

48. Betty Friedan Papers, Radcliffe Women's Archives, Schlesinger Library, Box 10.

49. Phyllis McGinley, *Sixpence in Her Shoe* (New York: Macmillan, 1964), 41, 47.

50. Judith Lynn Abelew Birnbaum, "Life Patterns, Personality Style and Self Esteem in Gifted Family Oriented and Career Committed Women," unpublished Ph.D. dissertation, Univ. of Michigan, 1971, p. 246. See Table 3, p. 106ff., for the statistical data on self-esteem among the eighty-one women.

51. Birnbaum data, case #105, Henry Murray Center, Radcliffe College.

Afterword

1. See Sara Evans, *Personal Politics: The Roots of Women's Liberation in the Civil Rights Movement and the New Left* (New York: Alfred A. Knopf, 1979), and Jacqueline Jones, *Labor of Love, Labor of Sorrow: Black Women, Work and the Family from Slavery to the Present* (New York: Basic Books, 1985), for information about the impression made on white women by the southern black women.

Appendix

TABLE 1. *Total Population and Household Size: 1790 to 1970*

Year	Total Population (Millions)	Households (Millions)	Individuals per Household
1790	3.9	0.6	7.0
1800	5.3	—	—
1810	7.2	—	—
1820	9.6	—	—
1830	12.9	—	—
1840	17.1	—	—
1850	23.2	3.6	6.4
1860	31.4	5.2	6.0
1870	38.6	7.6	5.1
1880	50.2	9.9	5.0
1890	62.9	12.7	5.0
1900	76.0	16.0	4.8
1910	92.0	20.3	4.5
1920	105.7	24.4	4.3
1930	122.8	29.9	4.1
1940	131.7	34.9	3.8
1950	150.7	43.6	3.5
1960	179.3	52.8	3.4
1970	203.2	63.4	3.2

Source: U.S. Census.

TABLE 2. *Occupied Housing Units and Home Ownership: 1890 to 1970*

Year	Housing Units (Millions)	Percent Owner Occupied
1890	12.7	47.8
1900	16.0	46.7
1910	20.3	45.9
1920	24.4	45.6
1930	29.9	47.8
1940	34.9	43.6
1950	42.8	55.0
1960	53.0	61.9
1970	63.5	62.9

Source: U.S. Census.

TABLE 3. *Children per 1,000 Women by Race: 1800 to 1970*

Year	Children under Five per 1,000 White Women[a]	Children under Five per 1,000 Black Women[a]	Children Ever Born per 1,000 White Women[b]	Children Ever Born per 1,000 Black Women[b]
1800	1,342	—	—	—
1810	1,358	—	—	—
1820	1,295	—	—	—
1830	1,145	—	—	—
1840	1,085	—	—	—
1850	892	1,087	—	—
1860	905	1,072	—	—
1870	814	997	—	—
1880	780	1,090	—	—
1890	685	930	—	—
1900	666	845	—	—
1910	631	736	2,806	3,237
1920	604	608	—	—
1930	506	554	—	—
1940	419	513	1,870	2,096
1950	580	663	1,828	2,089
1960	717	895	2,253	2,808
1970	507	689	2,285	2,976

Source: U.S. Census.

[a] Children under 5 years old per 1,000 women 20 to 44 years old. "Adjusted" and "standardized" data.

[b] Children ever born to women ever married 15 to 44 years old.

TABLE 4. *Domestic Servants: 1800 to 1970*

Year	Households (Millions)	Domestic Servants (Hundreds of Thousands)[a]	Servants per Ten Households
1800	—	0.4	—
1810	—	0.7	—
1820	—	1.1	—
1830	—	1.6	—
1840	—	2.4	—
1850	3.6	3.5	1.0
1860	5.2	6.0	1.2
1870	7.6	10.0	1.3
1880	9.9	11.3	1.1
1890	12.7	15.8	1.2
1900	16.0	18.0	1.1
1910	20.3	20.9	1.0
1920	24.4	16.6	0.7
1930	29.9	22.7	0.8
1940	34.9	23.0	0.7
1950	43.6	20.0	0.5
1960	52.8	24.9	0.5
1970	63.4	—	—

Source: U.S. Census.

[a] Ten or more years old.

TABLE 5. *Women in the Civilian Labor Force (Millions): 1890 to 1970*

Year	Total	Single	Married	Widowed or Divorced
1890	3.71	2.53	0.52	0.67
1900	5.00	3.31	0.77	0.92
1910[a]	7.64	4.60	1.89	1.15
1920	8.35	6.43[b]	1.92	—
1930	10.63	5.74	3.07	1.83
1940	13.01	6.38	4.68	1.96
1950	16.55	5.27	8.64	2.64
1960	22.41	5.28	13.61	3.52
1970	30.76	6.94	19.18	4.64

Source: U.S. Census.

[a] 1910 data not comparable with earlier or later censuses due to difference in basis of enumeration.

[b] Includes widowed or divorced.

TABLE 6. *Women in the Civilian Labor Force (Percent of Female Population): 1890 to 1970*

Year	Total	Single	Married	Widowed or Divorced
1890	18.9	40.5	4.6	29.9
1900	20.6	43.5	5.6	32.5
1910[a]	25.4	51.1	10.7	34.1
1920	23.7	46.4[b]	9.0	—
1930	24.8	50.5	11.7	34.4
1940	25.8	45.5	15.6	30.2
1950	29.0	46.3	23.0	32.7
1960	34.5	42.9	31.7	36.1
1970	41.6	50.9	40.2	36.8

Source: U.S. Census.

[a] 1910 data not comparable with earlier or later censuses due to difference in basis of enumeration.

[b] Includes widowed or divorced.

TABLE 7. *Life Expectancy (in Years) by Race and Sex: 1900 to 1970*

Year	Entire Population	Men	Women	White	Non-White
1900	47.3	46.3	48.3	47.6	33.0
1910	50.0	48.4	51.8	50.3	35.6
1920	54.1	53.6	54.6	54.9	45.3
1930	59.7	58.1	61.6	61.4	48.1
1940	62.9	60.8	65.2	64.2	53.1
1950	68.2	65.6	71.1	69.1	60.8
1960	69.7	66.6	73.1	70.6	63.6
1970	70.9	67.1	74.8	71.7	65.3

Source: U.S. Census.

Index

Printed in the United States
51610LVS00002B/134